1993

BY HARLAN CLEVELAND

Next Step in Asia (1949), with J. K. Fairbank, E. O. Reischauer, and W. L. Holland

The Overseas Americans (1960), with G. J. Mangone and J. C. Adams

The Obligations of Power (1966)

NATO: The Transatlantic Bargain (1970)

The Future Executive: A Guide for Tomorrow's Managers (1972)

China Diary (1976)

The Third Try at World Order: U.S. Policy for an Interdependent World (1977)

Humangrowth: An Essay on Growth, Values and the Quality of Life (1978), with T. W. Wilson, Jr.

The Knowledge Executive: Leadership in an Information Society (1985)

The Global Commons: Policy for the Planet (1990), with papers by M. Gell-Mann and S. Hufstedler

The Age of Choice (1990) (available only on computer disk)

Edited by Harlan Cleveland

The Art of Overseasmanship (1957), with G. J. Mangone

The Promise of World Tensions (1961)

The Ethic of Power: The Interplay of Religion, Philosophy and Politics (1962), with H. D. Lasswell

Ethics and Bigness: Scientific, Academic, Religious, Political and Military (1962), with H. D. Lasswell

Energy Futures of Developing Countries: The Neglected Victims of the Energy Crisis (1980)

Bioresources for Development: The Renewable Way of Life (1980), with A. King and G. Streatfeild

The Management of Sustainable Growth (1981)

Prospects for Peacemaking: A Citizen's Guide to Safer Nuclear Strategy (1986), with L. P. Bloomfield

BIRTH OF A
NEW WORLD

HARLAN CLEVELAND

BIRTH OF A NEW WORLD

AN OPEN MOMENT FOR
INTERNATIONAL LEADERSHIP

foreword by
ROBERT S. McNAMARA

Jossey-Bass Publishers · San Francisco

Substantial discounts on bulk quantities of Jossey-Bass books are available to corporations, professional associations, and other organizations. For details and discount information, contact the special sales department at Jossey-Bass Inc., Publishers. (415) 433-1740; Fax (415) 433-0499.

For sales outside the United States, contact Maxwell Macmillan International Publishing Group, 866 Third Avenue, New York, New York 10022.

Manufactured in the United States of America

The paper used in this book is acid-free and meets the State of California requirements for recycled paper (50 percent recycled waste, including 10 percent postconsumer waste), which are the strictest guidelines for recycled paper currently in use in the United States.

10% POST CONSUMER WASTE

The ink in this book is either soy- or vegetable-based and during the printing process emits fewer than half the volatile organic compounds (VOCs) emitted by petroleum-based ink.

Library of Congress Cataloging-in-Publication Data

Cleveland, Harlan.
    Birth of a new world : an open moment for international leadership / Harlan Cleveland ; foreword by Robert S. McNamara. — 1st ed.
      p.   cm. — (Jossey-Bass management series) (Jossey-Bass public administration series)
    Includes bibliographical references and index.
    ISBN 1-55542-511-9
    1. International organization.   2. International relations.
I. Title. II. Series. III. Series: Jossey-Bass public administration series.
JX1954.C545   1993
341.2—dc20

92-40189
CIP

FIRST EDITION
HB Printing   10 9 8 7 6 5 4 3 2 1   *Code 9317*

a joint publication in

THE JOSSEY-BASS
MANAGEMENT SERIES

and

THE JOSSEY-BASS
PUBLIC ADMINISTRATION SERIES

consulting editors
organizations and management

WARREN BENNIS
University of Southern California

RICHARD O. MASON
Southern Methodist University

IAN I. MITROFF
University of Southern California

CONTENTS

FOREWORD

EVERYBODY IS TALKING about "a new world order." From a lifetime of international experience and five intensive years (1986 to 1991) of personal inquiry worldwide, Harlan Cleveland shows why a new order is needed and how it's possible, describes its dynamics, suggests its limits, and prescribes for its organization and leadership. His is a practical and comprehensive action agenda for how to make the next stage of world history better than the last; that is, to make it a story of mostly peaceful change. The author argues, and I agree, that we face an "open moment" in world history. He suggests how to take advantage of this unique opportunity.

Harlan Cleveland has had a rich experience both as educator and executive. He has thought deeply and written persuasively about what it means to live in a global knowledge society in which thinking and learning provide most of the "added value." Both practitioner and philosopher of leadership, he is well placed to help us understand the changing styles and substance of leadership in the new world "disorder."

Birth of a New World analyzes what works and why in the politics of international security, trade, money, and the global environment. It then sketches a comprehensive strategy for what needs to be done to contain conflict without war, energize the bargaining about trade, prevent a "nervous breakdown" of the world money system, tackle the underlying "crisis of fairness," and manage a world environment that Cleveland calls *the global commons*.

The book also describes the leadership styles of consultation and consent that are beginning to displace more traditional systems of command, control, and coercion, and forecasts a parallel change in the style of global leadership by an open-ended "club" of nations led by the United States. But we Americans will need to adapt our attitudes and behavior to lead in a world where no nation or alliance or race or class will be in charge.

I first came to know Harlan Cleveland in the Washington of President John F. Kennedy, when I was secretary of defense and Cleveland was the assistant secretary of state working on *multilateral diplomacy,* that is, what to do and how to do it in the United Nations and half a hundred other international organizations to which the United States then belonged. We crossed paths frequently in the White House, as we tried to understand and consider the statements and actions of other nations — from China and Korea to Cuba and the Congo and the chronically touchy Middle East — and handled the various peace-and-security crises to which those nations gave rise. Clues to their reactions were found in the Byzantine politics of the United Nations in New York.

Harlan Cleveland was so often a reliable guide to the pratfalls and practical uses of multilateral diplomacy that President Lyndon B. Johnson later appointed him U.S. ambassador to NATO — the day-to-day American member of the political board of directors of the Atlantic Alliance. There, his capacity to think of military power and international politics as two parts of the same subject was especially handy — so much so that when President Richard Nixon was elected to succeed LBJ, he asked Ambassador Cleveland to stay on for a transition period that lasted almost half a year.

In the late 1960s, I became an executive in a very different business, as president of the World Bank. I found that Harlan Cleveland also had experience in administering aid to developing countries. Just after World War II, he managed large U.N. relief and rehabilitation efforts in Italy and in China. Returning to Washington in 1948, he managed aid to China, then all U.S. foreign aid in the Far East; by 1952, as assistant director for Europe in the Mutual Security Agency, he was responsible for managing in Washington the fourth year of the four-year Marshall Plan for European recovery.

When he first left government service in 1953, Cleveland began to fashion an alternate career as scholar and writer on world politics, international economic relations, and public administration. Since then, he has divided his time about equally between executive leadership (not only in government but in academia, with two deanships and a university presidency) and hard thinking about management and leadership at home and abroad. *Birth of a New World* is the eleventh book he has authored.

People who can get things done, and who also think hard about what to do and how to do it, are rare enough. Even rarer are those who can express their insights in lucid prose. The coverage of this book is extraordinarily broad, but Harlan Cleveland's capacity to deal with the situation as a whole is equally extraordinary. He discusses complex policy issues, such as arms control, global warming, and the world monetary systems, with readable informality.

"We are looking for something new — organization, structure, concept," said Valéry Giscard d'Estaing, former president of France, not long ago. "What is strange is that, for the moment, there is no thinker who is suggesting a possible course." Mr. President, meet the author of this book.

Washington, D.C.   ROBERT S. MCNAMARA
January 1993

ROBERT S. MCNAMARA is former president of the Ford Motor Company, former U.S. secretary of defense, and former president of the World Bank. His most recent publication is *Out of the Cold: New Thinking for American Foreign and Defense Policy in the 21st Century.*

FOR JOHN MUSSER

a great heart and a global view

*My country is the world
and my religion is to do good.*
—Thomas Paine, 1792

PREFACE

We have it in our power to begin the world all over again. A situation similar to the present, hath not appeared since the days of Noah until now. The birthday of a new world is at hand.

Thomas Paine wrote that in 1775. With perhaps a little less hyperbole, we have every right to feel today that we are again watching the birth of a new world. And since our own past efforts helped bring this new world to life, we have both the thrill and the responsibility to take seriously the new choices and chances in the 1990s and beyond.

It is a very open moment in world history. The last historic chance for systemic change remotely to be compared with this time of our lives started in 1945, not long before today's baby boomers were born. That new beginning produced the United Nations Charter, freed a billion people from colonial rule, jump-started the economies of Western Europe and Japan, codified universal human rights, launched the idea of development aid for poorer countries, and forged a democratic alliance without peacetime precedent.

"May you live in interesting times." In ancient China that counted as a curse. It still seemed so to the elderly Communists, immured in the Great Hall of (a Few of) the People in May 1989, learning the hard way that if the masses are educated in anything, they will sooner or later get interested in politics.

   The rapid spread of knowledge in the 1980s, culminating in these "years of democracy," not only caught a generation
of Communist leaders by surprise. In the non-Communist world,
it also blindsided a generation of experts on the management
of international relations. Their favored categories and modes
of thinking quite suddenly fell flat when analyzing the new state
of affairs. They could no longer rely on the comprehensive mind-
set they had developed, or at least learned in school, that defined
peace as the confrontation of military alliances backed by mutual
terror between the United States and the Soviet Union; *progress*
as the deployment of every inventable new technology, with Nature in the service of humankind; *growth* and *equilibrium* as the
twin goals of economic activity; and *development* as the trickle-
down outcome of transnational business and foreign aid.

   Suddenly the very idea of superpower status, based on
the possession of huge stockpiles of usable weapons, seemed
almost quaint — even though most of that explosive power was
still lying dangerously around. Suddenly the Warsaw Pact went
the way of SEATO, CENTO, and other forgotten euphemisms
for big-power satellite systems, and the North Atlantic allies were
scrambling in victory to find a rationale to stay together to deal
with instabilities to the east and south of the traditional "NATO
defense perimeter." Suddenly, in the changing knowledge environment, the ethic of quantitative growth seemed passé, and
widespread resentments of unfairness required world economic
management with more social conscience than the funds and
banks established by economists devoted to equilibrium had
managed to deliver. Suddenly the backlash from Nature and
from an emerging ecological ethic made it imperative to rethink
the impacts of human activity on the natural environment and
to invent new means of human self-control.

For those of us who watch and read the news of the world and
are exhilarated by the pace of change, these "interesting times"
are a great time to be alive. We are witnessing peoples who have
been fettered by despotism and distress quite suddenly finding
that they have a choice, if they insist on choosing.

   For the many peoples who have declared for democracy

since 1989, the tasks of self-governance are even harder than the angry eruptions that led to this point. (Remember that the French took a century and a half to transform their revolution into a stable democracy.) Still, after the changes of 1989 to 1992, the world will never be the same.

Whether this historic time of choice turns out to be more blessing than curse depends on what we — millions of us in diverse cultures in various parts of the world — do to build together a civilization that will, as the United Nations Charter puts it, "promote social progress and better standards of life in larger freedom."

Purpose and Audience

Birth of a New World, then, has two objects: one is to present an upbeat way of thinking about this extraordinary time of our lives. In an oversimplified phrase, the key to all the sudden happenings around us is *the spread of knowledge* — rapidly expanding literacy, rapid growth in the numbers of educated people, and rapid increases in newspaper and magazine circulation, radio listeners, and television watchers. My other purpose is to suggest — based on five years of "rethinking" while world politics was turning handsprings — an across-the-board agenda: how most fruitfully to use, for human needs and purposes, this open moment of world-scale ferment.

The book is for anyone who is concerned with the state of our world and wants to help shape a positive future: those in government and international affairs; current and future public administrators and corporate executives; people in private enterprise and nonprofit agencies; and anyone who, by voting, loving, and planning ahead, wants to help mold the new world now being born.

Background of the Book

In the spring of 1986 — when the Berlin Wall still looked solid, the dissidents in the Communist countries were still crying in the wilderness, and China's Gang of Four was still in living

memory—I put in the mail letters to a couple of dozen especially imaginative people in North America, Europe, Latin
America, Africa, Asia, and the Pacific. The letters were invita-
tions to join in an ambitious, international, nongovernmental
effort to "rethink international governance."

Acting for three colleagues (Lincoln Bloomfield, Geri
Joseph, Magda McHale) and myself, I proposed in our invitation letter that we and our colleagues "examine together, in its
parts and their relations to each other, the international system
as a whole." Suppose, we said to our correspondents around
the world, that we were assigned together to be an international
"postwar planning staff" in the midst of a great war or global
crisis. Wouldn't we feel obliged to break out of our hardened
categories and think globally about an international system that
spans security, development, economic management, human
rights and responsibilities, the diversity of cultures, the migration of peoples, and the protection of the global environment?

The trouble was that human civilization could not, this
time, afford war as the stimulus to hard thinking about peace.
So at our first gathering in November 1986 we agreed that we
would presume to do "postwar planning without having the war
first."

Astonishingly, every person invited to this party accepted
with enthusiasm—even though we were not able to offer them
consulting fees, only travel expenses, congenial colleagues, and
an exciting chance to rethink the agenda for peaceful change
in an unruly world.

We had all had experience in government and intergovernment dealings. On the basis of that experience, we judged that
governments and committees of governments could not be expected to start this kind of root-and-branch rethinking. Except
in times of deep crisis, such as a great depression or a war, government leaders are, paradoxically, too "responsible" for things as
they are to take the responsibility for charting system change.

The best bet was therefore to assemble for this purpose,
from around the world, under nongovernmental auspices, an
ad hoc group of wise and experienced rethinkers who would work
together in a manner that did not engage whatever professional

responsibilities they might otherwise be carrying, to sketch a credible, workable system of peaceful change.

When we started in the mid 1980s, it was inconceivable that either a Soviet or a Chinese colleague could play such a wide-open game of make-believe. Two Eastern Europeans, a Hungarian and a Romanian, did agree to join in — along with rethinkers from Belgium, Canada, Chile, Colombia, Egypt, France, India, Indonesia, Israel, Jamaica, Japan, Kenya, South Korea, Mexico, Morocco, Singapore, Spain, Sweden, Switzerland, Uganda, the United Kingdom, and the United States. Altogether, over its four-year span, thirty-one people from these twenty-four countries were members of what we simply called "The Group," which was assisted by a dozen close consultants and uncounted others who helped by listening, reading, reacting, and writing as our work went on. (The way we tackled our self-generated task, a list of the international meetings held and of our cosponsors at each phase of the project, and a list of the published writings spun off along the way, are spelled out in the section titled "Genesis of the Book" at the end of the book.)

Much of the diagnosis in the early chapters of the book and most of the prescriptions that follow in the later chapters are the result of intensive interaction with this international network of wonderfully stimulating colleagues. At our last full meeting together, held in Barcelona in October 1989, just as the walls were tumbling down all over Eastern Europe, members of The Group decided that a "consensus statement" risked being too brief and too bland to do justice to the depth and breadth of our work together. They proposed that I write my own version of the strategies and structures that we had discussed. I accepted this mandate with some diffidence, both because I knew how hard it would be to write and because so much of what I wrote would have to be the unattributed insights of others.

By 1990, as the passion for political choice spread with the spread of knowledge round the globe, what had seemed in the mid 1980s an engrossing but somewhat academic exercise suddenly looked both urgent and opportune. I found that I was writing on a moving wall. The pages of history were turning by themselves.

A first draft was completed just as the Gulf crisis erupted, Saddam Hussein became a household name, and the U.N. Security Council pulled itself together for its first major collective security action, with all five of its permanent members in concert, in the forty-five years since the Charter was signed. Our "postwar planning" had to take account not only of the Cold War that had dissipated so fast and the nuclear war that wasn't but also of the first regional war of the new era and its unforeseen aftermath. Meanwhile, long-suppressed cultural identities, a new politics of separation, and fresh awareness of what human actions were doing to the global environment challenged our earlier hopeful assumption that knowledge was more likely to draw peoples together than to split them apart.

Yet in the resulting rewrite I have found more nourishment than ever in the philosophy of international cooperation that emerged from our work together. More confirmed than upset was our sense that the global spread of knowledge was the prime mover in the rush of passing events. Confirmed also was our analysis of what had worked, and why, in the international system built during the late 1940s by those who were (as American statesman Dean Acheson, with pardonable immodesty, said of himself) "present at the creation."

Our analysis of how spreading knowledge and information technologies had fused together the traditional categories called *security, economics, development, environment,* and *leadership,* looked even better in the early 1990s than it had in the 1980s. The world-scale functions of the future we had identified as requiring fresh thinking and new international machinery seemed even more urgent in the garish light of oil-well fires in Kuwait, resurgent ethnic rivalries, fragmentation of the former Soviet Union, an extended worldwide recession, and the still-widening gap between rich and poor.

Overview of the Contents

The first five chapters of *Birth of a New World* describe the tidal waves of change that make both necessary and possible this century's "third try" (the League of Nations and a UN hobbled by the Cold War count as the first two) at organizing a disorderly world.

Chapters One and Two describe how spreading knowledge about the advantages of political choice and a worldwide "fairness revolution" toppled top-down totalitarianism. In Chapter Three I argue that the model for what is miscalled "world order" cannot be a worldwide nation-state; indeed, national governments are themselves leaking power to cities and other subnational communities, to transnational corporations and associations, and to groups of governments working on global dangers and desires. What actually works in international cooperation, profusely illustrated in Chapter Four, is functional pieces of peace glued together by common interest and powered by modern information technologies. Chapter Five derives from all this some moral and political guidelines for the next mutations in the management of peace.

What then follows is fresh analysis and a fistful of prescriptions on world security, the world economy, world development, and the global environmental commons:

- Controlling exotic weapons—nuclear, chemical, and biological (Chapter Six)
- Selecting and deploying "activist neutrals" as peacemakers, peacekeepers, peace-enforcers, and operational humanitarians (Chapter Seven)
- Organizing free trade fairly, sharing technology, managing the money supply, and moving toward greater stability in exchange rates among the world's currencies (Chapter Eight)
- Building an international system to promote "growth with fairness" in developing countries, establish standards and arrange bargains to meet basic human needs, use the huge debt overhang as an opportunity, and invent ways of using taxes, not "aid," to raise new funds for development (Chapter Nine)
- Using the "trusteeship" idea already built into the UN Charter to manage human behavior in the global commons—the oceans, the atmosphere, outer space, and Antarctica, the "sharing environments" where neither the laws of war nor the traditions of market economics seem to be useful guides for cooperative action (Chapter Ten)

Who can lead, govern, manage a world with nobody in charge? That's the question posed in Chapter Eleven. The nucleus of a Club of Democracies already exists — an open-ended club expanding in membership with the spread of government by consent. It's not an international organization; it has no secretariat or headquarters; practicing what the NATO allies used to call "a habit of consultation," its best description is MIT professor Lincoln Bloomfield's phrase: a "coalition of the willing." In the years just ahead, only the United States is in a position to serve as its "chairman of the executive committee" — if the United States can manage its own affairs well enough to take the lead again in building a world community that works.

I have not interrupted the text with footnotes. But the section titled "Sources, Notes, and Comments" contains the clues and references — the source of many ideas, books, and articles where fuller discussion can be found, and who said or wrote some particularly trenchant comments. The section is organized by chapters; within each chapter the notes are arranged in the same order as the points in the text to which they apply.

Now the more-than-ritual disclaimer: I took The Group's advice seriously and wrote my book, not theirs. I hope and believe it reflects many or most of their opinions; it certainly leans heavily on their facts and ideas. The draft of an early manuscript went to all the living members of The Group and to a number of special consultants who had helped us along the way. The result was a flood of insightful comments that enhanced both the accuracy and the vigor of this newer writing.

But for the whole story I have put together, and the many proposals for changes in the international system, I have to take responsibility — tempered by my gratitude to so many colleagues for the chance to sit at their feet and stand on their shoulders.

Minneapolis, Minnesota   HARLAN CLEVELAND
January 1993

ACKNOWLEDGMENTS

MY PREFACE DESCRIBES briefly, and the "Genesis of the Book" section describes in more detail, how a worldwide group of reflective practitioners and practice-minded scholars happened to come together between 1986 and 1989 to "rethink international governance."

The Group

The international "core group" for this wide-angle inquiry came to be called The Group, and is referred to that way in the text. The Group contained, at one time or another, thirty-one men and women from twenty-four countries. Two (John W. Holmes and Romesh Thapar) died during the four-year life of the project. There were no dropouts. All thirty-one are listed here, identified too briefly to suggest the extraordinary range of their experience and the quality of their individual and collective wisdom.

> I. H. Abdel Rahman (Egypt)
> Former Minister of Planning
> Founding Executive Director,
> U.N. Industrial Development Organization (UNIDO)

> Lincoln P. Bloomfield (United States)
> Professor, Political Science,
> Massachusetts Institute of Technology (MIT)

Jozsef Bognar (Hungary)
Director, Institute for World Economics
Hungarian Academy of Sciences

Margarita Marita de Botero (Colombia)
Member, World Commission on
Environment and Development ("Brundtland
Commission")

Albert Bressand (France)
Economist
Director, PROMETHEE

Noel Brown (Jamaica)
Director, Regional Office for North America
U.N. Environment Program

Harlan Cleveland (United States)
Former U.S. Ambassador to NATO
Dean, Hubert H. Humphrey Institute of Public Affairs

Ricardo Díez Hochleitner (Spain)
Fundación Santillana, Madrid
President, Club of Rome

Yehezkel Dror (Israel)
Professor, Political Science and Public Administration,
Hebrew University, Jerusalem

Mahdi Elmandjra (Morocco)
Former Rector, University of Rabat
President, Association Internationale Futuribles

Salvador Giner (Spain)
Professor, University of Barcelona

Bohdan Hawrylyshyn (Canada, Switzerland)
Scholar in Residence and former Director,
International Management Institute, Geneva

Ivan Head (Canada)
President,
International Development Research Centre, Ottawa

Carl-Göran Hedén (Sweden)
Professor Emeritus, Karolinska Institute, Stockholm
President, World Academy of Art and Science

John W. Holmes (Canada)
Counselor,
Canadian Institute of International Affairs

Geri M. Joseph (United States)
Former U.S. Ambassador to The Netherlands
Senior Fellow, Humphrey Institute of Public Affairs

Calestous Juma (Kenya)
Development Economist,
African Centre for Technology Studies

Masao Kunihiro (Japan)
Professor of Anthropology,
University of Tokyo

Hahn-Been Lee (Republic of Korea)
Former Deputy Prime Minister, Republic of Korea
Chair, Korean Institute for Science and Technology

R. Martin Lees (U.K.)
Former staff member, OECD and UN
Development Program
Consultant based in Paris

Jorge Lozoya (Mexico)
Economist, formerly with Collegio de México
Office of the President of Mexico

Mochtar Lubis (Indonesia)
Journalist. Associate Editor, *WorldPaper*
Director General, Press Foundation of Asia

Christian Lutz (Switzerland)
Economist. Director,
Gottlieb Dutweiler Institute, Zurich

Kishore Mahbubani (Singapore)
Former Ambassador to the United Nations
Foreign Office, Government of Singapore

Mircea Malitza (Romania)
   Former Ambassador to the United States
   Association of International Law and Relations,
   Bucharest

Magda Cordell McHale (U.K.)
   Director, Center for Integrative Studies, SUNY Buffalo
   Vice President, World Futures Studies Federation

Olara Otunnu (Uganda)
   Former Ambassador to the United Nations
   President, International Peace Academy

Juan Somavia (Chile)
   Executive Director,
   Instituto Latinamericano de Estudios Trasnacionales

Romesh Thapar (India)
   Former Adviser to the Government of India
   Editor and Publisher, *Seminar*

Sir John Thomson (U.K.)
   Former Ambassador to the United Nations
   Co-director, Twenty-first Century Fund

Jean-Paul van Bellinghen (Belgium)
   Former Ambassador to the United Nations
   Ambassador to the Court of St. James

Consultants and Advisers

During the four-year life of the International Governance Project, I had the opportunity to consult with many wise people engaged in "rethinking" in their own disciplines, specialties, professions, and cultural contexts. To name them all would double the length of this section. But I want to express my gratitude for the insights of some special people who attended one or more of The Group's workshops and sustained a lively interest in what we were trying to do. They range from graduate assistants and support staff to well-known experts and leaders in business, politics, and academia. They are listed here in alphabetical order:

Dean Abrahamson, Elmer L. Anderson, Kathy Bahma, Patrick Baudry, Richard E. Benedick, William Boyd, Anne Branscomb, Lea Burdette, Leone Carstens, H. Yvonne Cheek, Arthur C. Clarke, H. van B. Cleveland, Larry Condon, Gamani Corea, John P. Craven, Robert E. Dickinson, Sylvia Earle, Jens Evenson, Richard Farson, John Firor, John E. Fobes, Donald Geesaman, Luther Gerlach, Peter Gizewski, Michael Glantz, Scott Glinski, Peter Hansen, Willis Harman, Judith Healey, Masato Homma, Michael Horner, Brian Job, Nicholas Johnson, Vladimir M. Kotylakov, Robert Kudrle, Patti Mallin, Eleonora Masini, Robert Matteson, Sally Menefee, Edgar Mitchell, John and Betty Musser, Robert and Marcie Musser, Marc Nerfin, Rita Cruise O'Brien, Geoffrey Pearson, Jacques Piccard, Juan Rada, Sir John Rawlins, Victor Raymond, Philip J. Regal, Walter Orr Roberts, George S. Robinson, John Rollwagen, Wally Schirra, G. Edward Schuh, Russell Schweickart, Tommy Setchell, Jan Smaby, Edson Spencer, Timothy Stanley, Harold Stassen, Paul Strassman, Uno Svedin, Juliana Tanning, Janna Wallin-Haug, Thomas W. Wilson Jr., Burke Zimmerman, Marlys Zoren, and Charles Zraket.

Contributors

Altogether, the "rethinking" project cost a little more than a half-million dollars, in cash and in kind. On behalf of The Group, I want to thank the many supporters and cosponsors who believed in this effort and shared the sometimes controversial view that much more international cooperation is both required and achievable.

The initial planning was made possible by John Musser of St. Paul, Minnesota. Getting the project underway was funded mostly by the University of Minnesota's Hubert H. Humphrey Institute of Public Affairs from earnings on an endowment raised to establish the Chair and Center for World Peace in honor of Harold E. Stassen — once a youthful governor of Minnesota, the only surviving signer of the United Nations Charter, still a vigorous contributor to the national dialogue on international affairs. The endowment drive was launched by his colleague,

Robert Matteson, and carried on by the Humphrey Institute. When the endowment became large enough to support a full academic chair position at the University of Minnesota, other foundations and collaborators made possible the later phases of the "rethinking" process:

The General Service Foundation, Boulder, Colorado
The Joyce Mertz-Gilmore Foundation, New York, N.Y.
The Weyerhaeuser Foundation, Seattle, Washington
The United States Institute for Peace, Washington, D.C.
World Academy of Art and Science, Stockholm, Sweden
Spring Hill Center, Orono, Minnesota
The Hormel Company, Austin, Minnesota
International Management Institute, Geneva, Switzerland
Centre for Applied Studies in International Negotiations, Geneva, Switzerland
Charles E. Lindbergh Fund, Minneapolis, Minnesota
National Center for Atmospheric Research, Boulder, Colorado
Canadian Institute for Peace and Security, Ottawa, Canada
International Development Research Centre, Ottawa, Canada

Special Contributor

The debt to my wife, Lois, in the year of our fifty-first wedding anniversary, is incalculable. Her love has sustained a productive marriage and a peripatetic ménage, with enough patience and fortitude left over to work with a writer as skeptical editor and demon proofreader. As Paul the Apostle wrote to the Corinthians, love "beareth all things, believeth all things, hopeth all things, endureth all things."

H.C.

THE AUTHOR

HARLAN CLEVELAND, political scientist and public executive, is president of the World Academy of Art and Science and president emeritus of the University of Hawaii. He was founding dean of the University of Minnesota's Hubert H. Humphrey Institute of Public Affairs and became professor emeritus in 1988.

During World War II, Cleveland served as an economic analyst in the Board of Economic Warfare and as executive director of the economic section of the Allied Control Commission in Italy. Remaining in Rome after the war, he was deputy chief of mission for the United Nations Relief and Rehabilitation Administration (UNRRA), and in 1947 he became the last director of the UNRRA China Office, based in Shanghai. From 1948 to 1953 he was an official of the Marshall Plan in Washington, first building a crescent of foreign aid programs in the Far East, then serving the U.S. Mutual Security Agency as assistant director for Europe in 1952 and 1953. In 1953 he became executive editor, then publisher, of the *Reporter* magazine. In 1956 Cleveland was appointed dean of the Maxwell Graduate School of Citizenship and Public Affairs at Syracuse University.

During the 1960s Cleveland served as assistant secretary of state for international organization affairs in the administration of President John F. Kennedy and as U.S. ambassador to NATO under President Lyndon B. Johnson. He was chair of the Cabinet Committee on International Cooperation Year 1965.

Cleveland was president of the University of Hawaii from 1969 to 1974, and from 1974 to 1980 he developed and directed the Program in International Affairs of the Aspen Institute, with headquarters in Princeton, New Jersey. In 1979 he was appointed for one semester as the distinguished visiting Tom Slick Professor of World Peace at the Lyndon B. Johnson School of Public Affairs, University of Texas at Austin. During the 1980s he served two three-year terms as trustee at large of the University Corporation for Atmospheric Research in Boulder, Colorado.

A Princeton University graduate and a Rhodes Scholar at Oxford in the 1930s, Cleveland has served on numerous boards and is the recipient of twenty honorary degrees, the U.S. Medal of Freedom, and Princeton University's Woodrow Wilson Award. In 1981 he received (with Bertrand de Jouvenel of France) the Prix de Talloires, a Switzerland-based international award for "accomplished generalists."

BIRTH OF A
NEW WORLD

A HINGE OF HISTORY
THE EXPLOSION OF POLITICAL CHOICE

Freedom, like a genie that's been let out of the bottle, doesn't necessarily want to listen to the dictates of the person who uncorked the bottle.

— *Prime Minister Kazimiera Prunskiene of Lithuania, May 3, 1990*

THE ELEGANT ECONOMIST BARBARA WARD spoke of her time as a "hinge of history." The biosphere of our inheritance and the technosphere of our creation are out of balance, she wrote. "The door of the future is opening onto a crisis more sudden, more global, more inescapable, more bewildering than any ever encountered by the human species. And one which will take decisive shape within the life span of children who are already born."

Everything that has happened since Barbara wrote those words in 1971 reinforces their prescient wisdom. It was not as clear then as it is now that (in Roger Revelle's memorable image) we humans are conducting a giant geophysical experiment the outcome of which we cannot even guess.

Most of my friends in the world community of scientists don't think of themselves as revolutionaries. Many have long records of conservative voting behavior or above-the-fray neutrality in the politics of their own societies. Yet by exploring outer space, modeling the atmosphere and the oceans, pursuing the minutest particles of matter, deciphering the information in our genes, studying the working of our brains, and especially by linking computers to telecommunications, modern science and technology have set the stage for a revolution in the content and charter of world politics.

• First with atomic fission and then with nuclear fusion, we have developed the capacity to create such huge explosions

1

that we cannot figure out how to use them for military purposes or (in the case of fusion) how to control them for any other purpose. Meanwhile, with weapons already produced, the potential exists to commit something like civilizational suicide.

Along with the capacity to produce large explosions is the evolution of ever more complex industrial and military systems, all prone to the kind of cascading catastrophe that marked the events of Three Mile Island, Bhopal, Chernobyl, and the space shuttle *Challenger,* each of which was brought quickly into homes around the world by a proliferating global network of telecommunications.

• While physics was multiplying the power to explode, the life sciences were beginning to find out what goes on inside a cell, learning to move genes in and out of species, and melding genetics and chemistry to produce recombinant DNA. The visible consequences of biotechnology's "gene revolution" range from quantum increases in the productivity of plants and animals to practical ways for women to have fewer babies, proven ways to make human insulin from bacteria, promising ways to make protein cheap and abundant, and potential ways to detect and correct inborn errors of metabolism.

• The dawning intuition is that sometime in recent years, as environmental writer Thomas W. Wilson, Jr., puts it, "the works of human beings began to outweigh the works of nature in the global scheme of things . . . and the human race began to consume its own environment." The evidence is our destruction of so much without really meaning to destroy anything, including the genetic diversity of tropical forests, the purity of lakes and streams and inland seas and even the oceans, the quality of the air we breathe, and the balance of atmospheric gases that keeps our planet habitable.

It now seems much more probable than it did when Barbara Ward was writing that the buildup of carbon dioxide and other greenhouse gases in the global atmosphere could warm up the world enough to make Kansas a dust bowl and flood the world's seaports in an irreversible rising of the oceans. How soon this could happen, early or late in the twenty-first century, is still much debated — and depends on what we do about it in the meantime.

• Not even in the early 1970s, let alone in the 1940s, did we realize how the explosive marriage of computers and telecommunications would require us to rethink the very fundaments of our philosophy — rethink an economics based on the allocation of scarcities, rethink governance based on secrecy, rethink laws based on exclusive ownership, rethink management based on hierarchy.

The knowledge revolution came to a boil in the 1980s. But it climaxed a much longer story: of the 537 years since Johannes Gutenberg's Bible was printed in movable type; the 490 years since Nicolaus Copernicus and his mind-changing notion that the earth revolves around the sun; the 306 years since Isaac Newton's landmark book about universal gravitation; the 159 years since Charles Babbage's "analytical engine," forerunner of the modern computer; the 117 years since the telephone of Alexander Graham Bell; the 97 years since Guglielmo Marconi's wireless telegraphy; the 36 years since the first orbital satellite, *Sputnik I* — all leading up to the 1980s, when computers, space satellites, and telecommunications were fused in global systems with pervasive impact.

Many years ago I heard a story that became, for me, a metaphor for much of what has happened in my lifetime. A young army captain is passing his battalion in review under the critical eye of a senior general. The battalion commander gives his order in a conversational tone of voice: "Battalion march." The visiting dignitary leans over to give a word of advice: "Young man, you have to shout the order, so they all start at once." The captain looks back tolerantly at this relic of the age of administrative pyramids. "It's all right, General," he replies. "The word will get around."

It is precisely the spread of knowledge that makes necessary, because it is possible, a radical new way of thinking about world order.

It has been a long and eventful generation since the international system (the United Nations and its specialized agencies, the World Bank and the International Monetary Fund [IMF], established at Bretton Woods, the peacetime alliances and regional organizations) was put in place — one is tempted to say, "set in concrete." In that short span of time, the world to be governed has been transformed in ways and at a rate that were unimaginable in 1945.

Yet even then, in revulsion at the human tragedy of World War II, in alarm at the atom-splitting force that sobered their success, the leaders of the victorious Allies took thought and invented institutions without precedent in world history. They wrote the United Nations Charter and established a network of global organizations, some of which actually worked in handling special problems of global scope (weather forecasting, international civil aviation, electronic telecommunications, environmental monitoring, cooperative scientific research).

The United States, Canada, and Western Europe embarked on a huge recovery effort culminating in the Marshall Plan. They quickly included their main former enemies — first Italy, then Japan, then two-thirds of Germany — in the *perestroika* of that heady time. Before long they banded together in new kinds of peacetime alliances — a North Atlantic Alliance, a Western Hemisphere alliance known as the Río Pact, an alliance that linked Australia and New Zealand with the United States (ANZUS), and a bilateral alliance between the United States and a demilitarized Japan. Cooperating in the Security Council of the United Nations, they helped put together UN peacekeeping forces large (in Korea), medium-sized (in the Congo), and small (in the Sinai, Cyprus, and Kashmir). All this experience presaged the collaborations of the 1990s, beginning with Operation Desert Storm in the Mideast and the UN mandates in Cambodia and Yugoslavia.

And with more or less reluctance, they set 130 colonies free, codified international human rights, and started to act out the historically strange idea that richer nations have some obligation to provide technical and material help to their poorer world cousins.

Leaders of one major ally of 1941 to 1945, the ally that had suffered most, saw their destiny in a rapid separation from their wartime partners and a global competition with them for influence and ideology. To socialism with its emphasis on fairer distribution of the world's goods and its promise of a better life for all, the leaders of the USSR added the claim that state ownership, central planning, and collective farming were the way to build an economy both strong and fair, and the idea that political leaders should think of themselves as acting for those who do the world's work. They used spectacular science and technology to demonstrate their global reach (remember the worldwide impact of *Sputnik I* in 1957) and rebuilt an armed force that easily dominated Eastern Europe and ranked as the only real challenge to the only other nuclear superpower. This military and political gloss on the economics of Karl Marx persuaded (and cowed) many into believing that the Soviet Union was helping history toward a Marxist destiny.

For a time, many in the West doubted, as Alexis de Tocqueville had doubted 150 years before, that democracies could "regulate the details of an important undertaking, persevere in a fixed design, and work out its execution in spite of serious obstacles." But as things turned out, the vigor and attractiveness of life in the democratic, market-oriented West got through to those in the Communist, planned-economy East, who were deferring their gratification because their leaders told them it was necessary for socialist ideals. Close readers of de Tocqueville might have predicted this outcome from his long-ago insight — not in his best-known work, *Democracy in America,* but in a speech he made later on. "Democracy and socialism," he said, "have nothing in common but one word: equality. But notice the difference: While democracy seeks equality in liberty, socialism seeks equality in restraint and servitude."

Just after the Red Army strong-armed the uppity Czech government of Alexander Dubček in August 1968, a Paris cartoonist described in a single caption the Kremlin's 1989 dilemma. The drawing showed a group of students and workers standing on a street corner having a lively discussion about politics. In the background, two Soviet commissars were wringing their hands, and one of them was saying to the other, "The trouble with all these people's democratic republics is that they seem to be producing democratic republican people."

Just a year after that, I came home from Paris and Brussels after four years as U.S. ambassador to NATO. In a parting comment, Manlio Brosio, the wise Italian who was NATO's secretary general in the 1960s, predicted that peace would come "by osmosis," the gradual absorption of ideas through the porous membranes of ideology and nationhood. That was a good guess. Information about free institutions and wealth-creating enterprise had been leaking from West to East in Europe, with transformative results.

Quite suddenly in 1989 — more suddenly than anyone on either side of the Cold War had thought possible — political choice burst out all over. The "year of democracy" was touched off, as revolutions usually are, not by *les misérables,* the poorest of the poor, but by millions of educated people (to use the Chinese categories: students, workers, professionals, intellectuals) coming to realize that they had a choice, that their world didn't really need to be so low-ceilinged, so tunnel-visioned, so lacking in groceries and amenities and dignity and fairness.

The Chinese case is instructive but not because China's top-down reformers didn't like what they started and used tanks to suppress it; it is instructive because the story shows so clearly how economic openness leads to demands for political reform. In the late 1980s, China's political leaders as well as its millions of natural-born entrepreneurs rediscovered the incentive value of markets. Even more intriguing than what China's top-down reformers did was what they said about what they wanted to do. The new doctrine was a creative hash of Karl Marx and Thomas Jefferson, "with Chinese characteristics."

They called the new invention a *socialist commodity economy* or a *bargaining economy,* not capitalism; markets, they argued, had been around for several millennia before capitalism. From old-time Arab bazaars and Chinese opium marts to modern shopping malls, markets have been bringing buyers and sellers together to bargain for jade and drugs, for tung oil and hog bristles, for rice and fresh vegetables, for computers and compact disks. So China's leaders didn't speak of their rediscovery of market techniques as a Western import; it was more like a remembrance of things past.

What they rediscovered about markets is that they generate hard work, innovation, and hustle. In the bad old days, demand was projected by central planners and that much (or, usually, less) was produced under rigid quota systems. More recently, the official quotas were kept low enough so that an increasing amount of the nation's total business was subject to decisions not by econometricians but by buyers and sellers; whether the resulting markets were called *black* or *free* was a matter of taste. Even Deng Xiaoping, the ranking top-down reformer, said he was astonished at the rapid growth of small rural industries all over the country once local entrepreneurship was given its head.

But China's leaders discovered the hard way that they could not permit freedom of market choices to lead to freedom of thought and expression and at the same time maintain a rigid Communist Party monopoly on power.

The students who protested in Tiananmen Square in the summer of 1989 were taking their cue as much from Chairman Mao as from Thomas Paine. In the little red book now fallen into disfavor, *The Thoughts of Chairman Mao,* that old revolutionary urged the Communist regime's administrative leaders to remember that it is the masses (read *people*) who make the policy. Your job, he told them, is to get out, sniff around, and figure out where the masses are going, then describe that sense of direction, codify it, program and budget it, and organize to carry it out. Then, he added, you had better go back and check again with the masses to make sure you keep up with their changing sense of direction. Then you redescribe, recodify, reprogram, rebudget, and reorganize. This continuous cycle, this dialectic between you and the masses, said Mao, is the correct "theory of knowledge."

Whether or not they had studied this passage before it was dropped from their reading lists, the Chinese students in 1989 were playing the policy-making role of the masses. The leaders and cadres had started a semirevolution to blow life into a sluggish economy from the top. The students and the citizens attracted to their cause were saying that this was not enough, that initiative and productivity could only be the result of "letting many flowers bloom" (another Mao metaphor denied by his methods), encouraging people to take their destiny into their own hands.

In the end, the octogerentocracy of Beijing decided that enough was enough and had the loyal tank crews to make its crackdown stick. There is irony aplenty here. Psychologist Richard Farson guessed at the time that China's leaders must have been dumbfounded: they had opened their country to the world, doubled the nation's wealth in a decade, and experimented with market systems their critics miscalled capitalism. "And what did they get for it? Angry, protesting, thankless students. Then, like some parents in similar situations, instead of evaluating their success by the quality of discontent they engender, they became angry themselves and resorted to the massive repression for which their backgrounds had well prepared them."

In China as in the West, a dilemma worthy of Lao-tzu's passion for paradox had become uncomfortably obvious: those with visible responsibility for leadership are nearly always too visible to take the responsibility for change—until it becomes more dangerous to stand there than to move on. It is not a new idea: "I am a leader," Voltaire wrote, "therefore I must follow."

The key slogan, endlessly repeated in the square, was "democracy." Its content was far from clear: one student told a reporter he didn't know what democracy was, but he knew that China needed more of it. Neither Lenin nor Confucius got much play in Tiananmen Square, the great media event of May 1989. And even though 1989 was the bicentennial of the French Revolution and the inauguration of President George Washington, the metaphorical shots heard 'round the world from Beijing were not in their essence French or American either. They were the universal language of human rights, the multicultural language of people's aspirations to have a say in their own destiny.

Both the Soviet and Chinese strategies of "reform from within" were revolutions promoted—and, their leaders hoped, managed—from the top. The difference was that Deng Xiaoping thought he could have economic reform, even the openness needed to "let the market decide," while maintaining a monopoly of political power in one party dominated by a tight little group of lifetime associates, friends, and relations.

At first Mikhail Gorbachev was rhetorically clear that politics had to go hand in hand with economics. During those tick-lish days of May 1989, when he visited his Chinese peers in Beijing and found himself the darling of the students demon-strating for democracy, he put the matter bluntly to the elite assembled in the Great Hall. Soviet experience, he said, has shown that "economic reform will not work unless supported by a radical transformation of the political system."

The million Chinese just outside, in and around Tianan-men Square, were not permitted to hear Gorbachev's speech. They soon learned all about it from the radar effect of the elec-tronic media: stories filed with foreign news services were quickly played back to the students in the square by modern informa-tion technologies, producing the world's first fax revolution. But the demonstrators' educated intuition had already enabled them to reach a quick verdict: top-down reform will never go far enough to match the rising expectations it creates.

Leakage of information was a two-way street. It didn't take long for street-demonstration fever to bounce halfway around the world to Central and Eastern Europe. Although political change has moved swiftly in other times and places, it is hard to think of a historical moment with a comparable rate of acceleration. One observer said the ouster of a Communist party took roughly ten years in Poland, ten months in Hungary, ten weeks in East Germany, ten days in Czechoslovakia, and ten hours in Roma-nia. Real history does not come in such neat packages, but the remark helps remind us of that cascade of political surprises that filled our television screens in the autumn of 1989 and again in the autumn of 1991, when the Soviet Union itself fell apart and its republics started trying to pick up the pieces.

What is increasingly clear in retrospect is how much the tumbleweed of political change was blown across language bar-riers, national frontiers, and political obstacles by modern in-formation technologies. Telephones and fax machines, orbit-ing satellites, radio and television, and computers hitched to telecommunications supplemented, reinforced, and intensified that oldest and most trusted of communication systems, word of mouth.

As in Beijing, so in Europe's "Soviet bloc," it was not the miserably poor but feisty and frustrated educated people who set the parade in motion — once Gorbachev's Kremlin made clear that the lid was off and the bubbles would not be prevented from rising. Suddenly, the label *Communist* became as poisonous in public as it had long been in private. One after another, each in its own style but mostly with little violence, the peoples of Central and Eastern Europe discovered to their surprise that they were pounding on an unlocked door. They started pouring through, and before long some found themselves on the Western side of Berlin's Brandenburg Gate.

The abrupt turn of events was widely seen as a victory for "containment." George Kennan, the diplomat and historian who in 1947 proposed the "long-term, patient but firm and vigilant containment of Russian expansionist tendencies," now says the NATO military shield was not the main agent of change but rather the fact that the industrial democracies were so clearly outperforming the Soviet Union: "the realization upon the part of many intelligent people in the Soviet Union that the whole system was going downhill, that it was no longer competitive, that the capitalist countries were going far beyond it." From that judgment flowed in quick succession the turnaround in the Soviet Union, its jettisoning of Marxist economics, its tolerance for the breakaways in Eastern Europe, the flood of migrants from East Germany, the breaching of the Berlin Wall, the surprisingly bloodless breakup of the Soviet Union.

Vaclav Havel, the playwright who became Czechoslovakia's president, was asked on U.S. public television in February 1990 how he felt as a dramatist about the theatrics of 1989. It was, he replied with unrehearsed elegance, a "drama so thrilling and tragic and absurd that no earthling could have written it."

The central lesson of that time of our lives is clear enough: the people, not their leaders, were doing the leading. It's now time to start digesting this lesson. Herewith a few spoonfuls of fiber to speed our digestion.

• We were watching two contrasting and colliding urges: top-down reform and the bubbling of political choice from below.

In China the tight little group of top-down reformers—lifetime associates, friends and relations—hung on. The question is not whether they will succeed but when they will be supplanted.

In Eastern Europe some hasty declarations of top-down reform were wrenched from Communist leaders under the duress of placard-waving throngs. The bubbles of political choice rose and choked most of the old leaders; a few, notably in Romania, Bulgaria, Lithuania, and the Ukraine, survived the first wave of reform by agile apostasy, becoming overnight social democrats.

In the Soviet Union Mikhail Gorbachev kept having to adjust to the reform spirit unleashed by his advocacy of openness, which became an insistence on choice and self-determination with a life of its own. At first, Gorbachev was what a basketball coach might call a master of the fast break. In his early years as the Soviet leader, there were many quick-scoring transitions to the offensive basket. Routinely and repeatedly, Gorbachev outpaced other world leaders, especially Presidents Reagan and Bush, in proposing drastic arms reductions, protection of the global environment, a stronger United Nations. He took the initiative; his peers around the world were left asking themselves and each other, Is this guy for real? He was.

Later on, he failed to understand what every basketball coach teaches: the most important fast break is getting back under your own basket before anyone else does. His retreats under fire were sluggish. He kept thinking socialism could be repaired after his best and brightest advisers and most of the people he governed had consigned it to history's scrap heap. He hesitated to conduct the shakeout the featherbedded Soviet economy was obviously going to require. He appointed hard-liners whose failed coup against him was ironically the beginning of the end of the Soviet Union, and of Gorbachev's job.

The lesson from all three cases is that top-down reform will always be too little and too late; "the people" will all too easily get out ahead of the reformers.

• It is hard to think of a time in world history when the political leaders of powerful nations seemed so irrelevant to im-

portant outcomes. Well-known names, presidents and prime
ministers of the world's military powers and economic power-
houses, stared at the nightly news with ill-concealed astonish-
ment. The people power cavorting on the world stage after the
summer of 1989 had remarkably little to do with the customary
measures of power: weapons, armies, gross economic product.
More than anything else, the power of ideas was and is in play.

•   The impatient crowds were moved not by distant visions of Utopia but by spreading information about neighbors
who were obviously getting more goods and services, more fairness in the distribution of those goods and services, and firmer
guarantees of human rights than their own bosses and planners
seemed able to deliver.

This "demonstration effect," more than anything else,
heated political frustrations to the boiling point. The principle
is a familiar one. From time immemorial farmers have watched,
learned, and copied the farming innovations of their neighbors.
Business managers and bankers watch in horror as competitors
take their customers by working harder and being more inno-
vative—and then respond by imitating them.

What undermined the rulers of China was unstoppable
knowledge, especially among the educated young, of what was
going on in Japan, South Korea, Taiwan, Hong Kong, and Singapore. What caught up with the Communist leaders in Eastern
Europe and the Soviet Union was what went on in the democracies of Western Europe and North America. They observed
that people in the West chose both their leaders and their lifestyles and therefore seemed to be better fed and clothed, more
affluent, and despite all their problems, happier. The news of
this contrast readily leaked eastward—by the word-of-mouth stories of travelers, by the written word, by telephone and facsi-
mile, and especially by radio and television.

The major powerhouse in getting the word around is now
what futurist John Platt called "the TV dramatization of problems and fears and human needs. When some things become
vividly visible to millions, they become intolerable—a war, injustice, the death of seabirds. TV becomes . . . a conscience
machine, a sympathy and tolerance machine, across social and

geographic boundaries." For Eastern Europeans in the 1980s, TV was an envy-thy-neighbor machine, a machine that bred intolerance of corruption and foot-dragging by their own long-time leaders, who could not liberalize their policies fast enough to escape the viewers' wrath. Most of the leaders tried, in the end, to change their spots. But the protesters, seeing unaccustomed light at the end of the tunnel, condemned the very leaders whose sudden conversion made that vision possible.

Somehow, Mikhail Gorbachev kept saying in one way or another, we have got to mobilize our own people's sense of political enthusiasm and economic hustle by setting them free from the anxiety and apathy that come with being governed by secret informers and economic planners. Because nobody quite knew how to *manage* such a process from the top, leadership trickled away from the long-established bosses to leaders of local jurisdictions and interest groups (miners, science academies, retailers, bureaucracies, and the like) with a more immediate stake in getting decisions made and easing their neighbors' economic hardship.

• Top-down reformers keep trying to draw a line between safe and unsafe learnings. A century ago imperial China distinguished between "China's learning for essential matters" and "Western learning for practical matters." But how, these days, can a leader distinguish the practical from the essential, especially when the practical is so essential?

A good deal of science-based culture comes packaged with those "practical" imports. Embedded in modern technology are Western notions about limits to government, about freedom to discover and experiment and innovate, about workers' rights, about managers leading without being bossy.

• The toughest dilemma top-down reformers face is how to educate their people, especially their young people, without luring them into dissidence.

When it comes to politics, people who think are notoriously ornery and inventive. It doesn't even seem to matter much what they have been trained to think *about;* part of what they learn in every field of knowledge is the joy of creative choice. If the freedom to choose is so clearly essential to their specialist learnings, it's no big step to the conviction that freedom of political choice is not only attractive but also attainable. That's why the spread of education around the world erodes the pyramids of power and wealth and discrimination that look like granite but turn out to be porous sandstone, crumbling under pressure.

"The students" still don't know how to manage an economy or govern a society, but they notice that their elders are not very good at management and governance either. What they *are* clear about is the need to open what has been closed, reveal what has been hidden, substitute human choice for subhuman fate, and draw all manner of "untouchables" from the periphery to the center, where the choices seem to be made.

The determination of educated people by the millions to have a voice in their own destiny seems always to be resisted in the short run by those who already have it made. In the longer run, given the spread of knowledge, it seems to be irresistible — yesterday in the shipyards of Gdansk, in Wenceslas Square and the Soviet Academy of Sciences; today in the Soviet republics and South Africa and Latin American polities as different as Nicaragua and Chile; and tomorrow in monarchies, theocracies, and authoritarian systems such as the Gulf states, Iran, Iraq, Cuba, North Korea, Indonesia, and China, to name only the most obvious contemporary candidates for political change.

People who have grown up under democratic institutions are tempted to think they have a sort of map for the development of democracy — their own. In the United States, we recently took thirteen years (1976 to 1989) to celebrate the two-hundredth anniversary of our nobody-in-charge experiment, the Constitution of the United States. Yet we sense a fundamental difference now. Today's worldwide democracy movement is broader and deeper than the Declaration and Great Compromises of a handful of bewigged and brilliant men, upper class for their time, some of them still slaveholders, worldly well-read men presuming to speak (with impressive clarity and eloquence) for people everywhere.

Now women and men of all kinds and colors and modes of speech are sticking up for themselves, by the hundreds of thousands in one public square after another, by the millions when they get a chance to vote their own destiny. Their "established" leaders are behind them, way behind them, hurrying in breathless pretense that the new-style parades still need old-fashioned drum majors. Meanwhile, new leaders emerge, increasingly women as well as men, mostly educated people—journalists, writers, professors, labor leaders, entrepreneurs, civil servants, even some professional politicians—pushed into formal positions of power by the volcanic rumblings of the newly articulate crowds.

two

A WORLD OF DIFFERENCE
The Fairness Revolution

"Will you walk a little faster?"
said a whiting to a snail.
"There's a porpoise close behind us,
and he's treading on my tail."

—*Lewis Carroll,* The Lobster-Quadrille

The importunate crowds now pushing their leaders from behind are expressing a complex combination of hopes and fears. Their hopes are hitched to spreading aspirations about their human rights and rising expectations about their human needs. But the hopes are mixed with fears—of discrimination, exploitation, domination, conquest, or civil war—based on the clash of cultural identities.

The wet blanket of the Cold War dampened both hopes and fears. It was much used to justify political oppression. It soaked up resources that might otherwise have been invested in education and economic development. It squashed ethnic rivalries that interfered with the larger purpose of girding for another world war. The lifting of that wet blanket intensified the struggles for human rights and made possible a new war on poverty. But it also blew into flame the smoldering embers of religious and cultural conflict.

Throughout history the measure of fairness and the means of discrimination have always been access to civilization's dominant resource. In other times that meant the possession of the latest weapons—the caveman's club, the tribesman's spear, the early catapult, the feudal knight's armor. Since the invention of gunpowder it has meant the capacity to direct larger and larger explosions at those you don't like.

16

Among nomadic tribes, whether in Asia Minor or pre-colonial America, access also meant swifter and more dependable means of transportation. In human settlements it meant control of land and of construction materials to build fortifications. Later on the key resources were deemed to be minerals, especially those that could be converted into energy.

In the agricultural era, poverty and discrimination were explained and justified by the shortage of arable land; women and strangers could hardly be expected to share in so scarce a resource—even if the women did most of the work. In the industrial era, poverty and discrimination were explained and justified by the shortages of things: there just weren't enough minerals, food, fibers, and manufactures to go around, so those who got to them first felt no obligation to share them with anyone who couldn't wrest them by force from the early arrivers.

As information—abundant, shareable, instantly accessible—now becomes the world's dominant resource, what does that mean for the prospects of fairness? Surely it means that people who get educated to convert information into knowledge and wisdom, who hone their intuitive powers, who learn how to achieve access to information and (even more important) what to select from the information overload that threatens us all, will likely be better off and more fairly treated than those who don't.

But whether this really happens depends, in every family, tribe, neighborhood, ethnic group, and political jurisdiction, on whether individuals (and especially children) are encouraged to learn the basics of communication and computation, permitted to think for themselves, and rewarded for brainwork above all. Those decisions are mostly not "international relations"; they lie deep in the "internal affairs" of families, neighborhoods, local communities, cultural nations, and political states.

Fairness depends on education, which depends in turn on three kinds of decisions by governments (and in some degree by other "authorities"—religious, corporate, social, cultural—but ultimately by governments). One choice is whether authorities permit or forbid the right to think, speak, write, and publish unorthodox or unpopular thoughts. Another policy option is whether in each society the poor are systematically deprived of equal opportunity, especially the chance to learn how to process and communicate information. A third question is to what extent people are permitted by public policy to be treated as categories (ethnic outsiders, religious infidels, women, minorities) rather than as individual people with rights, and feelings, of their own. These three overriding fairness issues can be grouped under the labels *human rights, development,* and *cultural identity.*

The Issue of Human Rights

In the long history of human civilization, says Professor Elaine Pagels of Princeton University, the modern idea of *human rights* would have to be listed as "new business." The old business was rights *conferred* or *arrogated,* granted by God if that could be arranged but if necessary seized by force and maintained by claims of superiority on account of birth, rank, race, early arrival, or self-anointed citizenship, and ultimately by force.

It is true that the Code of Hammurabi saved aristocrats from being mutilated by their peers; and a citizen of ancient Rome, if condemned to die, could choose to be beheaded rather than tortured to death in the public arena. But even such rights as these were not inherent; they were handed down from higher authority. Not inalienable rights but the alienation of rights was the rule. Duties, not rights, were the substance of tradition for Hebrew, Chinese, Greek, Hindu, Buddhist, and Christian alike. The right called divine was typically privilege, that is, the right of the few to tell the many what to do and for whom to do it.

In Islam, the third "religion of the book," the Koran comes out for equity in property, fairness toward slaves, and generosity toward the destitute—but again, not as rights of the deprived but as duties of the more fortunate. In Marxism, too, the fourth "religion of the book" (the first to worship a book by an economist), the value of the individual is measured squarely by his or her contribution to the social order. Shortly before the Gorbachev era, a Soviet magazine accused Andrey Sakharov of "pathological individualism."

We may be living, even if we are not yet noticing and articulating, one of those profound shifts in human values that comes along once a millenium. The kernel of human rights was always there in the practice of a few: the civil disobedience that brought Daniel to the lion's den, the claim of the early Christians that Rome governed by transgressing the dictates of the divine, the resentment of oppression that drove the Puritans to America—all precedents for Mahatma Gandhi and Martin Luther King and Nelson Mandela and Lech Walesa and Vaclav Havel, who violated laws inconsistent with the inherent rights of human beings.

Only with the Enlightenment came widespread acceptance of the idea that every person has rights that are not conferred by society but must be recognized, even protected, by society. Today, three crowded centuries and many revolutions later, the content of these rights is codified in the UN's 1948 Universal Declaration of Human Rights and spelled out further in two unratified conventions. These are still debated, and no one's minimum list is anywhere fully realized. Yet we sense that this late-starting, primarily Western idea is on its way to universality. The idea of human rights, the notion that societies should be governed "as if people mattered," is so fundamental, so "natural," so obvious once revealed that it may just be the first revolution to achieve a global reach, the first world-class superstar in the history of political philosophy.

At the traditional core of international human rights are those dealing with security of the person. The heart of this collection of rights is freedom from the excesses of the state. In former Secretary of State Cyrus Vance's words, this means freedom "from governmental violation of the integrity of the person." Such violation includes torture; cruel, inhuman, or degrading treatment or punishment; arbitrary arrest or imprisonment; denial of a fair public trial; and invasion of the home.

In the UN's 1948 declaration and in numerous statements by governments, these "freedoms from" (that is, rights the state can guarantee by simply not mistreating its citizens) are bracketed with a couple of "freedoms to" that can only be assured by the state's affirmative action. These are an entitlement to the fulfillment of basic human needs (now usually defined as socially determined but culturally and geographically various minimums of food, shelter, clothing, education, and employment) and the right not to be discriminated against by reason of being different — a different race, a different belief, a different sex.

It is this fusion of "freedoms from" and "freedoms to" that sustains a human rights movement universal enough in its appeal and its application to qualify as a global political philosophy. It is this set of ideas that has produced an impressive body of international law and has burst forth in the democracy movements of 1989 and the early 1990s. It is best "enforced" by exposure, embarrassment, and the aroused opinion of relevant publics. No government, not even the totalitarian Soviets or military dictators or even the long dug-in South African authorities, seemed able to ignore entirely the ultimate enforcer that the U.S. Declaration of Independence calls "the general opinion of mankind."

The phrase *human rights* focuses our attention on what the individual should be assured by a society committed to democratic values. The phrase *democratic values* focuses our attention on how societies organize to promote and assure human rights. Both prisms are valid; neither excludes the other. The chain reaction of human rights and democratic values is proving to be explosive, and that explosive power is now somewhere near the center of world politics.

The Issue of Development

Despite the undermining of old power systems and the rude questioning of outworn assumptions, the political ice floes that are breaking up run mostly East and West. However, the deep and persistent development issue, the gap between rich and poor (among and within countries) is still frozen solid, with no warming trend in the forecast. What Mahdi Elmandjra, former rector of the University of Rabat, calls the "two-thirds world" of Asia, Africa, and Latin America does not yet have much to celebrate.

For more than forty years, from the earliest postwar relief to the latest "foreign aid," many concerned and intelligent people on five continents have been conducting a worldwide war on poverty, primarily by promoting economic growth. Yet by any measure one might use, there are more poor people in the world now than there were before we started. This is most glaringly true in Africa, where modernization has been the most sluggish, and in Latin America, where so much "development" has latterly been devoted to servicing old loans that by 1990 per capita income had slid back to 1970 levels. Even in Asia, where rates of economic growth are well above rates of population increase, poverty is capricious in resisting the technical fix.

This state of affairs is blameworthy, and there is plenty of blame to go around. Every country, "rich" and "poor," is organized to discriminate (in greater or lesser degree) against its own poor. By and large, the provision of "aid" from abroad has tended to reinforce whatever structures of discrimination already exist. If during forty years of development aid, the gap between the "rich and richest" and the "poor and poorest" has widened, the way assistance was provided has most probably been one cause of that effect. Outsiders, operating with the utmost goodwill, have often widened rather than narrowed the rich-poor gap inside.

Moreover, much "development assistance" has had less to do with warring on poverty than helping client governments build up their war-making capacities. Between 1977 and 1989, for example, the pattern of U.S. aid giving was grotesque: Israel and Egypt got 47 percent of U.S. aid to the world. In the 1980s U.S. aid, most of it military, to Central America rose so fast that it surpassed all U.S. aid to Asia. During the same decade, U.S. military aid rose from one-quarter to one-third of a dwindling total; if "economic support" (a euphemism for aid to reinforce the efforts of military establishments in developing countries) is added, that fraction would have been two-thirds.

This is not to say that foreign aid has been useless. On the contrary, tens of millions of people are doubtless alive today and hundreds of millions are better off because help came from friendly countries and international organizations. Especially in a few places where the input from abroad was massive and the local leadership was strongly motivated (some parts of

Europe; Japan, South Korea, Taiwan, and Singapore; and the modernized enclaves of other newly industrializing countries), economic growth has been hardly short of spectacular. And much of it has been achieved with comparatively fair distribution of the benefits, without destroying the cultural identity of the peoples who are helped.

Worldwide, however, other hundreds of millions have been left out of the development loop. Even where special efforts are put forward to direct outside assistance to the "village level," such inputs do not escape the hydraulic pressure of the social pumps that daily siphon resources from the marginalized poor to the already affluent in the larger cities of every country on earth.

Until recently, neither the leaders and voters in democratic societies nor the leaders of societies governed without consent felt an acute obligation to think hard about, let alone discuss out loud, the incapacity of the world community to meet the basic human needs of everyone born into the human race. We were saved from such fundamental thinking by an ideology; an ideology usually *is* a psychologically satisfying substitute for thinking.

The ideology was "more," as expressed and measured by economic growth. Quantitative growth of goods and services — especially goods and especially for "us" (those we were willing to include in the entitlement) — was seen, if not as an end in itself, at least as the primary means of satisfying human requirements and the pursuit of human happiness.

The underlying (if usually unstated) assumption was that if we could produce more and more wealth, everybody's basic human needs could and would be met sooner or later. Everybody should share in a common achievement ("more"); justice would thus be served, and we would all experience a sense of solidarity by sharing the good life together. As for participation, the drive needed to push economic growth might require management styles and political arrangements that would seem authoritarian in the early stages, but after a time economic growth would make possible the "luxury" of political democracy. Yet it was always likely, and has become the reality in recent years, that people wouldn't want to wait for the wealth to trickle down.

In its era, the growth ethic was an attractive and powerful vision. It pulled into its magnetic field not only the "advanced" societies of Western Europe, North America, Japan, Australia, and New Zealand. It also pulled in the planners and experts and business people and political leaders, the educated elite, of Asia, Africa, and Latin America.

The growth ethic was always flawed in two important ways. First, it promoted economic growth as the central purpose of life and work — a substitute for, not a means toward, the fulfillment of basic human needs and, beyond needs, a variety of human requirements. That was like saying that the purpose of a chemical company is to make chemicals, without reference to why or for whom the chemicals are to be made. Second, economic growth seemed to generate so much dirt, danger, disruption, and dissension. In the industrial world, growing awareness of damage to nature's systems produced the strong public resentments that coalesced in the "greening" of politics and industry.

In the name of growth, an aristocracy of achievement numbering in the millions took over from the older narrower aristocracies of birth and landed wealth. Tens of millions of people were well served, but hundreds of millions were left out. As the gap between rich and poor grew wider — inside countries even more than between countries — the trickle-down assumption that sustained the growth ethic for so long was discredited. As education spread, more and more young people came to understand how and why the outcomes were unfair; they felt excluded from "the system," and started wondering aloud why they were not participating in governing it. The uprisings of 1989 bear witness.

One of the world's authentic wise men, Soedjatmoko of Indonesia, defined the issue with thoughtful eloquence shortly before he died at the close of that watershed year 1989. The "development" problem, he said, is that "the rich in the developing countries have more in common with the rich industrial countries than they have with the fate of their millions of countrymen who continue to live in poverty." A large part of the industrial world and an important part of the developing world "live in an enclosed universe of work and entertainment that has been made possible by the communications revolution, the growth of the media." That universe has "very little to do with the problems of poverty. . . . It's a gap between those who have access to modern knowledge and those who don't, between those who have work and those who don't." He went on to warn of "massive population redistribution across the globe," as people from crowded countries seek access to the comparatively empty spaces (Soviet Asia, Australia, Canada, the United States) as a human right born of overpowering human need. And indeed, migration does keep growing as more and more people try to escape from poverty, military crossfire, and ecological hopelessness.

The core of development thus engages the "domestic affairs" of still sovereign countries. It encompasses not only economic arrangements inside countries, but also issues of social fairness and collisions of cultural identity. It is to this puzzle that a new strategy of development should be addressed.

We will return to this issue, with some suggestions for new international strategies, in Chapter Nine. Meanwhile, while giving one cheer for the bubbling of political choice on every continent, let's reserve two more cheers for what hasn't happened yet: the coming of democracy to other parts of those same continents, including the very large and very hard cases of China, Indonesia, and most of Africa; and the coming of development, or growth with fairness, to much of the developing world. The persistent crisis of inequity and the persistent puzzle of how to make democracy work are destined to become dominant issues among nations and within nations in the 1990s and beyond.

The Issue of Cultural Identity

Fairness is a familiar theme in the politics of modernization. It is far more eruptive when it is combined, as it now is in most societies, with resentments and reactions in the name of cultural identity.

In recent years, TV viewers in the West have been watching in awe and euphoria the breakup of the great ice floes of the Cold War. Some of the larger icebergs thus freed to float in the warmer waters of world politics have started in their turn to break up into smaller icebergs. The result may be almost as dangerous as the frozen antagonism of the two nuclear powers used to be.

What is most striking about that stunning series of events is not, after all, the cascade of conversions to democracy. It is the outbreak of cultural diversity, the boiling over of resentments in the name of almost forgotten or newly discovered cultural traditions.

On American university campuses across the country, the loudest student debates are about cultural fairness—demands by ethnic groups for separate equality, not for integration. Diversity has become the central issue of curricular change, of faculty recruitment, of student protest. What happened in 1991 on the campus of Stanford University stood as a metaphor for a national trend: Stanford had a traditional academic commencement exercise early that summer, followed by six ethnic graduation ceremonies. And this "equal but separate" trend in the United States was but a pale reflection of what was already happening around the world.

Sociologist Elise Boulding speaks of "the 10,000 societies living inside 168 nation states." Even this arresting way of putting it understates a complexity in which so many of the "10,000 societies" are transnational, in no sense "inside" the familiar political lines on our conventional world maps. There are multimillions of Overseas Chinese and disgruntled Russians in republics bordering Russia, millions of Hungarians and Romanians and Turks in other people's countries, millions of Catalonians and Basques and Kurds and Palestinians and Eritreans and Tamils and Ibos and Zulus and Tibetans, millions of Moslems and Hindus and Sikhs living in each other's laps in the Asian subcontinent, and millions of Quebecois and North American Indians who don't acknowledge as their "nation" the "state" in which they find themselves.

With Western Europe moving toward integration, the breakup of Yugoslavia heralded the Balkanization of the Balkans. In France there are said to be more practicing Moslems than practicing Catholics—a slippery statistic that depends too much on what the word *practicing* means. Mass migrations and differential rates of procreation are creating more and more societies where "everybody is a minority."

That has long been the basis for Hawaii's hothouse ethnic politics. It is in California's horoscope, too, and already reality on the University of California's Berkeley campus. Before long, "everybody is a minority" may be the story of political democracy in a couple of dozen U.S. states. This does not, by the way, mean that the metaphor of the melting pot is finally coming true in America. The durably distinctive cultures of this nation of immigrants from elsewhere — Anglo-Saxons, Africans, Scandinavians, Irish, Germans, Italians, Poles, Jews and Arabs from many countries, Chinese, Koreans, Japanese, Mexicans, Central and South Americans, Southeast Asians, Indians, Pakistani, Afghans, and so many others — are, along with a common language, national television, national sports, and nationwide technologies, part of the "American culture." The idea of a multiracial, multicultural society with both a national gist and a global perspective, pioneered in fits and starts by the United States, Canada, and Brazil, may prove to be one of the great social innovations of the twentieth century.

South Africa and black Africa are both searching for new dimensions of racial tolerance and racial sharing. Japan cannot be both a world power and an island of racial purity. India's future governance will have to feature a large measure of decentralized politics else what is now India, already chopped in three parts since independence from the British, could turn out to be several more countries.

What is *cultural identity?* The United Nations declared 1988 to 1997 to be the World Decade for Cultural Development, so there exists a UN definition, lucidly expressed in six languages in a 1987 document of the United Nations Educational, Scientific, and Cultural Organization (UNESCO). Cultural identity is "first and foremost our spontaneous identification as individuals with our linguistic, local, regional and national community and its specific values (ethical, aesthetic, etc.); the manner in which we absorb its history, traditions, customs and lifestyles; our feeling of undergoing, sharing or shaping a common destiny; the way we project ourselves into a collective self in which we continually see our own reflection, enabling us to build up our personalities through education and to express them in work which in turn affects the world in which we live."

The trouble with this definition is not only the glaring omission of any hint that the disparate "communities" had better cooperate with each other. Equally wrongheaded is the implicit assumption that each person is a member of only one culture.

Artist and futurist Magda McHale (Hungarian by birth, educated in Slovakia, living with a British passport in Buffalo, New York) argues that in the modernized world — and even in those societies that overtly resist modernization — nobody's cultural identity remains untouched by external influences. The identity of each of us is "like a collage, made up from fragments of different images, old and new, juxtaposed — creating a wholly new 'picture' that is well-balanced and pleasing," at least to ourselves. Each of us is "a slowly changing kaleidoscope of identities in a changing landscape of influences and circumstances. . . . Human beings constantly reshape their memories about their past, rearrange and reselect events and impressions to fit their present expediencies." The past is only prologue, not a forecast. According to this analysis, any "group culture" is only partly valid; some cultural bonds are largely fictional.

The net impact of modern information technologies on culture seems also to be promoting diversity. Some observers feel that a mass culture is developing; they point to the sameness of blue jeans, soft drinks, fast food, TV programs, and attack weapons around the world. I am equally impressed with the growing diversity: McDonald's and Kentucky Fried Chicken coexist in every world city with a growing variety of ethnic and regional cuisines, including French, Chinese, Mexican, Thai, Italian, and Vietnamese. The world's most information-intensive societies, which happen by no coincidence to be the industrial democracies, are (with one obvious Japanese exception) the most heterogeneous and fragmented in their cultural patterns. The new technologies, especially those (such as the telephone, cable TV, and personal computers) that enlarge the range of individual choice (with whom to converse, what to watch, how and where to work), make it possible to expand the range of individual options and increase the complexity of the collage.

Cultural tradition is often a drag on social change. This is not only true of antique customs, rituals, myths, and mores but also of narrow "modern" cultural mind-sets (the scientist's concept of proof, the economist's devotion to equilibrium), which inhibit the integrative situation-as-a-whole thinking that is the essence of policy leadership. Here is where information technologies (computers, satellites, and telecommunications fused in working systems) are especially influential in creating for millions of people a common awareness of the global environment and common norms such as the idea of inherent human rights.

Information technologies have also made it much easier to maintain communication among the like-minded regardless of geography. Global assertions of community, as in the Jewish diaspora and the Roman Catholic Church, are no longer rare; they are now matched by uncounted transnational advocacy groups and criminal conspiracies. Even leaders of cultural movements, such as the Shi'ite clerics of Iran, that take an antimodern stance, do not hesitate to use computers and audiocassettes and co-opt the TV news services to press their claims for ransom and recognition.

So, far from melding the world's rich diversity of cultures into an undifferentiated lump, the global technologies that show the world as one also help intensify a whirlwind of conflict among tribes, ethnic groups, belief systems, and *nations,* in the original, cultural sense of that word. André Malraux, the author who became France's minister of culture, was no neophyte on information technology. Yet before he died he made a prediction worth pondering: "The twenty-first century is going to be the century of religion."

Cultural diversity is enormously valuable. It is, as U.S. President John F. Kennedy said in 1963, what we should be trying to make the world safe for. It is also troublesome to majority elites and authorities, who respond to separatist ambitions with discrimination, suppression, even extermination. The worldwide pushiness of people for self-determination is just another case of their tendency to get out ahead of their titular leaders.

Cultural diversity is, however, on a collision course with two other values on which the twenty-first century will also have to be built. One of these is the clash of "group rights," asserted by ambitious cultural and racial communities, with the contrasting ideology of "human rights," individual and inalienable. In the latter view a person has rights not because he or she is a member of a nation, a group, a gender, a class, an ethnic category, or even a family but by virtue of having been born into the human race. The other challenge to cultural diversity comes from the outward push of modern science and technology, which makes it possible to think of the world as one — as a global market for goods and services and money, as an integrated biosphere to be monitored and protected, as a global community in which nuclear war and human hunger could conceivably be outlawed.

The strong desire to cleave to a "we" against an unfamiliar and presumably hostile "they" is among the most basic of human instincts. In world politics this urge creates many communities — bonded by ethnicity, religion, and ideology — whose "inward pull" is in tension with the imperatives of the scientific and technological revolutions of our time. These require an "outward push," the coalescence of wider communities to handle functions that cannot be tackled alone by even the most powerful nations or global corporations. Such functions are symbolized by the UN's peacemaking mediators and peacekeeping forces, the World Weather Watch, refugee relief, the control of infectious diseases, the safety systems for civil aviation, cooperation in agricultural research, the environmental cleanup of regional seas, and the concept of a global commons (the oceans, the atmosphere, outer space, and Antarctica).

At every political level the leaders' willingness to coordinate their problem-solving efforts with "foreigners" is constrained by the inherent, centripetal pull of sociocultural roots. People feel empowered by banding together with those they know against those they don't know. The tug of belongingness is what glues together every power structure from family to empire; people cherish their own ways and want to retain whatever freedom of action they can. "Politics gives people something, and somebody, to believe in," says Professor Yehezkel Dror of the Hebrew University in Jerusalem. "There's a desire for solidarity, and danger in solidarity. The leader's task is to be able to tell the difference."

This is the way people preserve their sense of individual worth in the face of the uncertainties of nature and the imper-

sonality of big institutions and big ideas — corporations, governments, rival religious doctrines, economic theories, and abstrac-
tions such as *world order*. This is why each cooperative move outward from neighborhood, village, state, or nation is in tension
with the natural inward pull of community. The burden of proof
is always with those who propose to coordinate the group's policies and practices with outsiders.

The pull of community equally applies to communities that
are joined by bonds other than geography, such as race ("the white
man's burden"), religion (fundamentalist movements, missionary
societies), professional solidarity (Olympic athletes, the international community of scientists), or common economic interest
such as the Organization of Petroleum Exporting Countries
(OPEC) and transnational corporations. It is tempting for the-
orists to see these transnational communities (or at least the ones
they approve of) as networks that undermine and might in time
supplant the geography-based sovereignty of the nation-state.
But communities of consanguinity, specialization, or like-
mindedness are hardly likely to be less narrow in their outlook
or less prone to analyze their interests in we-they terms than vil-
lages or principalities or nation-states that have had to bury a good
many local hatchets to achieve any sense of community at all.

Global village is thus an oxymoron, a contradiction in terms,
not the most creative way to think about a boundary-
transcending system of peaceful change for the next historic
period. Yet neither is reconstruction of the system likely to come
from the fragmentary worldview of nuclear physicists, resource
oligopolists, plant pathologists, religious fanatics, or stars of track
and field.

In sum, the centripetal pull of community, which gives
us all part of our valued identities, is part of reality; so also is
the value of each person as an individual; so also is the need
to shape more inclusive communities and institutions made possible by modern knowledge. What's unique cannot be universal. What's universal threatens and is threatened by what's
unique. So while we celebrate cultural diversity and the political change it is bringing about on four continents, we need to
think hard about reconciling it with both individual human rights
and global human opportunities.

three

THE FALSE ANALOGY
FAILURE OF THE NATION-STATES

The latent causes of faction are . . . sown in the nature of man. Since the causes of faction cannot be removed . . . relief is to be sought in the means of controlling its effects.

—*James Madison,* The Federalist

HUMAN HOPES AND EQUALLY HUMAN FEARS, plus new global technologies and even newer public awareness, have created the need for a new global agenda. That agenda comprises, first of all, the old issues in new guises: the management of change without violence, the settlement of disputes without war. It includes the management of a truly world economy now close to a nervous breakdown for lack of institutions that could make the business climate reasonably predictable. In two-thirds of the world, it requires new approaches to development that take into account not only needs for economic growth but yearnings for a fairer shake and passions for cultural identity.

The agenda now also highlights the management of inherently planetary environments (the deep sea, the ocean floor, Antarctica, the weather, outer space) and the protection of shared physical resources (soils, forests, fisheries, and fresh water) and the global natural cycles such as heat, moisture, and energy.

Collective and collaborative action on this range of issues requires rethinking what we mean by the word *international.* For all of them reach deep into what have been mainly the province of each country's "domestic affairs."

What makes a new international agenda necessary in all these domains is that it is now possible. Three hundred years of scientific discovery and technological innovation made possible the spread of knowledge, and the spread of knowledge is making

31

it possible for people nearly everywhere to make new political choices, choices about how they will be governed, by whom, and for what ends.

For these daunting new choices, the moldering institutions, fraying norms, and antique assumptions of the 1940s are going to require something more than cosmetic surgery. Aristotle observed that physicians learn what health is by studying bodies from which health is absent. We can learn a good deal by diagnosing, in a similarly skeptical spirit, why so many of history's "new world orders" didn't produce durable systems of peaceful change.

The pull of analogy is strong. Americans familiar with the development of the American nation-state tend to assume that a desirable world system can emerge as the next natural step along the lines of the American experience. In the American case, colonies became states, states a confederation, the confederation a federal union. Hence, some thinkers have thought, world order would have to mean the emergence of a super-sovereign power to tax, plan, and manage the world's people and erase the political jurisdictions that divide them from each other.

This idea of governance as control was not confined to Americans. In one form or another, the analogy of the nation-state has attracted most of the philosophers of world order. The architects of the Roman Empire, the Leninist work of revolution, the League of Nations, *Deutschland über alles,* Japan's East Asia co-prosperity sphere, and a hundred schemes for world government have all focused on architecture, structure, and authority and sought arrangements by which either a unitary sovereign or a committee of sovereigns would tax, plan, and manage a passive majority of peoples. Even the United Nations was taken by many to be a way station to world government, though the UN Charter's emphasis on human rights and the self-determination of peoples made it unlikely from the start that any one power or group of powers could long remain in charge.

The natural but mistaken view was that governing the world would be like governing a tribe or nation, only more so. The highest form of order had been the nation-state, and the nation-state had arrogated the power to govern by exercising the leadership of a few on behalf of (meaning, all too often, at the expense of) the many. Wouldn't governance at world level have to do the same? The extrapolation of history said yes.

Fortunately for human destiny, if disturbing to planners and managers, the expectations and ambitions of real-life men and women in this century proved too various for the static "structures of peace," with central authorities in charge of the taxing, the planning, and the managing. The notions about world order "architecture" that came out of World War II could not survive the urgent rush of science and technology, the mass movements of people, the rivalries of great powers, the ambitions of new nations, the awakening of submerged races and classes, and the importunities of plain people who came to consider their universal rights more important than universal order and organized to struggle for the blessings of modernization they felt were already overdue.

There is more to the cautionary moral of this story. Today, national governments themselves — with all their progressive taxes, central banks, and planning authorities — are demonstrably unable to cope. Those of us who presume to prescribe for international governance had better be very careful about using national government as a model.

The evidence is now overwhelming that every national government is beyond its depth. This is certainly true of the industrial democracies, plagued by inflation, unemployment, pollution, urban congestion, insecurity, drug addiction, and youthful crime. It was fatally true of the Soviet system, unable to feed its people and afraid to let them escape. It is true of the "China model," whose leaders used to speak openly about "ten lost years" of cultural revolution and political infighting, and after the Tiananmen crackdown opted to lose more years in fear of that explosive mix, young people and education. It is also true in most developing nations, unable to meet basic human needs or avoid the worst mistakes of the early Industrial Revolution.

Political leaders keep up a brave front, but their incapacity for decision making becomes more and more visible. Central

economic planning, popularized around the world partly by industrial democracies that did not practice it themselves, has now
been jettisoned by its main role models. Transnational companies, weathering the assaults of some sovereignties but welcomed
by others, have adapted their outlooks, policies, and practices
to life in an interdependent world far better than governments
have. A "new proletariat" streams across international frontiers
in enormous numbers. Ethnic and religious rivalries and subnational separatists threaten the integrity of long-established nations. The Soviet Union, Yugoslavia, Sri Lanka, South Africa,
Nigeria, Ethiopia, Jordan, Lebanon, and Canada were examples current and choice in the early 1990s.

Part of the trouble is that the traditional institutions of
national sovereignty are badly designed for the kinds of problems they now face. In the real world, the agenda for action
consists mostly of interdisciplinary, interdepartmental, and in-
terprofessional problems. Yet governments are not organized
that way. Their policy-making tends to be bounded by artificial
frontiers that survive from the history of rational thought (physics,
biology, economics, anthropology), from the history of government activity in simpler times (mining, merchant marine, for-
estry, the regulation of commerce), and from the historic professions (law, medicine, engineering).

In direct consequence, national government agencies in
the main still are not organized to handle problems that cut
across disciplines, specialties, and bureaucracies, to heighten
awareness of the interconnectedness of things, and to encourage
integrative training, staff work, and decision making. Instead,
every government is basically a collection of vertical ministries,
in which recommendations travel "up" and orders travel "down."
But everyone (including the inhabitants of these paper pyramids)
knows that complex decisions that work are mostly the product
of lateral negotiation—what we call committee work and the
Japanese call consensus and the Communists used to call (without really practicing it) collective leadership.

The other part of the trouble is that the kinds of problems national governments now face are so clearly international
in the scope of their causes and the reach of their effects. The

value of money, the swings of inflation and recession, the threats to the ecological systems, the production and distribution of wealth, the security of persons — and the flows of information, now the driving force of all of these — are ineluctably and increasingly international. Governments, even of the nations deemed "greatest" in weaponry or industry or science or land mass or population, find that the forces that drive change and threaten peace are connected more and more tenuously to the levers of power in their chancelleries and their capital cities.

A striking example of both troubles has been painfully apparent for two decades: the inability of the industrial democracies to develop an energy policy that is anything like a match for the problem they face in common. Before 1973, for example, no part of the U.S. government (and no international organization, either) was responsible for worrying about energy. The responsibilities for "oil" and "gas" and "coal" were scattered around as parts of the unstudied subject called "energy," which includes sunshine, cloud formations, ocean movements and temperatures, industrial technology, trade, monetary stability, home insulation, housing patterns, transportation, the mobility of populations, and much more. This obscured the fact that in the end the realm of energy is politics and the reach of energy is global.

Until quite recently, cheap energy powered industrial growth. Air and water were free. The environment was someone else's problem. The more "developed" the economy, the more energy it was thought necessary to use.

So by the early 1970s, per capita energy use in the United States came to be eight times the average for the rest of the world. This was no more regarded as a problem than the doctrine of exponential growth it fueled and reflected. The "problem" was thought to be on the supply side.

Before 1973, everyone knew what the "policy" was: to help make abundant supplies of energy available at the cheapest prices in order to expand economic growth (for any purpose) and raise the productivity of labor. For this, the institutional arrangements were entirely adequate. But they were hopelessly unequipped to deal with or even to think clearly about the crisis that emerged after 1973. In that year, led by the Arabs, most oil exporters clubbed together in a cartel called OPEC to raise prices—four-fold in 1973, eventually twelvefold. The big oil-consuming countries, which had invented cartels, were unable to sustain a posture of outraged innocence.

From the Arab embargo and OPEC's huge price hikes dawned a new consciousness that energy was now going to be expensive; that very large international flows of investment capital would be thereby reversed; that North America, Western Europe, and Japan were all dangerously dependent on Mideast oil; that oil might be a dwindling asset anyway in a generation; that exploiting coal and nuclear fission as the main short-term alternatives to oil raised scary environmental and security problems; that we were wasting energy and not developing fast enough the longer-term alternatives we would soon require.

Known reserves of oil in the mid 1970s were calculated to run out in a few decades. Early or late, massive substitution of other fuels was in the cards. The probable substitutes, in order of appearance, were natural gas, more coal, nuclear fission, oil from tar sands and shale, gases and liquids made from coal, renewable energy (sunlight, wind, tides, volcanoes, trees, plants, human and animal waste, and temperature differences in the tropical ocean), and nuclear fusion. Fusion was rightly judged to be a distant potential. "Renewables" were wrongly judged to be pie in the sky.

Not long after that, people began to worry seriously about urban smog, acid rain, and global warming—and to realize that oil and coal were the main culprits. (One potent symbol was that during the thirty-year payout of its mortgage, the average American household was responsible for the emission of a million pounds of carbon dioxide into the global atmosphere.) The market—rising prices—taught us all how to use less energy: between 1973 and 1986, total U.S. energy remained level, and carbon dioxide emissions actually dropped, while our economy expanded by almost 40 percent.

It has been all too obvious since the mid 1970s that the world could be in deep energy trouble without a clear focus on energy efficiency, a strong push toward renewable energy, and a whole new dimension in worldwide cooperation. Meanwhile, a good deal of energy conservation was put in place in the industrial countries; more oil was discovered; and the softening of world energy prices created the illusion that the problem had gone away. So here we are approaching the mid 1990s. What was going to be the "next fuel," coal, is now seen to have potentially enormous atmospheric effects not understood two decades ago. The nuclear power enthusiasts still haven't done their homework on safety, on radioactive waste disposal, and on nuclear proliferation. The attention of intergovernment committees and investment by governments in alternatives to fossil fuels are still dangerously dilatory and pitifully small. And the industrial democracies are more dependent on oil and on the volatile Middle East than ever.

The policy failure created an opening for leaders of the oil-producing countries too tempting to pass up: a chance for OPEC, prodded by Iraq, once again to set prices and ration supplies. Then in the summer of 1990 Iraq's President Saddam Hussein created another acute crisis by trying to swallow at a gulp its rich little southern neighbor, Kuwait, in an effort to control one-fifth of the world's oil production. The world's reaction to this first post-Cold War crisis is discussed in its security context in Chapter Six. The point here is energy policy failure as an egregious example of the impotence of the world's most "powerful" national governments, which couldn't look far enough into the future to govern with prudence in the present.

The earlier successes of nation-states had resulted from their capacity to assemble power in the hands of the few, to maintain an effective government monopoly on important decisions about governance, and to manage as domestic policy most of what affected the security and prosperity of "their own" people. Their current incapacity is the mirror image of their former capacities: the inability of the few to cope with the expectations of the many, the tendency of the many to take matters into their own hands, and the withering of domestic policy in the mistral of information and influence from "abroad."

Power is, in fact, leaking out of the national orders in three directions at once. (I will take my illustrations from current U.S. experience, not just because I have observed it most closely but because the "power spill" from Washington is, I believe, the precursor of similar trends in other "advanced countries.")

First, the vessel of national government leaks from the bottom, as the many get enough education to insist on participation in decisions affecting their newly understood rights and dimly understood destinies. In the United States the advocacy of openness, student protests, consumer lobbies, public-interest law firms, and the remarkable role of the citizen lobby Common Cause have all drained away from high officials in Washington the capacity to govern without telling people what they are doing. Indeed, the capacity to govern even in the open was weakened: the grass-roots tax revolt, starting with California's famous Proposition 13, lived on in the minds of elected officials long after most people had decided that the paralysis of the national government and the damage to the world standing of the United States and its currency were fates worse than taxes.

Long before the "Reagan revolution" had scuttled the federal government's role as the lead horse in domestic policy-making, hundreds of local communities had decided to adopt their own policies about population, growth, and environmental protection and to use their planning and zoning powers to mold their independent futures. And in the 1980s, the deliberate attrition of the federal government (except the Defense Department) induced a new spirit of leadership by governors as the states took more and more of the initiative on education, welfare, crime, and the environment. In the United States at least, the long history of accretion of power to the center in Washington is now clearly reversed. It was easy to spot similar trends in national governance on every continent, even before developments in Eastern Europe and the Soviet Union provided such extreme examples of people wresting power from their longtime leaders.

Power leaks out of national governments from the sides, too. Nongovernmental enterprise is typically faster on its feet, less constrained by national jurisdiction, and longer range in its planning than are government agencies. This is why trans-national business has been so successful: more than a third of "international trade" is now the internal transactions of inter-national companies. This is also why a growing range of func-tions, even those fully funded by government, are farmed out to nongovernment organizations. Advanced research and de-velopment, legal services to the poor, education and cultural exchanges, the U.S. Postal Service, tax collection (through the withholding device), and weapons production are only a few of many U.S. examples.

Some of the power to make policy has even leaked out to universities, research institutes and laboratories, think tanks and policy analysis groups, which each year provide a growing proportion of the strategic thinking, forecasting, and long-range planning used by governments. This trend is farthest advanced in the United States but is also now strongly in evidence in Western Europe and Japan. Some think tanks outside govern-ment are, of course, mostly or even wholly funded by govern-ment agencies; that is typically true of scientific academies even in the United States. But they "feel private," and the best of them are protected by the prestige of their thinkers from acting as instructed delegates of the governments that pay the bill.

The strategic brainpower focused by nongovernments on longer-range policy questions sometimes means that government officials, harried by daily crisis management and preoccupied with how their actions will look on the evening TV news, be-come the *announcers* of policy that is actually made outside the government.

Finally, national governments leak from the top into in-ternational arrangements, agreements, and agencies. This trend reduces a national government's discretion and control; it can-not act without consulting its partners, and sometimes (as in arms control) its adversaries too. Curiously, this does not neces-sarily, even usually, imply a loss of sovereignty. Sovereignty has never been an absolute claim; it has to be meshed with other claims. Combining sovereignties is often the only way for each partner to exercise its own.

The fruitful lessons of the UN's nearly half a century are found in its bits and pieces, its parcels of functional sizes and shapes wrapped around felt needs and discrete technologies. Some of these are in highly political arenas (UN peacekeeping forces, the codification of human rights, the unremitting pressure on South Africa to end apartheid). But most of the bright spots in international cooperation show up where new technologies make win-win games possible — and restrain the temptation of political leaders to score debating points instead of deciding to do together what can only be done together.

In assessing the record of international cooperation since 1945, it is best to examine not what the architects of world order said they wanted to construct but the institutions they actually built and what committees of instructed government officials and their staffs have been able, in practice, to do.

During the long generation since the United Nations was conceived, we have been building peace in parcels. The parcels are of functional sizes and shapes because they have been designed for the most part to be wrapped around discrete developing technologies. And where they worked, as we shall see in the next chapter, their success was heavily based on information technologies hardly dreamt of in the philosophy of those who were "present at the creation."

President Franklin D. Roosevelt, preoccupied with postwar planning even as he was leading a global war effort, was mindful of the sour comment of John Maynard Keynes that the failure of this century's first try at world order at Versailles was caused by the lack of "concrete ideas . . . for clothing with the flesh of life the commandments which [Woodrow Wilson] had thundered from the White House." That is why Roosevelt early developed the principle (which he practiced but was careful not to preach) that an ultimate pattern of peace must be put together over a period of time out of its major fragments. It was too much, he felt, to build a peace all at once, in a single stroke of diplomacy, from such a ruin as World War II might make of the world.

In the early postwar years, therefore, the planning for a new world was in bits and pieces, reaching into every specialized corner of the cooperating governments. The dynamics of specialist enthusiasm would be used to provide motive power for building the peace; peace would mostly take the form of international organizations for special purposes, for technical as well as political functions. A parallel strategy was adopted by Jean Monnet, who truly wanted a United States of Europe but started what became the European Community with a strictly functional first step, a European Coal-Steel Authority.

Even the central bodies established by the United Nations Charter tackled their assignments in bits and pieces. The Trusteeship Council didn't declare all colonies free on a date certain: rather, its members and staff prodded the few colonial powers to get on with decolonization. The colonial powers, hurried by independence movements in the colonies, came up with a variety of ingenious schemes for carrying out in differing ways at different times the policy of self-determination for more than a billion people that they had already agreed to when they signed the Charter.

Where this rapid political deregulation did produce violence, as in Kashmir, the Congo, Cyprus, and the Middle East, the elite club mandated to keep the general peace — the UN Security Council — has mounted more than two dozen practical peacekeeping operations. An interesting sidelight: the drafters of the Charter were so preoccupied with preventing Hitler-style aggression that they failed to provide for the kinds of peacekeeping in which the United Nations has actually engaged. Generals are sometimes chided for planning to fight some previous war; peacemakers are equally tempted to try to prevent it.

The United Nations' most universal organ, its General Assembly, was conceived as a recording device for common national decisions, with some latent authority to raise revenues. In theory it makes no decisions, only recommendations to its members. Yet it has gone far beyond a forum for ideological debate, to provide the legitimacy for far-reaching actions. These have included the creation of Israel, the independence of the Italian colonies, a new attitude toward population control, a universal (and ultimately effective) condemnation of apartheid in South Africa, treaties on the law of outer space and deliberate environmental change, a global weather-forecasting system, a shift in the political definition of *China,* and an emergency force in the Middle East—the first UN peacekeeping operation and the only one to be authorized by the General Assembly rather than the Security Council.

The General Assembly has also been a windy debating hall that reflects both deep divisions and sometimes surprising consensus in "the general opinion of mankind." It was the venue for a bitter dialogue about fairness (the 1970s debates on a new international economic order). It usefully aired codes of conduct for transnational business. It conducted a continuous conference on disarmament, which was largely ineffective as long as the superpowers thought the nuclear arms race and the global marketing of conventional arms was in their separate yet mutual interests. And it adopted the 1948 Universal Declaration of Human Rights, which creatively fused political rights (centered on the security of the person) with economic and social rights (centered on the meeting of basic human needs).

The General Assembly has also generated a series of agenda-setting world conferences, beginning with Stockholm 1972, in such "cut-across" categories as the human environment, population, food, the status of women (three big conclaves), habitat, water, and deserts and followed by the UN Conference on Science and Technology for Development and the huge 1992 convocation in Río de Janeiro on environment and development described in Chapter Ten. These "town meetings of the world" should not be judged by the carefully compromised "action programs" they adopt just before the delegates have to leave for the airport. They are best seen as generally quite successful efforts to push globally important issues onto the action desks of national governments. In short, they have provided problem-oriented sensitivity training on issues that have been neglected by national governments and international agencies because they were too interdisciplinary, too touchy culturally or politically, or merely important but not urgent enough to engage the attention of political leaders.

It has, of course, been easier to reach international agreements in the relatively "nonpolitical" arenas, where the UN's specialized agencies do their work. Here progress in one field of endeavor need not depend on simultaneous progress in the others. The compelling reason for the creation of each specialized international agency (each adding another fragment to the pluralistic pattern) has been the advance of science and technology. Whenever scientists achieved a breakthrough in what can be done by people for other people, it suddenly seemed outrageous not to be using for human purposes the new powers that new knowledge brought in its train.

Thus each new scientific discovery or technological innovation seems to require the invention of new international arrangements to contain, channel, and control it. A precept of business enterprise is that necessity is the mother of invention. But in the business of international cooperation, an inverse lesson emerges as well: technological invention is the mother of necessity.

There is now a rapidly growing list of functions that only credibly international (in some cases global) organizations or regimes can perform. Many of these "pieces of peace" are working more or less the way they are supposed to work. Wherever that happens, the blood of national governance gets a little thinner. So it's worth asking what's already working and why.

four

THE INTERNATIONAL SYSTEM
WHAT WORKS AND WHY

Many hands make light work.

—*John Heywood,* Proverbs

THE FIRST THING THAT COMES TO MIND when you think of world
affairs may not be love, or even tolerance, humanity, and cooperation. Most of the news about international cooperation is its
absence: distrust, suspicion, controversy, conflict, terrorism,
war. Collaborative success, what's actually working, is seldom
highlighted—on television, in newspapers, in the history books
our children read, or (let's face it) in our personal interest level.
The study and teaching of international relations usually focus
on what's wrong with the picture: riots and their suppression,
military takeovers, drug traffic, corporate raids, financial psy-
choses, arms races, wars and rumors of wars.

Yet if you stand back and look at the whole scene, you
see all kinds of international systems and arrangements that are
working more or less the way they are supposed to work.

• *Weather forecasting.* Beginning with a 1963 initiative of
the Kennedy Administration, the World Meteorological Organization (WMO) developed the World Weather Watch. It was
based on technologies just coming into use in the early 1960s:
picture-taking satellites, communication satellites, remote sensing satellites. These technologies were soon reinforced by supercomputers to help in large-scale modeling and to integrate
global data rapidly enough to be analyzed before the weather
itself had come and gone. They made possible a world weather
system that now daily merges observations from more than a
hundred countries, ships at sea, and balloons, with cloud pictures

and wind and moisture data from satellites. You now depend on that system every day of the year for guesses about what kind of environment the sky will produce during the next few days in your corner of the world.

- *Eradication of infectious diseases.* Diseases such as small-pox and diphtheria have been wiped out and malaria and others have been tackled by combining medical science with a massive worldwide public health information system. Coordinated through the World Health Organization (WHO), the system requires the continuous cooperation of almost every nation on earth. Next on this never-ending agenda: AIDS.

- *International civil aviation.* Planes of all nations use each other's air space, control towers, and airfields with astonishingly few mishaps. There is even an agreement that all communication between planes and controllers will be in a common language, English. The alternative to agreed rules of the game, negotiated through the International Civil Aviation Organization, would be mayhem compounded.

- *Allocation of the frequency spectrum.* The International Telecommunications Union (ITU) periodically assembles an all-nations gathering called "Administrative Radio Conference" to divide up the electromagnetic frequency spectrum among all users and purposes. (A modern wrinkle is to get agreement on a computer program, which then does the actual allocation.) This international public regulation makes possible an international market in radio and TV reception, satellite phone and fax connections. It also makes space probes and modern military communication possible. Without agreement to stay off each other's channels, astronauts would not be able to hear their ground controllers; pictures of international events, from political summits to athletic Olympics, would be so distorted they would not be sent; and you would not be able, on the telephone, to select out of the "noise" the familiar voices of your own family and friends.

- *Globalization of information flows.* Because computerized telecommunication works so well (often better among than within nations), systems have developed for instantaneous worldwide delivery of data twenty-four hours a day for purposes such as currency exchange, commodity markets, airline reservations, and the coverage of news and sports. These systems require a variety of hardware and software — and people trained to work together across political frontiers and time zones and able to react rapidly, accurately, and with a feel for the whole information system in which they are playing a role. The system is made possible in some degree by the deliberate actions of governments; but increasingly, the exchange of real-time information has taken on a life of its own, to which governments can only react after the fact, as in the fluctuating value of money.

• *Agricultural research for development.* A network of agricultural research stations, which started with the International Rice Institute in the Philippines, has made a big difference in farm productivity in developing countries as part of the success known as the "green revolution." The network is funded by a partnership of private foundations (which got the system started), government aid programs, and the World Bank. It is now working hard, through plant and animal breeding and genetic engineering, to follow up with a "gene revolution."

• *UN peacekeeping and peacemaking.* "Soldiers without enemies" have been stationed in many contentious corners of the world, including several parts of the Middle East, Cyprus, the Congo, Yemen, Kashmir, Irian Jaya (West New Guinea), and recently, Somalia, Cambodia, and what used to be Yugoslavia. UN observers and mediators (at times the secretary general himself or his personal representative) have been active in dampening conflict and sometimes settling disputes all around the world. These efforts started with the 1946 peace observation mission in Greece and have featured multiple peacemaking efforts in the Middle East, South America, and Southeast Asia and spot assignments in such places as Chad and the Dominican Republic. The secretary general of the UN played a critical role in defusing the Cuba missile crisis of 1962. More recently, personal representatives of the secretary general have helped to disengage Iran and Iraq from their long-running war in the Persian Gulf and to negotiate the withdrawal of the South Africans from Namibia, the departure of Soviet troops from Afghanistan, the formation of a coalition government in Cambodia, and the release of hostages from Lebanon.

- *Cooperation in outer space.* A generation ago the United Nations, with the agreement of the space powers, declared outer space and "celestial bodies" (including the moon) to be "the common province of mankind." There followed formal treaties on issues such as damage to the Earth and the return of errant astronauts and cosmonauts to their home countries. As space began to fill up, other kinds of international cooperation seemed necessary: banning bombs in orbit, keeping track of launches (which the United Nations does), carrying out agreements on access to data from space vehicles for weather maps and crop forecasting. A 1978 French proposal to provide the UN Secretary General with the capacity to observe military movements by satellite could turn out to be practical politics in the 1990s.

- *The Law of the Sea.* By an extraordinary act of consensus, the world's nations spent fifteen years rewriting ocean law in a book-length treaty, leaving only one loose end. When it all began, in 1967, the General Assembly declared the deep ocean and its seabed to be "the common heritage of mankind." In the years of multilateral negotiation that followed, the world's governments eroded that principle by permitting coastal states to reach out two hundred miles from their shores to take jurisdiction over "exclusive economic zones." For the sizable "hole in the doughnut" that remains, they agreed on a way of regulating the use of the seabed (the United States and a few other nations dissented on this one article). By unanimous consent, the governments of the world also provided for stronger environmental protection and for military and scientific use of the open ocean and of the important narrow places in the world's seas. The treaty is the most complex single document ever negotiated among nations; it even contains mathematical formulas, and it required the collaborative use of computer modeling. Despite the absence of a U.S. signature because of the seabed issue, the White House later declared that all the rest of the long treaty text had become "customary law."

- *The High Commissioner for Refugees (UNHCR).* This useful office (a single individual, not a committee of national delegates) was set up by the General Assembly as a way of recognizing a universal responsibility toward refugees and displaced

persons for whom new homes had still to be found after World
War II. Soon after the problem was solved for most of the displaced Europeans, refugee problems appeared on other continents. Today, with a very different ethnic mix of peoples, there
are more international refugees than there were forty years
ago—more than twice as many if people displaced inside their
own countries are counted. The UNHCR has done an ener-
getic and imaginative job as catalyst and coordinator, stimulating
actions that have saved many millions of people from international homelessness and many from disease and death. The
Nobel Peace Prize has twice been awarded to the high commissioner's office. In the 1980s, the office was less enterprising, but
new leadership in the early 1990s revived its reputation and expanded its role. The movement across nations of people in distress is now a permanent feature of the international landscape,
and UNHCR is needed more than ever before as a coordinat-
ing conscience of the world community.

• *The Ozone Treaty.* In 1974 two chemists first guessed
that human activities might be eroding the ozone shield that
protects humanity from receiving too much ultraviolet radiation from the sun. In 1987, only thirteen years later, fifty nations agreed by treaty to slow down the use of such ozone eaters
as chlorofluorocarbons (CFCs). The issues, says U.S. diplomat
Richard Benedick, were "staggeringly complex," the science still
speculative, the evidence of damage missing. Yet this remarkable achievement was possible because there was an international scientific consensus, information on the subject flowed
freely, the fact-finding process pulled in the nongovernments
(notably the industries using CFCs), and an active international
gadfly—the UN Environment Program (UNEP)—helped push
governments to set aside their conflicts on other matters and
cooperate on this one. The treaty itself was creative: it set emission targets but left to the market the task of reducing CFCs.
For reasons of fairness, those targets were tougher on the richer
countries than on the poorer ones and were left open for future
revision in a flexible and dynamic process. In the first five years
after 1987, most countries agreed to tighten the treaty restraints
on CFC emissions.

• *The Antarctic Treaty.* Every nation need not be in on everything. Twelve countries agreed in 1959 to suspend the pie-shaped national claims many of them had made to parts of Antarctica and to open up the entire continent for scientific research. They also proscribed any military activity, nuclear tests, or disposal of nuclear wastes in this frozen no-man's-land. Since 1959, six more countries have acceded to the treaty, and one more has become a full treaty partner. The resulting cooperation has produced some very important scientific work. For example, core samples of ancient ice provide a historical perspective that has been valuable both to space explorers and to the analysis of the prospect for global warming. The treaty process is unusual in that there is no international staff; all the political and administrative business is conducted at periodic meetings hosted by the member countries in turn. When the treaty was reviewed in 1991, all the signers stayed hitched and even added a fifty-year ban on digging for minerals.

These dozen examples are, I believe, clear cases of successful worldwide cooperation on global problems and opportunities, that is, clear cases of what works. The list omits arms control. As long as the Cold War was on, the outcomes of arms talks in and out of the United Nations were wholly disproportionate to the inputs of time and effort. The list is in any case far from exhaustive. It does not mention the extraordinary global contributions of the UN Children's Fund, or the spotty effectiveness of the World Bank and the rest of the UN's unfinished war on poverty. It omits the successes (albeit not without controversy) of transnational business, which have been making the world much more international than national governments find comfortable. It also omits the intriguing phenomenon of global media events such as Live-Aid, the Concert for Bangladesh, and "We Are the World."

Nor does the select list of one dozen include cases where the machinery creaked but many people worked hard to organize for tolerance, humanity, compassion, and cooperation. "More good may have been accomplished by people acting in the spirit of UNESCO than by the formal projects under its

approved program," says John Fobes, an American who served
as UNESCO's deputy director general. Besides, in many kinds
of international cooperation it is notably hard to measure "success," as in teacher training, or the promotion of human rights,
or the recapture and recording of cultural histories.

A few regional organizations have also chalked up some
outstanding successes. The North Atlantic Alliance certainly did
successfully the two main things it was invented to do: contain
Soviet military strength and provide a framework of close cooperation within which Germany could become resurgent without
reviving old European fears and rivalries. Since the late 1960s,
NATO has also been a working political caucus on how to make
peace with the Soviets.

The European Community, after two decades of iden-
tity crisis, finally got its act together and built a powerful common market. Thirty-four years after the Treaty of Rome, the
in-group of twelve countries drove toward much closer Western
integration in the draft Treaty of Maastricht (1991), agreeing
to establish a common currency, a device for harmonizing foreign policies, a European defense force, and a new range of social laws — and giving the directly elected European Parliament
a new set of teeth: the right to veto some executive actions. Having deepened their mutual undertakings, they then could deal
with the community's widening — and only just in time. By then
Scandinavians, "neutrals," East Europeans, and spinoffs from
Yugoslavia and the former Soviet Union were all clamoring at
its gates.

Outside Western Europe, only in one corner of Asia has
a geography-based organization (the Association of Southeast
Asian Nations, or ASEAN) shown a spark of life. Those in
Eastern Europe, Latin America, Africa, South Asia, and the
Arab League in the Mideast have never become major players
in international affairs. Some have been notably overstaffed and
underemployed; one, the Communists' Council for Mutual Economic Assistance, disappeared altogether. By contrast, networks
that link like-minded people wherever located, such as the oil
cartel, drug traffickers, the international community of scientists, Islamic fundamentalists, and the rich nations' club called
OECD (the Organization for Economic Cooperation and De-

velopment) have proved more cohesive, more durable, and more influential in world affairs.

One spectacular regional success has been the agreement to clean up the Mediterranean Sea. That once lovely body of water became so polluted during the postwar years that many thought its marine life was doomed and its appeal to tourists and residents would be greatly diminished. Goaded by UNEP, sixteen very diverse states bordering the Mediterranean, several of them officially at war with each other, agreed in 1976 to work out a plan of action to save its waters. In a decade and a half, parts of the Mediterranean began to look blue again.

Why does international cooperation work — when it does? Ten common threads run through the preceding dozen success stories, ten reasons why what works *works*. Taken together, they are the priceless ingredients for success in international cooperation.

1.   *There is a consensus on desired outcomes.* People who disagree on almost everything else can agree that smallpox is a threat to all, more accurate weather forecasts would be useful, enclosed seas should be cleaned up, civil aircraft should not collide, somebody should help refugees. For most of this century there has been no comparable consensus about trade or money or disarmament.

2.   *No one loses.* Each of the dozen successes turned out (sometimes after years of national head scratching and international negotiation) to be a win-win game. The Ozone Treaty would not have been so regarded if developing countries had not been given a break on how fast CFC emissions had to be scaled down. Every country washed by the Mediterranean would win if that enclosed sea, polluted in common, could be cleaned up in common. It is in each nation's interest to have channels of telecommunication unencumbered by the electronic transmissions of others. We did not begin to see real progress on disarmament (the 1989 "INF treaty" to eliminate a whole class of intermediate-range nuclear forces) until both the Soviet Union and the NATO allies concluded that their security would actually be enhanced by getting rid of dangerous but unusable weapons.

3. *Sovereignty is pooled.* Whenever a nation cannot act effectively without combining its resources, imagination, and technology with those of other nations, cooperation does not mean *giving up* independence of action but *pooling* it, that is, using their sovereign rights together to avoid losing them separately.

4. *Cooperation is stimulated by "a cocktail of fear and hope."* Fear alone produces irrational, sometimes aggressive, behavior. Hope alone produces good-hearted but unrealistic advocacy. Reality-based fear and hope, combined, seem to provide the motivation to cooperate. In the case of the Ozone Treaty, even a proven threat (let alone a speculative one) to the ozone layer by itself would have produced much scientific doomsaying and no political action. But once the major companies responsible for the CFC emissions got the message, they worked hard on alternatives. By decision time, Du Pont and others were pretty sure their research teams had found viable substitutes for CFCs, so they worked with rather than against the diplomats trying to negotiate a treaty.

5. *Individuals make things happen.* In the early stages of each of the success stories, a crucial role was played by a few key individuals who acted (whatever payroll they were on) as international people in leading, insisting, inspiring, sharing knowledge, and generating a climate of trust that brushed past the distrust still prevailing in other domains. On the World Weather Watch these were mostly scientific statesmen; on small-pox eradication, public health doctors; on the Law of the Sea, visionary lawyers including key players from the developing world; on the frequency spectrum, a few telecommunications experts who saw a connected world that cooperation could create and conflict could destroy; on outer space cooperation, lawyers and later some of the space travelers themselves with their metaphors about an undivided Earth.

6. *Modern information technologies are of the essence.* Needs for complex data processing and rapid, reliable communication seem to be common to the success stories in international cooperation. This suggests an interesting idea: the marriage of computers and electronic telecommunications is actually driving the world toward larger systems of cooperation. For example, the

new systems of measurement, modeling, and mathematics these technologies make possible have generated an "ecumenical movement" among the earth sciences, enabling experts to think seriously and systematically about very large environmental issues in the framework of a global commons.

7. *Nongovernments play a key role.* The recent story of international cooperation is replete with the contributions of scientific academies, research institutes, women's groups, international companies, and "experts" who don't feel the need to act as instructed representatives of their governments. Often the need for international regulation occurs first to people outside governments — scientists, for example, working on plant and animal genetics, atmospheric chemistry, biological warfare, and polar research. Most of the Declaration on the Human Environment, agreed to by governments at the Stockholm conference in 1972, was written in the summer of 1971 by a task force of people outside government, convened by the nongovernmental Aspen Institute, working closely with Maurice Strong, the secretary general of the official conference. Much of the real negotiation about concepts and language for the Law of the Sea Treaty, especially in its later phases, occurred between the official sessions at meetings of the Law of the Sea Institute, an international nongovernmental think tank based in Honolulu.

8. *Flexible, uncentralized systems work best.* The more complicated the task and the more diverse the players, the more necessary it is to spread the work around so that many kinds of people are improvising on an agreed sense of direction. The clearest case is, of course, the global flow of information about commodities, financial instruments, and money. Indeed, the essence of a market system is that decisions are uncentralized but compared and aggregated very rapidly in a central "marketplace." With modern information technologies, this no longer has to be a *place* but simply the simultaneous availability of the same information in thousands of dispersed computers. Even in activities that are inherently government functions, the complexities are best uncentralized. The World Weather Watch works well partly because, within standards and definitions agreed to by governments in WMO, the actual data gathering,

analysis, modeling, and forecasting is done not by an international bureaucracy but by national weather services and experts scattered around the world in atmospheric research laboratories and university faculties. Technical coordination and large computer capacity are supplied by three major system nodes in Russia, the United States, and Australia.

9. *Educated local talent is essential.* Especially where developing countries have major roles to play, cooperation works best when they use their own talent to do their part. The need to participate in global systems has, in fact, pushed developing countries to develop their own experts and system managers — and to secure aid from the technologically advanced countries in doing so. This is notably true in such fields as atmospheric research, epidemiology and public health administration, remote sensing from outer space, air traffic control, telecommunications, news services, agricultural research, biotechnology, and (for coastal and island states) the management of marine resources.

10. *The United States is a key player.* In all the dozen success stories, American initiative, research, resources, and entrepreneurial bias have been important factors. The other side of the same story is illustrated by the record of the 1980s: when the United States is "dead in the water," the international system is likely to be becalmed as well.

The world of the future will be different: most of the history reviewed here started in an era when the United States was the only nation that could take large initiatives requiring major new resources and an ambitious worldview. In the 1990s and beyond, global cooperative projects already depend partly on initiative and leadership from Europe and Japan as well. Important leadership roles will also be opening up for middle powers such as China, Canada, Brazil, India, Australia, and Nigeria. As systems for international cooperation grow out of their swaddling clothes, we can also look more and more to international public executives to play the kind of catalytic and energizing role that Secretary General Pérez de Cuéllar recently played in political and military issues and Maurice Strong and Mustafa Tolba, the first two executive directors of UNEP, played in threats to the global environment.

But having said all that, my guess is that in the matter of international leadership the past is partly prologue. The United States is still the only country with a global reach in every domain: political, military, economic, educational, cultural. Even among more equal partners, U.S. governments and non-governments may have to provide more than their share of the initiative to reshape the international system, even if the financial support and human enterprise for new forms of cooperation can now be more widely shared. We will return, in Chapter Eleven, to the puzzlement of leadership in what is bound to be a nobody-in-charge world system.

five

THE MANAGEMENT OF PEACE
Guidelines for the "Third Try"

The core function of governance is that of community learning at the world level; of organizing and facilitating that learning. After all, the learning capacity of a society determines its ability for sustained progress and development.

—Knut Hammarskjöld, 1990

A KNOWLEDGE SOCIETY is a learning society. We learned much about what to do and what not to do from the first two tries at world order, the League of Nations following World War I and the United Nations and other organizations that grew out of World War II. Now, at this open moment in world history, we have a chance to apply these learnings to the third try — without having the third war first.

As a part of our effort to "rethink international governance," MIT Professor Lincoln Bloomfield and I decided to set down in a systematic way some guidelines for what was not then being called a new world order. Were there basic flaws in the way the United Nations was conceived as the charter was written between 1943 and 1945? Are there some widely accepted norms — standards of civilized behavior — in which a "third try" could take root? Will new kinds of organizations be needed to carry a new kind of "try" into action?

The founders of the League of Nations and the United Nations — and most of the other advocates of governing institutions for One World — shared some bedrock ideas. Their "world order" would be peopled with universal organizations that would administer and, if possible, enforce universal rights and duties.

They would reflect a near-universal political will to band together to restrain and discipline outlaws and aggressors (in the image of Kaiser Wilhelm and Adolf Hitler). They would operate by the rule of law and would make decisions through a parliamentary democracy in which sovereign nations would be substituted for sovereign individuals.

These ideas have carried us part of the way toward a global system of peaceful change. Perhaps 10 percent of the way. They could not carry us further because the governance of a world community presupposes a world community. And as things turned out, the kinds of institutions that emerged from these noble conceptions didn't fit the kinds of world community that have begun to emerge in the last decades of this century. Why? The ideas were universal and the institutions unitary; but the emerging real-world community was pluralistic.

For the League of Nations to have succeeded would have required a club of the like-minded, determined to dominate. Even at its start in 1919 and 1920, the league did not attract a still isolationist United States. The members that did join the club soon found they had neither the power nor the will to deal with a growing band of outlaws: first, the Japanese militarists in Manchuria, then the Italian fascists in Ethiopia, then the German Nazis, with two-front ambitions in Europe. The doctrines of "peace" were frozen in a pattern of nonchange, nonmaneuver, nonnegotiation, and nonresistance — until resistance became the only remaining option.

In those days, what was to become a global fairness revolution was still kept dormant by colonial rule, economic dictation, and naval superiority. Meanwhile, the like-minded made some progress in creating a common language for talking about the weather, tracking communicable disease, and projecting Western-style labor standards. But most of humanity was effectively left outside the pale of the like-minded. Latin America, black Africa and Arab Africa, and continental Asia were quiescently dependent. This was true whether they were formally colonies, or protectorates like China and Siam and Ethiopia and most of the Western Hemisphere, or parts of a commonwealth still meriting the adjective British. As for the Soviet Union, it was still struggling to be born in Lenin's mold, preoccupied (despite Marxism's universal rhetoric) with infighting among the founding revolutionaries and the reality of a profound internal revolution.

Then the whole League of Nations structure was washed away in the tidal wave of a war that could not yet be technologically worldwide but managed to be effectively global.

The UN: Flawed Assumptions

The United Nations was what the stop-Hitler coalition called itself during World War II, the Allies preoccupied for the time being more by what they were fighting against than what they were fighting for. Those United Nations then gathered at San Francisco in 1945 to organize the postwar peace as well. They started with premises similar to the league's: a universal order enforced by universal institutions, reflecting universal rights and duties, demonstrating a universal will to band together against outlaws, operating by legalistic rules and pseudoparliamentary practice.

Those premises biased the outcome toward a status quo machine. Analyzing the "midlife crisis" of the postwar grand design, Knut Hammarskjöld (longtime head of the International Air Transport Association) observed that political leaders are often convinced "that once a political objective . . . is achieved . . . time will stand still, the world will not further evolve."

The world after 1945, however, was much more fluid, peace more obviously a function of change. Radical and universal changes were embedded in the UN Charter itself: self-determination of nations, human rights for everyone. Members of the war-winning coalition, split by the Cold War, promptly set about to exploit the rising political ambitions and rising economic expectations in the four continents in the service of their new rivalry. The postwar "architecture" of world order just wasn't built for the earthquakes that soon shook the UN's still fragile processes. Indeed, several of its founding assumptions were fundamentally flawed: so rooted in Western metaphors that they could not and did not survive once the stage was the whole world.

A first premise of the United Nations' founders was that the major powers, having won the war, could and would quash aggression by collective security. The prescription was right for dealing with the war that had just happened. But the global Cold War and the many regional conflicts that ensued were equally *hors de catégorie* to the United Nations Charter. Until the Iraq crisis of 1990, the typical reaction of the United Nations Security Council when a regional conflict was brought before it was (a) to avoid declaring anyone the aggressor, (b) to advise the combatants to stop fighting and talk, and (c) in some cases, to arrange for peacekeeping forces and third-party mediators, in other words, to use modes of interventions *not* explicitly provided for in the Charter. The main exception was the 1950 decision to oppose aggression in Korea, and that was only possible because the Soviet UN delegation was boycotting the Security Council that week on an unrelated issue and could not change its stance quickly enough to enter the council chamber and object.

Major power rivalries (the arms race between the United States and the Soviet Union, the NATO-Warsaw Pact standoff) and even major regional conflicts such as the decade-long Vietnam War and the eight-year war between Iran and Iraq were mostly ignored in the Security Council's agenda, by consent or insistence of those primarily involved. Lesser conflicts were either discussed without action (as happened for years on Vietnamese forces in Cambodia) or with automatic prejudgment (as when Israel or South Africa was involved). The nations that could do something influential about ending them were frequently not so inclined, and the rest of the world, like witnesses to murder on a city street, preferred not to get involved.

In a nuclear world we are probably lucky that universal collective security — an advance commitment by all to be involved in every breach of the peace — did not turn out to be a realistic doctrine. What is already overdue is the invention of permanent workable machinery for international peacekeeping and peaceful settlement.

A second flawed assumption of the UN's founders was that familiar legislative-type institutions could be reincarnated

at the intergovernmental level. Dean Rusk called this "parliamentary diplomacy"; it was partly his writing on this subject that established him as the thoughtful analyst of international relations
President-elect John F. Kennedy (who had never met Rusk) was
looking for as secretary of state after the election of 1960.

In a genuine legislature, clashing interests are fought out
bloodlessly, and some form of majority decides for all. A committee of sovereign states does not act that way.

When the Soviets defaulted on their assessed United Nations dues in the 1960s, the United States thought that a parliamentary body, even an international one, could be depended
upon to defend its own power to tax a member state. As it happened, I was then the person in the State Department responsible for making that judgment. I guessed wrong. Most members of the General Assembly scampered away from dunning
a superpower for overdue bills. And later, after a couple of turns
of the political wheel in Washington, D.C., the United States
also defaulted with impunity on the Charter obligation to pay
its dues — an obligation that supposedly has the force of U.S.
law under the treaty power of our Constitution.

It is interesting that whenever there is serious business
to be done, even in controversial domains, the members of the
United Nations tend to agree from the start to act by consensus.
This has been true, for example, of the Treaty on Principles
Governing the Activities of States in the Exploration and Use
of Outer Space, Including the Moon and Other Celestial Bodies; the negotiations on the Law of the Sea (up to the final vote);
and many actions by technical intergovernmental agencies.

This is even true, on occasion, of the Security Council: if
action is to be taken, the delegates of the five "veto" powers keep
talking until they arrive at an agreement. If agreement is reached,
a vote formalizes what everyone already knows. If no agreement
is possible, a vote is sometimes avoided. Voting is a good way
to take a snapshot of a disagreement; but voting is not very useful in bonding sovereign peoples to do something together.

A third notion of the UN's founders underlay their decisions about economic and monetary management, including the
Bretton Woods agreement setting up the World Bank and the

International Monetary Fund. It was to treat equilibrium as a goal in itself. The economist's "equilibrium model," a Newtonian analogy to the idea of stasis in the physical sciences, assumed that market turbulence will — and should — come to rest in a natural state of balance between or among opposing forces of demand and supply. But much of the international economic agenda of the past forty-odd years has turned on issues of equity, not balance.

Most of the leaders of the world's disadvantaged majority did not want stasis; they wanted dynamic change toward a fairer world. They didn't even want freedom of trade, of money exchange, of the seas, or of communication. They correctly divined that the "free" environments work out most profitably for the technologically strong — that is, for the countries and companies most able to add value to and thus produce wealth from these systems and resources. As other industrial countries have encroached on United States domestic and foreign markets, in autos, steel, grains, transistor electronics, computer chips, and color television, many Americans have also been persuaded that fair trade might be less damaging than uninhibited freedom.

A fourth assumption of those who created the present international system was that nation-states would be the only really important actors on the international political stage. Since the founders of the postwar world were all leaders in their own national governments, this was a natural professional deformation. But it led to a major distortion: the effort to treat issues among sovereign states, in committees of instructed representatives, as though domestic and international questions could be clearly differentiated from each other. Increasingly, of course, they cannot. The content of most international affairs is now efforts by countries to influence each others' "domestic" affairs. That is what negotiations on arms control, trade, overseas development assistance, radio frequency allocation, air traffic control, and so on, are all about.

The story of leakage through porous national frontiers is also the story of the growing influence of nongovernmental movements and organizations, global corporations, commodity cartels, and transnational organizations of all kinds, including, at the malign extreme, international crime, drug traffic, and networked terrorism. Future international cooperation will have to work far more explicitly with nongovernmental bodies, which compared with all but the largest states often dispose of more power, act with more flexibility, and are clearer (because more focused) in their purposes.

Fifth, the United Nations system was devised by Westerners nurtured in a tradition of optimism about the inevitability of progress and the perfectibility of man. The inference was that international organizations should be considered way stations to supranational government.

In 1948 the General Assembly overwhelmingly endorsed a United States plan to turn over to an international authority the nuclear facilities then exclusively in American hands. The enterprise was to be administered without a great power veto. The Soviet Union rebuffed the offer, while moving to develop its own nuclear weapons. That spared the United States Senate from having to decide whether the American people really wanted to divest themselves of the bomb that had just shortened the war with Japan.

For a time, discussion focused on proposals for limited world government, such as the Clark-Sohn plan, which called for enough central power to enforce a process of disarmament but home rule for other functions. Such ideas were discussed among intellectuals but were never taken seriously by governments; they would have required far more consensus and sense of community than has existed in the postwar decades. And they were always vulnerable to fears that a world government might itself become oppressive. One key question always seemed unanswerable: "If I don't like the world government, or it doesn't like me, where do I go then?"

International Norms and Standards

The object of the third try is not "world order." That has too often seemed to mean defense of the status quo by those who are temporarily the most powerful. The object of this new try is to ensure peaceful change in a world made safe for diversity.

Nobody is going to be in general charge. Just as the American colonists were fed up with autocratic kings, the world's people (when they get a chance to express themselves) seem to have had enough of czars, dictators, commissars, bosses, and privileged authorities of many kinds. The problem, then, is not to build structures of authority and privilege (which usually go together) designed to be rest stops on the highway to world government. The problem is to put in place processes appropriate to the management of pluralism.

International governance need not be in conflict with national sovereignty. Our search is for ways in which nations and their citizens can pool their collective learnings in win-win systems for shared purposes without homogenizing their cultural identities.

Some shared purposes — common norms and standards — are already widely accepted:

- Territorial integrity
- The inviolability of diplomatic missions (the violations are dramatic because they are rare)
- The nonuse and nonproliferation of nuclear weapons
- The immunity of civilian aircraft and ships (a few brutal attacks and tragic accidents have served to strengthen norms against hijacking and firing on innocent craft)
- An obligation to help refugees
- The inadmissibility of colonial rule
- The unacceptability of overt and officially sanctioned racial discrimination
- The undeniable equality of women
- The full menu of human rights described in the 1948 Universal Declaration of Human Rights and reinforced in the Helsinki Final Act of 1975

Wide acceptance in principle isn't universal compliance in practice, of course; but it's a step in that direction.

Most of the world's people, and even their governments, might now agree on some even further-reaching norms. In the third try, the problem is how to make them operational.

- A third world war is wholly impermissible, and nuclear weapons need to be made irrelevant to political conflict.
- Local conflicts should be insulated from outside involvement whenever possible to prevent their escalation. (However, clear cases of aggression, such as Iraq's takeover of Kuwait, will still engage the obligation of all members of the United Nations—and of the UN Security Council—"to take effective collective measures . . . for the suppression of acts of aggression.")
- The lives of innocent bystanders should not be used as political bludgeons.
- The quality of human life worldwide must be protected from catastrophic degradation of the atmosphere and the biosphere.
- No child in the world should go to bed hungry.

A clear distinction should be made between two tiers of international cooperation: the more centralized public policy decisions with universal participation, where debate is encouraged and agreement is reached on standards, norms, goals, and codes of ethics; and the more operational processes, where many different enterprises and authorities can do their own thing, acting within the framework of the agreed upon standards and norms but without the need for centralized decision making, heavy regulatory regimes, or large international bureaucracies. In some cases, especially in the world economy, the operational level will be a market system.

(This distinction between the collective establishment of norms and standards and the dispersed bargaining, sharing, and clearing is poorly described by the much misused word *decentralization*. In a decentralized system the control is still in a central office; it is the center that decides how partial controls will be exercised by subordinate authorities, and it keeps track of them through a central accounting system. This is why I use the word *uncentralized* for a system in which many "flowers" are encouraged to bloom, many "points of light" stimulated to shine. Learning works from the bottom up.)

A review of what works in today's world drives us to belated recognition of the crucial role played by major nongovernments, including corporations whose decisions affect people's lives and fortunes, professional associations whose expertise educates and informs, religious movements with their unique capacities for love or hate, the distinctively international scientific community, and advocacy groups that mobilize people for behavioral change. The main nongovernments (not necessarily "accredited nongovernment organizations" but those that are major actors in real international relations) need to be brought into the planning and decision making in ways that reflect their real-world roles.

Some global issues require actions by millions of individuals, families, and small groups. There will be an important role for the mass media in spreading the word and developing wide accord as a basis for political cooperation.

The experience of the postwar years suggests that when governments want to record their disagreements ("divide the house," as Western parliamentarians say), they resort to voting. When they have to work together to make something different happen, they increasingly decide from the outset to act by consensus. In the many cultures accustomed to practicing decision making by consensus, the word *consensus* does not mean "unanimity." It means something more like "the acquiescence of those who care (about the particular decision), supported by the apathy of those who do not."

Almost none of the "functions of the future" discussed next requires all the world's people or all nations' governments to be involved. In practice if not in theory, most international cooperation, even inside organizations with universal membership, involves only communities of the concerned, what Lincoln Bloomfield was the first to call "coalitions of the willing." That is as it should be. Those who can and will act must take whatever action is to be taken. If a collective task is to be accomplished, it cannot be subject to acquiescence by the least relevant or least cooperative member of the world community or by the most apathetic one. In matters affecting the globe we all share, however, those who do act have an inescapable obligation to explain what they are doing together and why. So we also need open consultative forums where stakeholders not operationally engaged can nevertheless be heard.

The "Extranational" Principle

Some of the ideas in the rest of this book for reorganizing and reenergizing the international system can be accommodated in organizations and processes that already exist. Essentially, these are clubs of sovereign governments, universal or regional or functional, served by "international civil servants" appointed by the governments acting as a group, sometimes drawing in "experts" acting in their personal capacities, and funded partly by assessments that vary according to the governments' ability to pay and partly by "voluntary funds" to which only some of the club members contribute.

This description is generic; it describes the United Nations and its specialized agencies, the World Bank group of agencies, the world's main regional alliances, and dozens of ad hoc intergovernment clubs established for technical cooperation in matters ranging from water rights to copyrights. There are exceptions to this general pattern: the International Labor Organization, for example, makes room at its committee table for people representing labor unions and business associations. Refugee issues are entrusted not to a committee but to the high commissioner; this adds a degree of flexibility, but in practice the government delegates appointed to "advise" the High Commissioner's Office pull pretty hard on its budgetary purse strings and thus act almost like a board of directors. The Antarctic Treaty, as noted, never established an international secretariat. By and large, however, the postwar pattern, from 1945 until today, is the committee-of-sovereigns-with-a-staff.

In the 1990s and beyond, what needs to be done among countries is not mostly committee work by instructed representatives of governments. The UN pattern is too often a formula for sluggish response and inefficient follow-through and sometimes a prescription for paralysis. This is especially true when committees of sovereigns that are set up to get something practical done are used instead as mini–general assemblies, with technical experts arguing about the future of the Palestinians or South Africa or Cambodia or other issues they cannot do anything about.

We have seen that the UN pattern can often be made to work if the conditions are right. But each of the world-scale functions of the future — among them watching and averting international conflict, mobilizing peacekeeping forces and peacemaking teams, regulating trade and investment and money, deterring terrorism and international crime, promoting scientific research, channelling technological innovation toward human needs and purposes, educating and training people to be both specialists and integrative thinkers, helping the world's poor "get rich by brainwork," assuring fairness and protecting human rights, and regulating the exploration and use of the global commons — requires an international capacity to act and thus more flexible and dynamic systems than we yet have in place.

In each of these fields we will need institutions at both tiers: norm setting and execution. For norm setting, there is no getting away from committee work. But the need is urgent for state-of-the-art equipment for monitoring and analysis and the most imaginative and sensitive people to help committees arrive at viable norms and set well-thought-through targets and standards on which governments and nongovernments can and will act in their own spheres and jurisdictions. In the future, moreover, some of the committees will need to include people not only from national governments but from international nongovernments, which have to be consulted about the international norms and standards if they are expected to be guided by them.

Beyond the norm-setting committee work, when it comes to getting things done, we can no longer depend on heavy permanent international staffs responsible to large councils of government delegates posturing with an eye to how they will look back home. What is the alternative? In the 1970s, in the midst of the worldwide debate about proposals for a "New International Economic Order," I assembled under the nongovernmental Aspen Institute an international group to consider the elements of a rich-poor "bargain" among the nations. Our consensus report was then ahead of its time, but perhaps it is not so today. It seemed then, and it still seems, that there is need for a new kind of international institution, better able than committees of sovereigns to organize executive action but without the dangers to

fairness and human rights of entrusting international functions
to a single general-purpose world authority.

It was the French member of that earlier group, Georges
Berthoin, who first named this intermediate social invention the
extranational institution. Here in updated paraphrase is how we
described it, with European experience as the nearest analogy,
in our 1975 report entitled *The Planetary Bargain:*

> The extranational principle is illustrated by the way
> the European Community is supposed to work.
> Reaching for the supranational star of Jean Mon-
> net, the Europeans fell short. But in falling short,
> they invented something new: an executive com-
> mission operating at the political level, which in-
> ternationalizes much of the initiative for action with-
> out derogating from the ultimate power of the
> governments who have, in effect, loaned their sov-
> ereignty to the Commission for specified purposes.
>
> The European Commissioners are not "in-
> ternational civil servants." They are, for the most
> part, former ministers, accustomed to operating at
> the "cabinet level." They are appointed for a term
> of five years by their own governments, but are not
> removable by their own governments — only by all
> governments acting by unanimity [which has never
> happened]. They are therefore in a position to deal
> with government leaders as personal equals, not as
> secretaries serving committees-of-sovereigns from
> below. [This distinction was clarified for me when
> I heard Secretary of State Dean Rusk, in a rare mo-
> ment of exasperation, say to UN Secretary General
> U Thant, "Who do you think you are, a *government?*"]
>
> Under the Treaty of Rome it is the Commis-
> sion, not the member governments, which takes the
> initiative in proposing "European" policies and ac-
> tions. (What's European is defined in the Treaty.)
> It is also the Commission which carries on the
> necessary consultations with nongovernmental or-

ganizations (trade union groups, agricultural lobbies, and the like) and with the directly elected European Parliament. After these very public consultations, reported and debated in the media, the
Commission's revised proposals are submitted to
the Council of Ministers, which acts for governments in approving or rejecting it. But (another interesting innovation) under the Treaty the Council cannot edit or rewrite what the Commission has
publicly proposed. It has to be voted, in the glare
of publicity, up or down.

Let's not be misled by a descriptive analogy. In earlier
days the European Commission did not take full advantage of
its potential; more recently it has become a dynamic driving
force toward tighter economic, monetary, and even political links
among the West Europeans. The European Community's strong
magnetic influence is now felt in Eastern Europe too. Our purpose here is not to judge how the ingenious arrangements in
the Treaty of Rome have worked out in practice, though even
when they were not working well, they were a great improvement over several hundred years of European wars. Besides,
the unfinished business of European integration is vastly different, and for all its complexities probably easier, than the global
issues involved in the "third try."

So please, if you can, drain this description of its Euro-
peanness, and consider the suggestive key elements of this social invention, the extranational organization. There is, first,
the collective nature of the executive leadership, which gives
some assurance that a wide spectrum of viewpoints will already
have been brought to bear on its thinking before important executive initiatives are taken. Because of their experience and
standing in their own countries, the commissioners are likely
to have informed judgments about what the political traffic will
bear back home. Because they have, in effect, a guaranteed five-
year term, they can go beyond the conventional wisdoms of current national governments, find common ground among them,
look farther ahead, act more boldly. They are both obligated

and empowered to analyze problems and formulate policies from an international point of view. They are able to float ideas and consult with nongovernments in the open, and by so doing they can frame the terms of the public discussion and debate to which governments then have to tune their political antennae.

Perhaps the most ingenious device of all, when the governments do finally get to consider a commission initiative (after everyone else has been publicly heard from), the ministers in council cannot edit. If they don't want to bless the initiative, they have to toss it, publicly, back into the public arena where the consensus for it was developed in the first place.

The point is not that one such institution should tackle all these functions. Quite the contrary. The point is that for each "function of the future" special processes will be needed—and that the extranational form of organization may be the best bet in arenas that require a combination of international policy analysis, international policy consensus, international policy decisions, and an international "watching brief" on how policies are carried out, by market or managed mechanisms or some creative combination of both.

Before moving on, let's sound one cautionary note: the only real-life extranational organization, the European Commission, is less democratic (that is, less directly responsible to the governed) than most national governments we call democracies. In the Treaty of Maastricht (1991) the European Parliament, already directly elected, was given a new set of teeth: the power to veto some executive actions. But the executive (the European Commission) is appointed without the advice or consent of the European Parliament. The European Community still has a long way to go before it resembles a federal democracy.

International Taxes

In the past, even those international programs widely agreed to be essential have been plagued by chronic funding crises. It will be necessary to develop international income streams that do not depend on annual soul-searching by half a hundred governments.

Buying a world of peaceful change will be much less expensive than the threat or use of force. And there are plenty of international systems and transnational transactions that depend for their viability on a managed peace. The stake they share in a world peaceful enough to make possible the transporting, communicating, and transacting should be reflected in the prices we all pay for such services.

The recommendations of several international commissions that have studied the shortcomings of the international system, including the *North-South* report by the group chaired by former West German Chancellor Willy Brandt and *Our Common Future,* the report of the World Commission on Environment and Development chaired by Prime Minister Gro Harlem Brundtland of Norway, have included the still heretical suggestion that international taxation is part of the solution. One of these, our Aspen Institute consensus report *The Planetary Bargain,* advocates an international development tax. We describe the idea this way:

> Rather than trying to pump life back into the worn-out policy of year-to-year decisions by individual governments on how much to appropriate and to whom it should go, what is needed is a flow of funds for development which are generated *automatically* under *international control.* . . . The idea of international taxation (on ships for the use of international waters, on international air travel, on passports, on international telecommunications, on ocean fisheries) is a hardy perennial, but we believe it should be treated as an idea whose time has come.

One version of this idea would link development funding to the creation of Special Drawing Rights (SDRs) by the International Monetary Fund. But SDRs are supposed to be a device for creating monetary stability and should therefore be created at irregular intervals, at moments when more international liquidity is needed. Such a system would starve international development (or whatever other function was to be

supported by such international revenue) whenever world liquidity did not justify the creation of new international money
(as frequently occurred in the 1970s and 1980s).

As a matter of common sense, fundraising for international functions should bear most heavily on those activities that
benefit most from a peaceful and predictable world environment.
Travel, transport, communication, and international transactions are the obvious candidates. As a frequent international
traveler and communicator, I see no reason why I shouldn't pay
a tithe of my passport fee, a fraction of the price of my airplane
ticket, or an override on my bill for telephoning, faxing, or sending data across international frontiers to help fund the privilege
of moving myself and my thoughts around in a world that will
become much more unfair, more turbulent, and more dangerous if the international system doesn't "work."

Another easily understood device is a tax on the use of
a part of the global commons. Rent for a parking stall in geosynchronous orbit; licensing fees for the exploitation of resources
in the deep ocean, on the seabed, and on the continental margin; an easement for work in Antarctica; payments for the international transfer of genetic resources; fees for transborder
data flows and especially on international financial transactions;
a tax on the deliberate emission of "controlled substances" (CFCs,
carbon dioxide, methane, and so on) intended as a disincentive
(like tobacco and alcohol taxes) as well as a revenue measure —
the list is limited only by the human imagination.

Over the years, a good deal of thinking has been done
on this subject. No national government or major international
leader has effectively espoused it. Sooner or later, someone will.
Whoever does so first will make an unforgettable contribution
to a workable system of peaceful change.

A Practical Pluralism

What do these "third try" guidelines, including the extranational
principle and the need for international revenue streams to sustain international capacities to act, imply for the future of the
varied organizations set up in the 1940s and 1950s to manage
the "second try," and especially for the United Nations? The

future always has to be grafted onto the past. So the UN Charter is the obvious starting point. Years ago a diplomat assigned to the United Nations in New York gave me an important clue. "There's nothing wrong with the first five pages of the Charter," he said. "It's those following fifty pages of procedure that get in the way."

It is not quite accurate to say that the fifty-two pages that follow the Charter's soaring Preamble and its first chapter ("Purposes and Principles") deal only with procedure. Article 55 defines the economic and social "conditions . . . of peaceful and friendly relations" and cements into international law the idea that "human rights and fundamental freedoms" anywhere are the concerns of governments everywhere. Article 73, dealing with "peoples who have not yet attained a full measure of self-government," asserts that "the interests of the inhabitants of these territories are paramount." This is the cornerstone of the greatest achievement under the Charter so far: the abolition of colonial rule.

It is true, however, that the elaborate procedural "architecture" of the United Nations as an organization has often interfered with the pursuit of its members' declared common purposes, as set forth in those few paragraphs. (The text of the Preamble, Chapter I, and Article 55 of the UN Charter are reproduced, as a timely reminder, in the section called "Sources, Notes, and Comments.")

As we have seen, a good many UN-based forms of international cooperation have been working fairly well. What is interesting, and suggestive for the future, is that the agencies and processes that have worked in practice are those that adhered to the Charter's purposes and principles but played fast and loose with the Charter's procedures. For example: the UN's successes in peacekeeping (stepping in between belligerents) and peacemaking (mediating and conciliating what the fighting might be, is, or was about) are not spelled out in the Charter's "fifty pages of procedure." But they are clearly consonant with the Charter's purposes "to ensure . . . that armed forces should not be used, save in the common interest" [Preamble], and "to be a center for harmonizing the actions of nations in the attainment of these common ends" [Article 1(4)].

Another example: the Charter describes voting procedures. But these apply only when votes are taken. The Charter
does not require voting, and as we have seen, most of the successful actions taken by UN agencies have been agreed upon
"by consensus." When votes have been taken in these cases, they
have been to confirm earlier consensus agreements or to get on
the record what has not yet been fully agreed upon, as with the
Law of the Sea treaty.

A third example: the Charter's "procedures" describe an
organization of members who can only be governments. The
"parties to a dispute" are only governments. Judging from the
Charter text, "threats to the peace, breaches of the peace and
acts of aggression" come only from governments. International
terrorism was not unknown before 1945; nor were international
nongovernment cartels, for crime or drug running or other more
superficially respectable purposes such as currency speculation
and commodity price-fixing. These were apparently not thought
of as peace security issues; we know better today.

Not until the drafters reached Article 71 did it occur to
them that nongovernmental organizations might need to be
consulted—and then only on economic and social matters, not
peace and security issues or trusteeship policy or international
law. Even the chapter on the secretary general assumes that international staff work would be done only by UN employees.
Yet the history of the last forty-seven years is replete with evidence that nongovernments have often taken the lead in making and carrying out international policies, with the UN's official
members catching up late if at all. Most systematic training for
UN peacekeeping has been done by the nongovernmental International Peace Academy. Much of the mediation and concilia-
tion undertaken by the secretary general has been done by people
loaned to him or engaged by him outside the "international civil
service" or even by volunteers with no formal UN affiliation.
Most of the useful fact-finding and "searchlight" publishing on
violations of human rights guaranteed by the Charter has been
done by such nongovernmental gadflies as Amnesty International and the International Commission of Jurists.

Many of the proposals advanced in the rest of this book

can result in strengthening the United Nations if that doesn't mean trying to breathe life into the aging and enfeebled parts of the UN system that aren't working. Strengthening the United Nations means taking its purposes and principles very seriously but, to carry them into action, building within the framework of the Charter fresh institutions that reflect the probable realities of the twenty-first century.

Viewed in this way, the United Nations is needed more than ever. Any international convention of lawyers asked to rewrite the Preamble, Chapter I, and Articles 55 and 73 of the Charter would not likely do nearly as well in defining the need to make change peaceful and make peace changeable.

What is needed is to develop new work ways — bypassing not the Charter's stated purpose but some of its outdated processes — in order to:

- Fashion a world security system "to make the world safe for diversity" (Chapters Six and Seven)
- Regulate world markets to make them not only efficient but fair (Chapter Eight)
- Generate a worldwide growth-with-fairness push powered by something more dynamic than grudging aid and bad loans (Chapter Nine)
- Negotiate fair and workable planetary bargains about the human environment, which is a global commons (Chapter Ten)

A sensible system of peaceful change for more people than ever before in world history is a feasible goal. Some steps in its direction already have been taken — piecemeal, the practical way. The guiding principles have made themselves apparent. The puzzle, complex but not insoluble, is how to move — no doubt untidily, in a zigzag course — toward carrying into action what the past half-century has taught us, by trial and error, in theory.

Our task in the 1990s is strikingly similar to the one successfully confronted by Thomas Jefferson, James Madison, and the other founders of the United States. They managed to develop a new way of thinking about the governance of a large diverse and developing nation. They then wrote general rules for durable institutions crafted to ensure that no one would be in general charge.

The real-life management of peace worldwide seems bound to require a Madisonian world, a world of bargains and accommodations among national and functional factions, a world in which peoples are able to agree on what to do next together without feeling the need (or being forced by global government) to agree on religious creeds, economic canons, or political credos. A practical pluralism, not a unitary universalism, is the likely destiny of the human race.

six

A NEW WORLD DISORDER
The Erosion of Superpower

One definition of peace is well-managed conflict.
—*Kenneth Boulding, 1990*

IN THE 1990S, FOR THE FIRST TIME since the anarchy of the early Middle Ages, no national leaders dominate world politics, or are even trying to dominate, or think they are dominant when they are not. The overblown ambitions of Charlemagne, the Holy Roman and Spanish and British empires, the Germanies of Kaiser Wilhelm and Adolf Hitler, the Japanese militarists, the Soviet Union of Lenin, Stalin, and their successors have all fallen by the wayside. Also rapidly obsolescent is the mystique that the Atlantic-oriented West is the world's big brother and the related axiom that the United States is its rich uncle.

For a forty-year instant of history, nuclear weapons persuaded nearly everybody that two nations merited the status of "superpower." Very large explosions then proved to be militarily unusable as instruments of global domination.

One of the superpowers tried to hold the world's last empire together in an alliance of duress. It bet so heavily on military power and got so far behind in everything else that it finally gave up the struggle to be Number One, or even Number Two. The other superpower also bet heavily on the kinds of military power that couldn't seem to be applied in real-life military situations and couldn't even be brandished without appearing to bully. But its other wagers were more widely spread, on science and enterprise and freedom and international cooperation: the Marshall Plan, the North Atlantic Alliance, economic aid to former enemies, global advocacy of human rights and freer trade, the fusion of computers and telecommunications to create the global knowledge society.

The world of the 1990s and beyond is fundamentally different from anything in our cultural memory of international relations. No "power" has the power to undertake on its own responsibility "to make the world safe for diversity." It is already apparent that a nobody-in-charge world will be more volatile and more crisis-prone than the potentially fatal yet eerily stable confrontation of nuclear-tipped superpowers glaring at each other from their hardened silos.

The former colonial powers, new and old, did not merely release two-thirds of the world from political dependence, economic exploitation, and a strategic role as pawns in a global rivalry. They largely abandoned it. *Independence* often came to mean "neglect."

In the early nineties both "Wests," Marxist and capitalist, turned in shock and apprehension to their own troubles: sharpened social conflict at home, competition with world neighbors, fear of migrants and refugees, resentment of the discarded yet ambitious pawns.

In Eastern Europe and the republics of the former Soviet Union, democracy and economic development will be a predictably bumpy road. Communist China's approach to modernization, the double track of education and repression, guarantees a restless and unstable partner in the international system. Internal strife and regional rivalries in South Asia will keep Kashmir, the Indus Valley, Sri Lanka, and other conflicted places in the news. In the Mideast old hurts and new hates, combined with the geological maldistribution of wealth, seem bound to keep monarchs and despots, rich leaders and poor peoples, fundamentalist and modernized Moslems, and Jews and Arabs reaching for each other's throats. In Africa much development, enterprise, and modern governance are still in a losing race with poverty, tribalism, population growth, incompetence, and corruption. Latin America's great potential and rich resources will still be at risk unless the democratic trend of the eighties can be consolidated in the nineties. There and elsewhere, the producers and sellers of addictive drugs continue to make war on civilization. Only in East Asia is there a crescent of bright spots, but even there economic growth runs far ahead of "consent of the governed."

And looming over the global scene, making every problem less soluble and every solution less hopeful, is the continuing rapid growth in the numbers of people—born into a new world where, because the West has won, everyone is entitled to freedom of speech and of worship, freedom from want and from fear.

The First Test

The dismantling of the Berlin Wall in the autumn of 1989 was a metaphor for the end of an era, and therefore the beginning of another. The world, in T. S. Eliot's phrase, was "throbbing between two lives." It didn't have to wait even a year for a first broad hint of its new life. Iraq's invasion of Kuwait on August 2, 1990, provided the first descriptive metaphor for the puzzles of the post-postwar era. The metaphor was mixed, as befitted a world of mixed cultures, mixed ethnic and religious loyalties, and mixed ideologies about international governance. But the fundamental nature of the global political change was illustrated by the newfangled world reaction to Iraq's old-fashioned move to swallow at a gulp its rich little southern neighbor.

Iraq's longtime dictator, Saddam Hussein, was no dummy. He had a good basis for believing that much of the world approved of his military buildup. The Soviet Union had sent sophisticated military equipment, with technical advisers to help Iraqis learn to use it. Successive French governments poured sophisticated military equipment into Iraq and even lent a hand in the building of a nuclear fuel facility that only a bold Israeli air raid brought to a halt. Iraq in the 1980s had replaced Libya as Brazil's largest market for military exports. Argentina had provided Iraq with a secure site for building missiles. The United States had increasingly tilted toward Iraq in its eight-year war with Iran and was facilitating the sale of military equipment up to the week before Iraq's invasion of Kuwait.

Iraq's leader must also have assumed—his adult life had

been conditioned by the Cold War—that the rest of the world would be incapable of getting together in the United Nations to stop him. In the late forties he may even have watched in youthful fascination as Israel's David Ben Gurion took over territories Arabs thought were theirs, planning his military operations for five-day spurts because he rightly guessed it would take the UN Security Council about five days, each time, to tell Israel to cease fire and negotiate. (This is not idle speculation; it's what Ben Gurion told me was his strategy, when as a magazine editor I interviewed him in 1955.)

But Saddam Hussein guessed wrong about the post–Cold War world. The Soviets pulled the plug on their longtime military aid to Iraq within hours of his invasion of Kuwait. The Americans, who got less than 5 percent of their oil from Iraq and Kuwait combined but had to import 46 percent of their bloated needs for oil from abroad, swiftly decided on an embargo. The Japanese and the Europeans, despite their much heavier dependence on Mideast oil, quickly did likewise.

Then the United Nations Security Council, which had wrung its hands ineffectually on such issues as this while the Cold War was on, decided to activate the seldom-used Chapter VII of the UN Charter, ordering a total embargo of oil and all other "commodities and products originating in Iraq or Kuwait exported therefrom," the import of "weapons or other military equipment," and "transfers of funds to Iraq or Kuwait," including foreign investment. The next day, Turkey joined in with a crucial decision to cork the pipelines that conveyed more than two-thirds of Iraq's oil to a Turkish port in the Eastern Mediterranean for transshipment to consumers around the world.

The Arabs, doubly split (haves and have-nots, royal families and military strongmen), provided a test of the old adage that courage is directly proportional to distance from the problem. But after a week of royal hesitation, King Fahd of Saudi Arabia asked for help. Forces designed to enforce the UN sanctions and deter another invasion almost immediately began to arrive. Later the same week, twelve members of the Arab League, led by Egypt, said they would join in sending help to Saudi Arabia.

Never in modern history had there been so broad and rapid a world consensus on mandatory action against an aggressor. The sudden consensus was helped along by the Soviet Union's anxiety to cooperate with the West — and the fact that China had no ideological or national stake in using its UN veto to hold out against the near-universal condenmnation Iraq's leader had brought down on his country.

The consensus was also partly produced by the intense round-the-clock coverage of the crisis on worldwide television. James Schlesinger, a former U.S. secretary of defense, paraphrased Clausewitz: "TV is the extension of diplomacy by other means." The spread of democracy had brought a taste for openness in many places not previously plugged into the global information system. For television's newspeople, global *glasnost* created new and attractive markets.

The widespread outrage had little to do with sympathy for Kuwait, an enclave of coastal desert floating on one of the world's largest lakes of oil. It would have been hard to find a rationale, in the new climate of pluralism and participation, for why such unearned wealth should be controlled by a tribal monarch. Indeed, the decaying monarchies around the Persian Gulf seemed unlikely to be enduring features of the political landscape. The curious thing about the Iraqi action was how out of step this drama was with theatrics in other parts of the world — a despot attacking a dynast, "the people" cast only as casualties and refugees.

The international coalition — and the U.S. political consensus — almost came apart during a few weeks of clumsy unilateralism late in 1990. In that interlude President George Bush doubled the U.S. troop strength in the gulf without consulting either with allies or with the U.S. Congress.

For most of history, solo American-flag military adventures have been à la mode. But in recent decades the use of U.S. troops in multilateral operations with many flags has been the way to avoid domestic political trouble about overseas commitments. For forty years the NATO alliance and the UN-sponsored American force in Korea had popular support both wide and deep. The Vietnam War was tagged early by U.S. opinion

as made in America and failed when domestic support for it
petered out. There are recent exceptions to this multilateral
preference: Grenada, Panama. But a U.S.-only adventure es-
capes a domestic political backlash only if it is wound up in a
week or two.

To protect the operation in the Persian Gulf, the United
States soon returned to the United Nations and to multilateral
diplomacy, the key to consensus both in American politics and
in coalition building. The stage was set for "Desert Storm." Once
the coalition ran out of patience, the force assembled in the gulf
proved overwhelming: the air war lasted forty days, the ground
war four days. The principle of collective security was vindi-
cated. All the problems that had produced the crisis remained.

The Iraqi dictator still held sway, though more in his own
backyard than in the region as a whole. His yearning for exotic
weapons — nuclear, chemical, biological, toxin — was unabated;
UN inspections merely revealed the margin by which Western
intelligence had underestimated what a developing nation can
accomplish when it has enough help from its more developed
friends. After a short international rescue effort, most of the
Kurds and Shi'ites were left alone with their persecutors — for
a damaging time being. The monarchies to the south were no
more democratic, the users of energy to the West were no less
oil-dependent, the Arab-Israel rivalries were no less intense, and
peace in the gulf itself no more secure than before the "decisive" victory.

Yet this new eruption in that chain of political volcanoes
called the Middle East, leading to the first test of cohesion in
a world without a Cold War, did clarify the agenda for international governance, neglected for so long while scholars, political leaders, the big private foundations and think tanks, the
military-industrial complex, and the peace movement were all
preoccupied with strategic nuclear war and U.S.-Soviet relations.

That new agenda to make the world safe for diversity comes
in five packages of actions, each closely related to the others:

1.   Radical disarmament and durable deterrence of nuclear
     weapons — and making sure that nuclear weapons of all sizes
     and shapes remain unusable and unused

2. Deterring the use of other exotic instruments of frightful-
    ness—chemical and biological weapons, and missile deliv-
    ery systems—which are easier than nuclear weapons to
    come by and more readily usable in limited ways
3. Organizing to anticipate, deter, and mediate regional con-
    flict, manage crises, mediate ancient quarrels, isolate those
    that cannot yet be settled, stop wars when they break out,
    and restore peace when it is broken
4. Strengthening international systems for responding to "hu-
    manitarian" crises inside as well as between countries—
    "security" threats to those targeted by terrorist threats, lured
    by drug addiction, caught up in human rights disputes,
    pushed from their homes as refugees, or visited by sudden
    disasters natural and unnatural
5. Developing a wider and more flexible system of world
    leadership: a "club of democracies" whose members are will-
    ing to act in differing groupings for different situations in
    dissimilar regions pursuant to the purposes, if not always
    using the procedures, of the UN Charter

The first four baskets of measures, considered in this chapter and the next, all have to do with *world security,* rather narrowly defined as armed conflict or other conditions that threaten
security of the person—the business of armed forces, police, and
other emergency workers.

The fifth basket requires a broader discussion of the nature of leadership in a nobody-in-charge system; it will be considered in Chapter Eleven, after we have given attention also
to the nervous tension of the world economy (Chapter Eight),
the politics of poverty (Chapter Nine), and the protection of our
planetary environment (Chapter Ten).

Inching Toward Nuclear Common Sense

It is clear now, even to governments, that a nation doesn't need
many very large potential explosions in its arsenal to conduct
an altogether credible information game, a game of threats and
deterrence of threats in which the military objective is the mind
of the adversary, not his territory or industry or population.

Nuclear threats and their deterrence are wars fought with ideas
and impressions, with knowledge of what adversaries could do
and uncertainty about what they might do. Thinking of nuclear
threats and deterrence not as piles of hardware but as an information game shines a fresh light on requirements for the numbers and kinds of weapons the game is about.

When the first two primitive atomic weapons, products
of nuclear fission, were dropped on Hiroshima and Nagasaki
in 1945, both scientists and political leaders rushed to judgment:
nuclear weapons are ultimate weapons, and those who possess
them deserve to be called superpowers. More than four and a
half decades later, two facts stand out.

One fact is that the world was hugely supplied with nuclear
weapons. In 1945, the world's inventory was three of them; two
were used in Japan. By 1989 there were nearly fifty-seven
thousand—representing, according to longtime weapons counter
Ruth Sivard, "an explosive force equivalent to 1,200,000 Hiroshima bombs—or at least 1,000 times greater than all the firepower used in *all* wars since the introduction of gunpowder six
centuries ago." Another way of expressing this mind-numbing
number is to calculate that 11 megatons of explosive energy were
released altogether in World War II, the Korean War, and the
Vietnam War; the explosive energy yield of 1989's nuclear arsenals was something over eighteen thousand megatons.

Close to 98 percent of this firepower was deployed by the
United States and the Soviet Union: about 55,500 nuclear
devices, large and "small," with average yields thirty times that
of the Hiroshima bomb, the explosive power of 160 million Cher-
nobyls, were aimed at each other's forces, allies, and populations.

Robert McNamara, who as U.S. secretary of defense from
1961 to 1967 presided over much of this mutual buildup, later
declared it to be grotesquely out of proportion to any sensible
concept of deterrence. He openly took his share of the blame for
the "incremental decisions" that brought the powers called su-
per to the dangerous heights from which it was so hard to clam-
ber down. "Each of these decisions, taken by itself, appeared rational and inescapable. But the fact is that they were made without
reference to any overall master plan or long-term objective."

In a second tier of explosive power were France (450 weapons in 1989), Britain (300), and China (350), overt members of the nuclear club. Some other nations had either exploded a "peaceful" device indistinguishable from a weapon (India) or had unacknowledged nuclear capacities (Israel, South Africa, Pakistan). Still others showed clear signs of wanting to develop nuclear weapons potential (Iraq, Brazil, Argentina, North Korea), either by parlaying nuclear electricity programs (the "plutonium path") or by what had become the preferred route, that of enriching their own or stolen uranium in remote factories with the help of international smugglers of nuclear materials and facilities.

The other big fact is that since those first two bombs, no government or even nongovernment had actually found a military use for the size and character of explosion that atomic fission and fusion have made physically possible. Their sole function had been to serve as a latent threat, especially to deter comparable explosions set off by someone else.

It is true that while Nikita Khrushchev was general secretary in the Kremlin, he threatened nuclear firing forty-one times. Vice Admiral John Marshall Lee, in reporting that count, also revealed that since the Nagasaki bomb the United States had seriously considered using nuclear weapons some twenty times, in crises ranging from Iran to Korea to Vietnam to Cuba to the Persian Gulf. But both of these lists were already ancient history. After the braggadocio of Nikita Khrushchev departed the Kremlin, even brandishing nuclear weapons went out of style. Despite some loose-lipped nonsense about "nuclear war fighting," both in published Soviet military doctrine and in Washington during the early Reagan years, the world's best strategic analysts had failed to come up with a practical way to use such unprecedented explosive power to serve their national interests. By 1990 ordinary citizens by the millions, like the child in Hans Christian Andersen's fable, could see that the nuclear emperors were unclothed.

The gap between myth and reality was nowhere more obvious than in NATO military plans. They had long been based on the doctrine that the North Atlantic Treaty Organization

(meaning mostly the United States) would strike first with nuclear weapons if a Soviet attack with conventional weapons
threatened to overwhelm Western Europe. This idea had been
inherently unbelievable for more than two decades. I served in
Paris and Brussels as U.S. ambassador to NATO (the U.S.
member of NATO's political board of directors) from 1965 to
1969; I did not believe even then that an American president
would really make such a "mutual suicide" decision, and I found
almost no one in Europe or indeed in Washington who did not
also privately admit to serious doubts. Nevertheless, the uncertainty of U.S. behavior in an emergency was at the core of the
nuclear deterrent; no one in responsible office could suggest it
was not that uncertain after all.

In the 1970s some people in a good position to know began to speak out publicly—once they were out of office. Admiral Noel Gayler, a former commander in chief of the Pacific
theater, was one of the early voices to question out loud the military relevance of nuclear explosions. Robert McNamara told
an Aspen Institute seminar in the 1970s that neither of the two
presidents he served as secretary of defense in the 1960s (John
F. Kennedy and Lyndon B. Johnson) would have used a nuclear
weapon first. And Henry Kissinger, shortly after ending his tenure as national security adviser to President Richard Nixon and
President Gerald Ford's secretary of state, gave a speech in London that questioned the whole first-nuclear-strike dogma, dampening NATO's declaratory strategy with a heavy blanket of fog.

In effect, that strategy died in the 1960s but wasn't buried
until July 1990, when the North Atlantic Council made official
the nonofficial consensus: NATO went from *first use* to *last resort*.
The next stop on that train would necessarily be no first use,
and the one after that would be no use at all except to deter
the use of nuclear weapons by another.

Even when the United States was still thinking about deterring an implacable foe, there were public estimates of strategic weaponry needed for stable mutual deterrence on the order
of 10 to 15 percent of existing stockpiles, or a couple of thousand strategic weapons at most, not tens of thousands. In 1988
Richard Garwin, IBM's veteran expert on weapons policy, pro-

posed an interim goal of 95 percent reductions, leaving the United States and the Soviet Union with one thousand warheads each (counting all kinds of delivery systems) and the United Kingdom, France, and China with two hundred warheads each. Parallel thinking in the Kremlin was reflected in Gorbachev's increasingly skeptical remarks about the usefulness of nuclear weapons. By 1990, McNamara was writing that nuclear deterrence required a few hundred warheads at most, and the relevant number might prove to be in the teens.

We were inching toward rationality by downgrading nuclear weapons as symbol and substance of power. Yet over the years arms control negotiations had developed a leisurely rhythm of their own. Political leaders on both sides felt the need to satisfy their internal critics that precise and timely information would show beyond a doubt that there was no cheating. Verification was the boulder in the path toward radical reductions. Yet once overkill capacity is seen to be irrelevant to deterrence, what matters is what it would take to obliterate the adversary if deterrence were to fail, not how many times the rubble can be bounced thereafter.

A Worldwide Nuclear Puzzle

By the early 1990s, U.S.-Soviet negotiations about nuclear arms control had already gone about as far as they could go, which was not far enough to change the East-West balance: both sides still planned to keep far more weapons than they could conceivably use. Chipping away at the huge numbers of deliverable warheads made for a radical change. But the change was a transformation of intentions, not of capabilities to maximize damage to an enemy.

The first major changes were still in the Gorbachev era, and the first step was the agreement to get rid of a whole class of nuclear weapons: those of intermediate range. For the Soviet Union, these had been primary instruments of threat to Western Europe; Gorbachev agreed to eliminate a total force of 2,150 weapons. President Reagan agreed to stand down 550 comparable U.S. weapons designed to be based in Europe as part of

NATO's counterthreat to the East. (Some of the U.S. nuclear warheads were quickly recycled as gravity bombs for use in F-16 fighter bombers, and in this new incarnation they were promptly returned to the European theater.)

Meanwhile, negotiators were still working on a deal about the larger, longer-range "strategic" weapons. The bargain was finally struck in July 1991 after fifteen years of talks; each side agreed to stand down 4,500 of its most powerful intercontinental weapons.

Late in 1991, after the abortive coup in Moscow that was the beginning of the end for Gorbachev, another arms control agreement promised the withdrawal and destruction of 11,000 Soviet and 5,500 U.S. short-range weapons intended for "tactical" use in a European war. Again, American experts assumed that some of the nuclear fuel in the U.S. weapons could be readily recycled for use in weapons not yet proscribed by arms control agreements. Once the Soviet Union became a tenuous Commonwealth of Independent States and the Russian Federation emerged as its main nuclear successor state, Russian President Boris Yeltsin was ready to go much further in jettisoning nuclear warheads — even sidestepping the idea, central to all prior arms-control negotiations, that neutral nuclear deterrence required the two "sides" to maintain a rough parity in deliverable warheads of comparable power.

On June 17, 1992, President Yeltsin during a visit to Washington agreed with President George Bush to cut back about two-thirds of the remaining Russian and U.S. stockpiles of long-range missile warheads. Using as a base a total of about 11,250 such warheads on each side, the Russians agreed to cut theirs to 3,000 by the year 2003. The Americans would cut theirs to 3,500 at most. Yeltsin's negotiators thought that the 2003 deadline could be moved up to the year 2000 if the United States helped Russia defray the cost of destroying its missiles.

The new bargain — when and if it is carried into action — would wipe out the traditional core of Russian first-strike capacity, which consisted of land-based missiles able to deliver ten warheads at once to U.S. targets hundreds of miles apart. The United States would have to give up its own much smaller force of ten-warhead MX missiles but would be left with its most advanced multiple-warhead missiles, based on Trident submarines — though each submarine could only carry four missiles instead of the eight for which it was designed.

This abandonment of parity, in favor of the United States, was not as dramatic as the numbers suggest. Roger Hilsman, once the top intelligence officer in the U.S. State Department, calculates that the Russians would need only "about 200 warheads to destroy the 70 U.S. metropolitan areas containing more than 50 percent of the American population." The United States would need "about 300 warheads to destroy the much larger numbers of urban areas containing 50 percent of the Russian population. . . . [A] nuclear war fought with each side having 3,000 to 3,500 warheads for intercontinental missiles is not much of an improvement over a nuclear war fought with each side having 12,500 warheads. Either way both sides could easily lose half their people and almost all their industry."

So the Bush-Yeltsin bargain in the summer of 1992, even if carried out without cheating on either side, would leave in place as many as ten times the number of nuclear weapons required for the "mutual suicide" pact that still (except for changeable intentions) defined strategic deterrence between Washington and Moscow.

Meanwhile, the word about nuclear unusability was spreading worldwide. A generation ago, scholarly advisers in the United States were telling their political leaders that by the early 1990s there would be twenty-five to thirty-five "nuclear weapons states." Those forecasts did not nearly come true. At least part of this outcome must be attributed to doubts about how such weapons could possibly be used in particular situations: where in the Indus Valley or Kashmir, how in the crazy-quilt map of the Middle East, at what point in arguments about frontiers or rivers or trade practices in Latin America, it would be clearly helpful to a national cause to set off an explosion many times the size of the Hiroshima bomb. It must have occurred even to China's leaders, overt members of the nuclear club, that such an explosion would be unhelpful if not ruinous in dealing with the threat that was giving them nightmares, which was on their own streets.

In part, the sluggish rate of nuclear proliferation for more than four decades can also be traced to the roadblocks constructed by the nuclear powers: international inspection by a UN agency of nuclear power plants, which produce as a by-product the raw material for nuclear weapons; and the Nuclear Nonproliferation Treaty (NPT), which 137 countries had been shamed into signing. But that impressive global array did *not* until 1991 include even France or China. And still in 1992, signatures were missing from a few ambitious governments that had not yet thought through the consequences of nuclear use: India, Pakistan, Israel, South Africa, Brazil, Argentina, and North Korea.

These countries on the nuclear threshold, or across it without saying so, constituted a new peacekeeping puzzle. We knew that two-sided deterrence, between superpowers with superweapons, did seem to "work," unattractive though it was as a definition of world peace. We had no idea how some of the more complicated regional relationships would be affected by the threat, much less the use, of nuclear weapons. If, for example, North Korea were to decide overtly to join the nuclear club, both South Korea and Japan might well look again at the restraint they had shown. Both had the scientific and industrial know-how to develop deliverable nuclear weapons if they wanted to.

The threshold countries not only did not adhere to the NPT; they were also not members of the nuclear suppliers group, the club of nuclear "haves" intended to prevent the export of nuclear weapons and what it takes to make them. What that implied was spelled out in a 1990 report by the nongovernmental Aspen Strategy Group: "It has been said that while every nation wants a nuclear weapon, once it gets one it tries to deny others the same capability; but before that nation becomes committed to the cause of nonproliferation it makes a mistake. For example, the United States helped the British, the French helped the Israelis, the Soviets helped the Chinese, who in turn helped the Pakistanis. . . . [T]he likelihood of more 'mistakes' grows."

The "mistakes" were often lapses in control by governments of exports by private companies. A University of Wisconsin nuclear watch group told a too typical story: West German firms, while their government dozed, sold Pakistan a multimillion dollar plant to enrich uranium to weapons grade; German firms also sold Pakistan special steel, electronics, and high-precision milling machinery for manufacturing nuclear weapons. When Pakistan decided to go for a tritium-based fusion bomb, it bought the design for a tritium-making reactor from German firms, which also supplied a giant tritium purification plant and some tritium to test it. "A civilian use of the tritium gas produced by the plant," said the German prosecutor who investigated this illegal export, "is not plausible." German laxity in helping South Asians develop the capacity to obliterate each other was impartial: in the 1980s an ex-Nazi operating out of Dusseldorf helped India recover from a shortage of heavy water by shipping it 250 tons, enough to help make forty bombs a year.

Yet there was hope in the early 1990s in the raw fact that despite all the wars and rumors of wars since 1945, no government had judged a nuclear weapon to be so clearly advantageous as to explode one in anger.

What was true of governments was also true of nongovernments. In forty-seven years no terrorist group had yet brandished, let alone used, a nuclear warhead. The largest terrorist explosions on record had been in the range of two tons of TNT, small enough to fit into a medium-sized truck, yet explosive enough to blow up the King David Hotel in Jerusalem and the University of Wisconsin's mathematics and physics laboratory and to kill 241 U.S. Marines in their ill-protected barracks in Beirut. Two tons of TNT is not even close to the bottom end of the range of the smallest "tactical" nuclear weapons. If even the wackiest people in world politics couldn't figure out how to use nuclear weapons for real, maybe they were not, in any meaningful military sense, weapons.

The irrelevance of nuclear weapons was especially striking in the failure of national governments to control their borders. Large arsenals of explosive power did not protect even the superpowers from border-jumping migrants or large-scale drug running. Terrorists were also not frightened of nuclear weaponry and for the same reason that the urban guerillas in Beirut were unimpressed when the United States deployed a battleship off the Lebanese coast to deal with them.

Admiral Lee, who worked on the military usability of nuclear weapons for a national security study I managed in 1984, concluded that nuclear weapons are not "a follow-on to such decisive but finally manageable changes as the stirrup, gunpowder, and aircraft." "The nuclear weapon," he wrote, "is not a step in development, or even a revolution, but has taken us into a totally new era where nuclear conflict between states has lost all relevance to their political objectives."

The dawning recognition that nuclear weapons are unusable left plenty of room for smaller but still very destructive explosions. The irony was that regional wars, even with conventional weapons of growing power and accuracy, came to seem "safer," even to those engaged in them, once it seemed clear that their local actions wouldn't "lead to nuclear war."

That was how matters stood when the bubbling of political choice hurdled the limits of top-down reform and the Soviet Union disappeared, to be succeeded partly by its Russian Republic and partly by the fragile Commonwealth of Independent States. For the new state of affairs no strategic doctrine existed, and the relevant homework on what to do next was sparse. None of the brightest strategic thinkers had dreamed of a chessboard on which one side's queen would abruptly melt like the wicked witch in *The Wizard of Oz*. The old rules of the game, including the intricate calculus of arms control, the mutual espionage, the verification agreements, even the "hot lines" and "crisis communication centers" to avert confrontation and avoid errant missile launchings, suddenly seemed very old-fashioned. Yet the old nuclear puzzles remained: the latent explosive power of nuclear weapons, the big powers' doubts about their usability, the danger of their being stockpiled or even used by others.

The new nuclear puzzle comes in two parts. One is how to scale down fast the grotesque oversupply of existing weapons in the United States and in the Soviet Union's successor states. The arithmetic and technology of this gargantuan task may be hardened into calculations and processes before these words can get into print. In the broadest terms, however, we are looking at defusing and then destroying more than fifty thousand weapons, while protecting very large populations from radioactive waste that no one in the first half-century of the nuclear age has yet figured out how to throw safely away.

In tackling this task, the old ways — arms control treaties between adversaries, backed up by national means of inspection — are clearly unsuitable. Some of the Western negotiators would harbor the haunting thought that the Cold War might not turn out to be over after all. They would insist on building trust by complex systems of national verification. The other negotiators, from Russia and its nuclear neighbors, would be looking over their shoulders at their own internal politics overheated by issues of cultural separatism, Moslem identity, and regional autonomy.

Both to get the job done in a hurry and to reassure the world that it is being responsibly done, a special international agency is needed, one staffed mostly but not wholly by experts from the countries that own the weapons to be destroyed, which happen also to be those that hold the five permanent seats on the UN Security Council. The new emergency agency should be established by the Security Council, mandated for this one purpose for a limited time (as the UN's largest-ever agency, the United Nations Relief and Rehabilitation Administration [UNRRA] after World War II), and provided by the nuclear powers with the full technical and financial support it would require.

The other part of the new nuclear puzzle is how to deter those national leaders who are not yet convinced that nuclear weapons are unusable as military or even political instruments. Here the beginning of wisdom is for the overt nuclear powers to act out their own convictions: to sweat down fast their own large dysfunctional stockpiles, in the first instance to the levels needed to deter their use by another. Only in this way will the nuclear powers persuade others to accept and confirm their nonnuclear status.

As long as some leaders who still don't get the point remain, enough nuclear weapons will have to remain available and also be deliverable on orders from Washington, Moscow, London, Paris, or Beijing to ensure rapid retribution against any nation's leadership that uses a nuclear weapon for any purpose anywhere.

An attack on one is an attack on all, says the North Atlantic Treaty; it is up to each signatory to decide what to do
if that happens. A similar principle of collective security can
now be applied worldwide: *the first use of a nuclear weapon should
be ruled in advance, by the United Nations Security Council, to be an
attack on civilization itself.*

If a nuclear act thus warned against were to happen, it
would not be good enough for the Security Council just to plead,
"cease fire and talk." Any nation or group of nations should then
be able to act, under the self-defense-and-collective-defense provisions of Article 51 of the UN Charter, to discipline the miscreant without asking all the others first. The certainty of judgment combined with uncertainty about whence its enforcement
might come would be the deterrent.

The perilous but constructive ambiguity of known nuclear
capacities but uncertainty about how and when they might be
used has served as a deterrent in Europe for nearly half a hundred years. It is time to apply this learning in other continents
as well.

A final comment on nuclear common sense, based on my experience as an American once deeply involved in the nuclear
strategy that is now so outdated. I will start with an idea tossed
off by Russian President Boris Yeltsin while traveling in the
United States early in 1992. This idea is so radical that it almost
passed unnoticed. He said that what we all should really do about
nuclear weapons is get rid of them altogether.

As a rhetorical flourish this idea has a long and distinguished history. Adlai Stevenson campaigned against nuclear
weapons when, running hopelessly against President Eisenhower
in 1956, he decided (against the advice of advisers) to "talk sense
to the American people." In the 1960s the Soviet leader Nikita
Khrushchev, for whom rhetorical flourishes were the stuff of life,
regularly proposed "general and complete disarmament"—when
he wasn't threatening to bury the United States, incinerate the
orange groves of Italy, or reduce the Acropolis in Athens to radioactive ash. In the 1970s President Jimmy Carter targeted the
elimination of nuclear weapons as a major goal. So did both

Mikhail Gorbachev and Ronald Reagan at their Reykjavik summit in 1986 — until Reagan's handlers tugged at his coattails, explaining how dangerous it was for the president to talk peace as if he meant it.

Yet espousal of mutual and total disarmament played a practical part in getting arms control negotiations started in the 1960s. The strategy the United States adopted then (some of us called it nuclear jujitsu) probably should be revived in the 1990s. A short personal story will illustrate what I mean.

My job in the administration of President John F. Kennedy was assistant secretary of state for international organization affairs, responsible for U.S. policy in the United Nations. Our gladiator at the United Nations in New York was Adlai Stevenson. Historian Arthur Schlesinger was one of the top assistants to the president. On Saturday, August 5, 1961, the three of us joined President Kennedy for a ride off Hyannisport in his motor launch *Honey Fitz* to talk over the upcoming agenda for the General Assembly of the United Nations — Kennedy's first full exposure to hard-ball UN politics. Schlesinger (in his great biography of JFK, *A Thousand Days*) recalls the day as "gray and dreary." My warmer memory is of a smiling Jackie serving us Bloody Marys.

Stevenson, for whom getting rid of nuclear weapons was still top priority, wanted to make sure the young president shared his strong feelings. But Kennedy was no long-range strategist; he was the tactician incarnate. For him, disarmament talk was psychological warfare. Stevenson, in anguish, abandoned the ritual form of address. "Jack," he pleaded, "you've got to have faith."

It was the wrong approach to Mr. Pragmatic. An embarrassed silence fell over our little policy picnic on Nantucket Sound. Trying to repair the damage, I took a different tack.

"Mr. President," I said, "the problem is this. The Soviets have for years been getting away with murder, coming out for 'general and complete disarmament,' while we've been advocating 'next steps.' Lots of people are coming to think we're less interested in peace than the Soviets are. If you now, as a fresh voice in this global debate, come out for 'general and complete

disarmament' as our ultimate goal, there won't be anything left
to discuss with the Soviets at that level of abstraction. What will
be left to discuss will be 'next steps.'"

The president's quick mind had no trouble with this tactical calculation. "Okay, that makes sense," he replied, and we
went on to other topics.

Before long two certified hard-liners, John J. McCloy and
Valerian Zorin, had negotiated at the United Nations a Soviet-
U.S. agreement to get rid of all military forces in stages if everyone else would too, within an enforceable system of world law.
That did indeed lead to talks about next steps. Despite the dramatic intermission of the Cuba missile crisis, the first step, a
nuclear test ban treaty, was on track within two years of JFK's
policy decision aboard the *Honey Fitz*.

Destroying all nuclear weapons sounds Utopian, but it
is not an irrational goal, considering how hard they are to use
and how dangerous they are sitting there unused.

Translating that simple idea into commonsense policies
will be exceedingly difficult. The atom was hard enough to split;
it will be impossible to glue it back together. Experts can do
almost anything with modern inventions except disinvent them.
Not even the political leaders with the most reason to envision
a nuclear-free future—those of Britain, China, France, Russia, and the United States—have done so as yet. Today's and
tomorrow's Saddam Husseins may not soon realize that nuclear
use is the ultimate suicide machine.

So do we consign the "no more nukes" goal to the dust-
bin of "impractical" human aspirations? That would not be my
answer. Most of the world's political leaders will continue to assume that nuclear weapons are valuable as long as American
leaders act as if they are. A United States of America willing
to forswear nuclear weapons as soon as all others do would have
the best of both worlds in disarmament politics: the highest moral
ground and the strongest bargaining position.

Meanwhile, two actions in the Security Council—(1) to
mandate an international agency to destroy more than 90 percent of the world's nuclear weapons and (2) to declare any nuclear
use a punishable act against civilization—would move the world
much faster toward nuclear common sense.

Curbing Chemistry and Biology

My grandmother had two kinds of handkerchiefs: "some for show, some for blow." The downgrading of nuclear weapons put them primarily in the show category. That focused world attention on weapons not yet clearly suicidal: the products of modern chemistry, biology, and genetic engineering, which were invented with intent first to frighten but if necessary to use. The potentials of chemical warfare (CW) and biological and toxin warfare (BTW) are especially frightening, amplified beyond their inherent dangers by fears of the unknown.

Chemical weapons—incapacitating agents such as mustard gas and superlethal agents that attack the human nervous system—have the longer history and are more developed. My father, a U.S. Army chaplain, died eight years after World War I from the aftereffects of a German gas attack. The horrors of gas warfare were well advertised during and after the war and came to be joined in the public mind with the "killer flu" epidemic of 1917 and 1918, which claimed more than twenty-five million lives and dramatized the human damage that spreading lethal infections could inflict. By 1925 this worldwide revulsion led to the Geneva Protocol, now signed by 130 states; it rules out the use in war of asphyxiating, poisonous, or other gases and of bacteriological methods of warfare.

Unlike the openly discriminatory treaty to discourage new countries from joining the nuclear club, the Geneva Protocol seeks a total ban on their use. It makes no invidious distinctions between large nations and small, rich peoples and poor, military powers and weaker states. It served for a long generation, through World War II and the Korean War, as a solid worldwide norm of international behavior. It contains, however, no means of policing the forbidden weaponry, no sanctions to prevent its use, not even a procedure for handling complaints.

In the 1960s scientists began to ring alarm bells. Egypt had used chemical weapons in Yemen. The United States used harassing chemical agents and chemical defoliants in Vietnam. More than six thousand sheep were accidentally killed by a nerve gas in Utah in 1968. That same year, the United Kingdom proposed a "more comprehensive and forceful treaty" in place of

the Geneva Protocol. Talks about this idea languished until
chemical and biological warfare were separated; chemical weapons were serious business, biological weapons were still the stuff
of research papers and science fiction. (That is no longer true,
but it was then.) By 1972, therefore, a treaty was quickly drafted
and agreed to (it has been signed and ratified by 110 states, and
signed by 24 others), banning the development, production, and
stockpiling of biological and toxin weapons and requiring that
any existing stocks be destroyed within six months of the signing of the treaty.

The norm is crystal clear: "to exclude completely the pos-
sibility of bacteriological (biological) agents and toxins being
used as weapons." The BTW treaty proscribes the development
of offensive weapons, but research leading up their development
is not covered. As with the Geneva Protocol, no sanctions or
arrangements for verification were put into the treaty; indeed,
the wide consensus may have been produced by the widespread
assumption that such weapons were militarily useless because,
as one study put it, they were "uncontrollable after release, unde-
pendable in action, and gave rise to unpredictable consequences."

This regime seemed to have universal support for a decade or so. Then, in the early 1980s, the alarm bells started ringing again. A 1979 epidemic of anthrax at Sverdlovsk, in the
Soviet Union, was attributed by the United States to an accident in an illicit BW facility. And U.S. sources charged that
a toxin known as yellow rain had been used by Vietnam against
the Hmong people and Cambodia and also by the Soviet Union
in Afghanistan. These widely advertised "findings" never achieved
a scientific consensus and may well have been untrue.

There was no international regime (except the toothless
Geneva Protocol) to restrain chemical warfare, and Iraq started
to use mustard gas and cyanide agents not only against Iranian
troops—from 1984 without admitting it, after 1988 boasting
about it—but also to terrorize its own Kurdish minority. The
Iraqi threat to use chemical weapons against Iran's cities may
well have been one of the factors that persuaded Teheran to agree
to the UN Security Council's call for a cease-fire. In Geneva,
negotiations about banning CW dragged on through the 1980s
but by early 1992 had not yet produced a treaty.

The revolution in biotechnology made BW look more practical as well. In the early 1970s a UN expert group had already guessed out loud that "deliberate genetic steps may be taken" to change the characteristics of microorganisms for BW purposes. A report done in 1990 for the Stockholm International Peace Research Institute (SIPRI) by American and Swedish experts describes the chilling import of this technological "advance":

> In nature only minute quantities of toxins are produced by a relatively small number of microorganisms, plants, and animals. . . . [But] present day genetic engineering techniques can be used to develop microorganisms capable of producing toxins having promise for weaponization, while modern fermentation technologies enable their production in bulk. Toxins are from hundreds to thousands [of] times more toxic than the nerve agents; produced in sufficient quantities and appropriately "packaged," they could be used to substitute for a nerve gas or to serve as a virulent adjunct to conventional, chemical, or nuclear weapons.
>
> Turning to BW, biotechnology offers to the armorer the tools for overcoming the technical limitations that have so far precluded biological weapons from being militarily useful. If there were a military interest in doing so, pathogens could be genetically engineered to increase their virulence; to circumvent the target's immunodefenses; to enhance the BW agents' hardiness so they store better, are more "packageable" in munitions and, once released, resist environmental stresses, such as drying and ultraviolet radiation; and conceivably, if far-fetched, to direct their actions against specific sectors of the population ("ethnic weapons").

Closely related to these exotic ways of killing people is the technical "progress" in getting the lethal agents to the people you want to kill. A 1990 report by four experienced experts for the Aspen Institute called ballistic missiles a "proliferation multiplier"—that is, once nuclear, chemical, or biological weapons can be delivered with accuracy and surprise, they become a more attractive buy for countries that want to threaten their neighbors. "Missiles offer a relatively cheap way to break the stalemate which has developed between strike aircraft and layered air defenses." Fourteen developing countries had ballistic missiles, according to the 1990 report; half of these had missiles with ranges of greater than two hundred miles, and twelve of them were listed as "suspected chemical weapons states."

The developing countries with missiles have mostly imported them ready-made from sponsors in the industrial world and also, increasingly, from other developing countries with big military programs. Argentina, for example, got from Iraq the famous French-made Exocet missile that destroyed a British warship early in the war over the Falkland/Malvina Islands. By 1991, twenty developing countries had the capacity to make chemical weapons; a Central Intelligence Agency guess was by the year 2000, fifteen "Third World" countries would be producing their own ballistic missiles.

Dozens of countries can now play in the new game of exotic threats against each other if they want to badly enough. A few ballistic weapons will not be hard to come by. The dual use of so many chemicals makes any nation with a petrochemical, fertilizer, pesticide, or pharmaceutical industry a potential producer, and supplier to others, of chemical weapons. Bacteriological agents and powerful toxins will still require sophisticated scientists and engineers plus well-equipped facilities with elaborate safeguards; but the amounts required to mount a terrorist threat can be small and readily hidden in laboratories that look like something else.

The "general opinon of mankind" would certainly favor banning all these exotic weapons. What can be done to convert that consensus into worldwide policy and international action in the face of a comparatively few but very stubborn holdouts?

The regime to discourage proliferation of nuclear weapons was more successful than experts thirty years ago thought it could possibly be. It rested on popular revulsion against "ultimate weapons," was confirmed in the candidly discriminatory Nuclear

Non-Proliferation Treaty and was reinforced by inspection of nuclear power plants whose by-product could become fuel for nuclear weapons, inspection carried out by a special UN agency, the International Atomic Energy Agency (IAEA). For chemical and biological weapons, the revulsion is so widespread that a nondiscriminatory ban is on the books. But verifying compliance is inherently so much more difficult that it was bypassed altogether for bioweapons and toxins, and on chemical weapons it led to decades of fruitless negotiation between experts permanently resident in Geneva.

The blunt truth, obscured by the forbiddingly technical language of discourse, is that an airtight inspection system for chemical and biological weapons would have to be very large and complicated, employing thousands of experts in many different disciplines. It would be expensive: perhaps a dozen times more costly for chemical weapons than the IAEA's inspection of nuclear facilities. It would also be far more intrusive than international inspection of nuclear power, oil spills, civil aviation, or environmental damage. It just seems that the conventional approach—detailed treaties backed up by international inspectors—is unlikely to be a match for the inherent leakiness of scattered facilities, some of them as secret and remote as the Libyan plant discovered in 1990 or Iraq's oversized cannon project that was hidden for so long from prying eyes.

When it comes to missile technology, the approach so far has been a suppliers' cartel. There is no treaty, but seven industrial countries—Britain, Canada, France, Italy, Japan, the United States, and West Germany—decided in 1987 that they would "restrict exports that could contribute to the acquisition of nuclear capable missiles." It is another openly discriminatory regime. There is no international inspection; each government uses its own export controls to do its part.

Such an arrangement could work if all the suppliers joined in. Missiles are extraordinarily complicated machines; it is no mean feat, says the Aspen report, to make sure all the hundred thousand precision-crafted moving parts in a Pershing II missile are in perfect working order. What is lacking in the case of ballistic missiles, however, is a widely agreed taboo.

Is there no light at the end of these dangerous tunnels? The first and most important checkrein is still wide popular revulsion. The second is transparency: to maximize the probability that violations of widely agreed norms are quickly and widely known. The third is to make violations extremely dangerous to a violator, guaranteeing that crime doesn't pay.

Except for missiles, the revulsion exists. Chemical, biological, and toxin weapons are closely linked in the public mind. In all the talks about them, the starting assumption has been that all states should forgo their military use. Can this near-universal revulsion become a practical nonproliferation regime? Once the norm is clear, it is possible to make sure that most violations of a widely agreed taboo are quickly and widely known. Governments cannot do this. The international community of scientists can.

An intriguing proposal was floated by microbiologists Raymond A. Zalinskas and Carl-Göran Hedén, in the SIPRI report cited earlier. The Biological Weapons and Toxins Convention of 1972 contains in Article 10 a promise, never carried into action, that governments signing the treaty would "undertake to facilitate, and have the right to participate in, the fullest possible exchange of equipment, materials and scientific and technological information for the use of bacteriological (biological) agents and toxins for peaceful purposes."

If Article 10 is taken seriously, the conscious community of scientists thereby created would likely know whatever is being done in the field, for peaceful *or* other purposes. "[T]he probability of illicit activity being detected is low unless practitioners themselves are the ones who take the responsibility for oversight. . . . [T]he detailed practice of science is largely outside the control of governments . . . it takes an expert to catch an expert."

What's needed here is to activate Article 10 by pushing the widest exchange of biotechnology; Zalinskas and Hedén propose that this task be entrusted to the International Council of Scientific Unions (ICSU), whose membership "spans the width of science": seventy-five national academies and councils of research, twenty international scientific unions, and twenty-six other scientific organizations. The ICSU does in fact have an outstanding record of constructive activity in molding a proactive international community of scientists — working with yet independent of governments. In the atmospheric sciences, for example, an ICSU group of science statesmen helped initiate the World Weather Watch and organize the Global Atmospheric Research Program (GARP). More recently a next generation of scientists pulled together the striking international scientific consensus that is now the basis for practical actions to limit the emission of "greenhouse gases" and slow the global warming trend in the twenty-first century. The ICSU already has an active committee on biotechnology; altogether it is well placed to be the lead organization for promoting the cooperation of scientists in a global attempt to suppress biological and toxin warfare.

In the case of chemical weapons, at this writing there is at least a chance that a more formal treaty will emerge from the marathon technical talks in Geneva. Producing a CW agent means putting together, in sizable quantities in a facility quite likely to be noticed, a number of "precursor" chemicals that cannot be assembled without the kind of coordination that leaves a visible paper trail. So in a CW regime there might be something for outside inspectors to work on. But the task is at best complex. The Geneva Protocol did not bother with verification; it fits easily on one page. The Chemical Weapons Convention, coming to its sluggish boil in Geneva, filled 142 pages by 1990 and may become another book-length document, like the Convention on the Law of the Sea, before the negotiators can assure their political masters that it is ready to be ratified.

Whether or not a formal treaty is achieved, an international consortium of scientists will need to keep a close watch on toxics and toxins. The international flow of information about actions widely viewed as illicit is critical to deterrence.

Beyond public shame and embarrassment, to which some leaders will always be impervious, there remains a third sanction: to make sure that "acts against civilization" carry an unacceptable cost to the outlaw. Some armchair strategists propose an eye for an eye. A month into the Iraq crisis of 1990, before British troops joined the desert force, the *Economist* of

London advised the United States to "give as bad as it gets": if mustard gas is used by Iraqis, mustard gas should be used on Iraqis; "if they used the more deadly nerve gases, they could expect a shower of VX or SARIN." In real life, however, no political leader or military commander could be hog-tied by so mechanistic a strategy.

Here, as in the case of nuclear weapons, a world consensus can be expressed through the UN Security Council: *the use of chemical or biological weapons is declared in advance to be an act against civilization.*

Not all who agree with the expressed UN principle will be available to bell the cat, but for a coalition of the willing, a wide range of options should be kept open. It is arguable that the retribution should fit the crime: certainly the capacity of the violator to wage war with exotic weapons — nuclear, chemical, and biological and the missiles that can carry them to other people's countries — should be promptly removed by international action. The threat to world security and human rights is such that the ancient and still sometimes honorable principle of nonintervention will be set aside; else the victim might be civilization itself.

seven

WORLD SECURITY
The Role of Activist Neutrals

*Political society exists for the sake of noble actions,
and not of mere companionship.*

—*Aristotle,* Politics

EVEN DURING THE COLD WAR, with peace frozen in Europe, 122
wars elsewhere killed some twenty-two million people. These
wars, and the many civil conflicts the war counters didn't count,
have killed, maimed, and displaced at least as many more.

When the Cold War's wet blanket was removed, millions
of dozing disputants awoke from a long sleep with their cultural
memories unimpaired: "Now, where were we? Weren't we about
to bash in our neighbors' heads?"

Spin your globe at random and stop it with your finger.
If you're touching dry land, you may well be pointing to a zone
of present or probable conflict. In Africa, tribal hatreds are still
at boiling point in the Sudan, Somalia, Ethiopia, Mozambiq, e,
and Liberia. In the Middle East and around the Persian Gulf,
arguments about procedures for peace veil renewed preparations for war. Indians and Pakistanis are still wondering about
how they could use nuclear weapons to settle disputes in Kashmir and the Indus Valley. In Afghanistan, the pullback of the
superpowers has merely "Afghanized" the conflict. The Balkanization of much of the Eurasian continent has begun with
the breakup of Yugoslavia and, in the former Soviet Union, the
victory of republicans who may or may not turn out to be democrats. Tamil Tigers in Sri Lanka, Shining Path guerillas in Peru,
drug dealers masquerading as freedom fighters, criminals dressed
up like bankers—there is no end to the trouble ahead in the new
world disorder.

The eruption of long-dormant political volcanoes has produced an acute requirement for *activist neutrals*. In conflicts among and within countries, they are the bone marrow of civilized society. They are not neutral about individual human rights or cultural human diversity or the global human opportunities opened up by modern science and technology. Above all, they are not neutral about violence; their bias is that there is always a better way than murder to settle a dispute. Their activism for peace is made possible by not taking sides in violent quarrels, by trying to anticipate and prevent violence before it breaks out and to restore the peace when it is broken.

The instruments of activist neutrals range from public embarrassment and moral suasion through economic sanctions to "soldiers without enemies" placed between combatants and ultimately to collective military action to halt aggression or to deter acts against civilization such as the use of exotic weapons.

The activist neutrals are peacemakers public and private: conciliators and bargain makers, mediators and advocates, judges in courts and juries of public opinion. Once upon a time they tended to be national leaders, as when U.S. President Theodore Roosevelt lured the Russians and Japanese to Portsmouth, New Hampshire, to settle their war in 1905. Increasingly today, they are two kinds of people: public international officials and international nongovernments — private citizens banding together across national frontiers to act more rapidly or boldly than is possible for either bureaucrats or politicians.

In the first year after the Cold War, Javier Pérez de Cuéllar of Peru was already showing what a UN Secretary General's calculated courage can accomplish in suspending wars in such varied regions as East Africa, the Persian Gulf, Southeast Asia, and Central America. The UN's next Secretary General, Boutros Boutros-Ghali, was an unusually international person: a Christian citizen of Egypt, an Arab national with a Jewish wife. He had a variety of role models to emulate, ranging from the timid and passive neutrality of Austria's Kurt Waldheim in the 1970s to the life-risking dynamism of Sweden's Dag Hammarskjöld in the 1950s. It was Hammarskjöld who, while visiting Soviet leader Nikita Khrushchev at the Black Sea resort of Sochi in

1957, just after the Soviet Union launched the world's first orbital satellite, best described the nonpartisan stance of the activist peacemaker. "I'm like your *Sputnik*," Hammarskjöld argued. "I was launched from a Swedish platform, but now that
I'm in orbit I belong to no country."

Crisis Management

The anticipation, deterrence, peacekeeping, mediation, and con-
ciliation of international conflicts — and increasingly of some "internal" conflicts too — are a shared international responsibility.
So is mitigating the human misery to which they give rise. The
international community, which for these purposes must act as
a community, needs to get much more seriously and profession-
ally organized to cope.

The science and art of crisis management depends, as conducting a war does, on skills in command, control, communications, and intelligence. Mostly behind a curtain of secrecy,
it has grown up in the governments of a few major military
powers. Yet rapid, accurate, and widely disseminated information is its essence. Transparency, as we have seen in the control of the spread of exotic weapons, is itself a deterrent. The
need is for a pool of international data bases, communication,
and information processing that can be available to governments
and nongovernment watch groups for anticipating and helping
to resolve both international disputes and "internal" conflict that
slops over into international politics.

The rapid spread of information technology makes it likely
that a more than adequate flood of information can be organized
and disseminated to all comers from a central analysis house
related to the United Nations. An analysis and research staff
is, indeed, already in place: the UN Office of Coordination of
Research and Collection of Information (ORCI), which is experimenting with a computerized data base and conflict analysis system known as CASCON, developed at MIT by Lincoln
Bloomfield and Allen Moulton. It may well be true, as Bloomfield argues, that "the more automated the information the less
contentious it may appear to skeptical or technophobic officials."

Modern information technologies are, however, a very mixed blessing. I have worked with computer-mediated communications (don't believe anyone who says he or she has mastered them) for a decade already. Each time I work myself out of a glitch that holds me incommunicado for minutes or hours or even days, I find myself wondering how I could be sure, if I were commander in chief or even a platoon leader, that all the computerized wonders and communications miracles that are now the key to military strength will work as advertised by the vendors, even after exhaustive testing in noncrisis simulations.

If the hardware does work to perfection (a dangerous assumption for any human artifact; U.S. experience with the space shuttle bears witness), it can produce and process prodigious quantities of information. Not access but sorting is the toughest part of any management information system. The more automatic the system, the more readily it produces information overload. Selecting from what's merely interesting what is relevant to today's decision is the bottleneck in any information system serving people who have to analyze and act in a hurry.

The human brain is still our most useful computer, but it is also our softest software: it gets tired to the point of shutting out new information ("I ain't farmin' now as well as I know how," the farmer said to the county agent) and unfamiliar ideas ("The problem is already too complex; let's not complicate it further," the executive said to the researcher). The owner of a tired brain will tend to narrow the circle of consultation to exclude uncomfortable peers likely to ask for more rethinking. Examples abound in any U.S. president's relations with the Congress of his time. Psychiatrist Mottram Torre, who studied the dangers of disability in high office, wrote that one of them is the tendency, especially in crisis conditions, to "conserve energy by projecting the blame to others."

After watching two U.S. presidents through a dozen peace-and-security crises, I got interested in some past cases where presidents had not been feeling well at moments of destiny: Franklin Roosevelt's performance at Yalta ("He won't take any interest in what we are trying to do," Churchill complained),

Woodrow Wilson's tactical rigidity on the League of Nations issue when he was bedridden yet still president, Abraham Lincoln's damaging hesitations during the first year of his presidency ("When hurried by the pressure of rapidly, uncontrollable circumstances and events, he tended to become . . . inwardly indecisive," wrote one historian.)

No matter how good the crisis information delivery system, its priceless ingredient is the brainwork of the people who select what information to use and which part of that to believe. The prime qualities needed are intensely human: reflective judgment and flexibility and rapid adaptability to conditions the planners didn't think to program into the machines — which, despite the hype about artificial intelligence, are not "intelligent" but merely hyperinformed.

Not long before the Soviet Union evaporated, President Gorbachev organized a Moscow seminar to see what could be learned from comparing notes on the Cuba missile crisis of 1962. Some of those who were responsible participants in the management of that conflict (still the closest the world has come to nuclear war) took part in the seminar. Robert McNamara's 1990 report on the dialogue is illuminating: "Khrushchev did what he did, and Kennedy responded as he did, because each leader, his associates and his people were captives of the gross misperceptions and deep-seated mistrust which underlay the Cold War." Crisis management, McNamara concluded, is "dangerous, difficult, uncertain . . . we must direct our attention to crisis avoidance."

Early Warning

Given the leakiness of information, broad hints about any substantial war preparations, troop deployments, naval and air dispositions, and even the buildup of supplies in anticipation of a crisis will be known by someone, not necessarily or even probably by spies. I was privy to the products of U.S. clandestine intelligence for a good many years, and I seldom saw a piece of information that was so different from what was available in the public domain that it was worth the risk of getting caught

procuring it. Usually available are known indications that make
a decipherable pattern if they are put together by skilled analysts.
(The skill of the analysts is directly proportional to their capacity to avoid discarding surprising information because it doesn't
fit their settled preconceptions.)

Moreover, space satellites that can "see" through clouds,
day or night, now provide a way of keeping track of most mili-
tary-related movements (though not, of course, scientific research
or small-scale technologies). Already in 1990, readouts from the
French SPOT satellite and some Russian satellite observations,
as well as data from U.S. remote sensing and weather satellites, could be bought by anyone who could afford them. Advanced reconnaissance satellites, which can read from outer space
the numbers on automobile license plates, should now be made
part of an international early warning system that alerts not a
handful of intelligence analysts but the worldwide community
of political leaders and diplomatic and military advisers — as well
as a global radio and television audience — about military moves
that could be the prelude to premeditated war.

In 1978, Bloomfield and I suggested in an Aspen Institute report a U.S. initiative for a satellite monitoring function
to be carried out by the United Nations. It fell on deaf ears in
the Carter administration but was picked up by a French expert we had consulted and passed along to French President
Valéry Giscard d'Estaing, who floated it in a major address to
that year's UN General Assembly on Disarmament. The notion was that such a capability, producing information spread
in the open by the United Nations, might in itself deter military solutions and incline governments toward trying nonviolent
resolution of disputes. At the time, the world was not ready for
publicly authorized spies in the sky. Perhaps now it is an idea
whose time has come.

Arthur C. Clarke, the imaginative scientist who also has
been a best-selling science fiction writer, proposed a variant:
the public "spy satellites" would be operated by Canada, Sweden,
and Japan ("the only nonnuclear space powers — not to mention the only [historical] target for nuclear bombs"). Perhaps,
he added, "even the fanatically neutral Swiss might be induced

to join such a project." "We would enter," Clarke argued, "what has been aptly called the Age of Transparency. Like most people, many nations would not like to live in glass houses. They may not realize the extent to which they are already doing this. . . . As the Age of Transparency dawns, political and military wisdom will lie in cooperating with the inevitable."

Transparency can also be enhanced by energizing international nongovernments to monitor and warn of future conflict. Nongovernment "searchlights" have been especially good at shining on violations of human rights: the work of Amnesty International, based in London, and the International Commission of Jurists, based in Geneva, are outstanding examples. An international satellite monitoring agency, as proposed by France, could even contract to nongovernments much of the work of assembling the hardware and making the observations, which (for maximum visibility) would be published for the world to see by the UN agency itself.

Almost instantaneous multichannel communication by satellite makes it possible to bring a local conflict, even in a "remote" region, to world attention overnight. This cuts both ways. In terrorist scenarios, for example, worldwide attention may be just what the kidnappers or hostage snatchers want. (We will return to this issue shortly.) But rapid information exchange can also speed up consultation within a community of the concerned: computer teleconferencing can mobilize a response as rapidly as those consulted can make up their minds. And response time in the command and control of far-flung international peacekeeping forces can be greatly reduced.

The Always Available "Third Party"

Conflict resolution, whether in a family, a local community, or between states, generally requires a third party, someone able to analyze the issues independently, willing to talk frankly with and listen hard to both (or, in complex disputes, several) parties concerned.

UN secretaries general and their personal representatives have been more or less active in this role (depending on the per-sonality and courage of the incumbent) at important moments of recent world history. Dag Hammarskjöld was willing to plunge into the blood-soaked mess in the Congo (now Zaire) when in 1960 independence from Belgium induced a civil war with a potential for a Soviet-U.S. war by proxy. His personal representatives, Ralph Bunche and Conor Cruise O'Brien, and the UN's largest peacekeeping force thus far reunited the country and helped the powerful outsiders decide to keep their distance. (The crisis also cost Hammarskjöld his life in a mysterious Congo plane crash and led to a quarter-century of chronic budget trouble for UN peacekeeping.)

U Thant was willing to intervene in the U.S.-Soviet crisis over the Cuba missiles, appealing to both sides not to deepen the nuclear danger by a direct naval confrontation. It was that UN appeal Nikita Khrushchev was answering when he announced that Soviet ships and their escorts would turn around and not challenge the U.S. picket line of destroyers that had "quarantined" Cuba. (The untold story is that the letter the secretary general sent to Khrushchev was drafted in the U.S. State Department. The United States badly needed this activist neutral's bold move, which enabled the Soviet leader to save face by responding to an international plea, not capitulating to an adversary's demand.)

In more recent examples of a UN secretary general as the always available third party in international politics, Javier Pérez de Cuéllar and his personal representatives were key players in the complicated choreography that enabled the Soviet troops to slide out of Afghanistan, helped turn off (though without settling it) the war between Iraq and Iran, brought the four warring factions together in Cambodia, and took over the peacekeeping role in what used to be Yugoslavia after the European Community shrank from that ticklish task.

Pérez de Cuéllar's calculated courage in such cases as these led him to recruit people of extraordinary tact and skill to serve as his personal representatives. One was a former U.S. secretary of state, Cyrus Vance, who shuttled in and out of Yugoslavia and paved the way for a UN force there. Another was Giandomenico Picco, the Italian who helped stop the eight-year war between Iran and Iraq, then negotiated the last of the Western hostages out of Lebanon.

There is clearly a chronic and continuing need for this kind of international service. After nearly half a century of experience, it makes no sense to keep treating this as an *ad hoc* function. What's needed is a panel of people able, ready, and willing to represent the world community as mediators and conciliators in efforts to avoid violence, mediate conflict, settle disputes. These would be trustworthy individuals known for their integrity, designated and approved in advance for this role, who could be dispatched at a moment's notice by the secretary general on his (perhaps in future *her*) initiative or at the direction of the UN Security Council.

Such a panel of conciliators would have to be large enough to contain people from many cultures and all world regions, people with experience in public and international affairs, persuasive personalities with independence of spirit and skill in human relations. They would not be full-time international people employed by the United Nations—except as consultants when called to active duty. Rather, they would be distinguished persons of assorted nationalities and skills (including language skills), carrying on with their own responsibilities in their own countries as professional arbitrators, lawyers, scientists, professors, labor leaders, business people, nonprofit executives, retired diplomats, international agency officials, or whatever. But each would agree ahead of time to drop almost overnight whatever he or she normally does and act instead for the community of nations in defusing or resolving an international conflict.

To avoid holding up emergency action by arguments about the qualifications of possible mediators, they should already be in place, appointed to the panel by the Security Council on the recommendation of the secretary general. Appointment would thus be a signal personal honor as well as a potentially heavy personal responsibility in matters of life and death. Members of this distinguished panel would doubtless be put to work also by regional organizations trying to bring about peaceful change in their own jurisdictions.

The widespread need for available third parties is not a substitute for the formal processes of mediation, arbitration, and adjudication described in the UN Charter's "fifty pages of procedure" and the Statute of the International Court of Justice. These are still alive, but not particularly healthy. The United States further weakened the World Court in the 1980s by its unwillingness to submit to the Court's jurisdiction on its covert actions, notably the mining of harbors in Nicaragua. But toward the end of the decade, as the Cold War abated, both the United States and the Soviet Union said they would place several of their disputes before the Court. And in 1989 the United States Senate, breaking with a long tradition of reluctance, agreed to compulsory arbitration on a wide range of trade disputes. The World Court may find its calendar filling up with issues touching trade and investment, the Law of the Sea, terrorism, and narcotics traffic.

But let's face it: this very Western idea that international politics can be subordinated to arbitration rules and courts of law hasn't played very well on the world stage. The formal laywer-dominated mechanisms are not attracting very much of the world's dispute business, partly because so much of the world's work is no longer even conducted by governments. Most international law is being made not in court but out where the problems are, made by people who do not think of themselves as making law or setting precedents but are simply doing what needs to be done: commanding armed forces, practicing diplomacy, buying and selling things, moving information around, and resolving conflict case by case in a chronically turbulent world.

Peacekeeping and Peace Enforcing

The UN's peacekeeping function has been cited (in Chapter Four) as an example of what works. It shares with the High Commissioner for Refugees the distinction of a whole UN function having been awarded the Nobel Peace Prize.

Peacekeeping has come to have a special meaning, and it's important to be clear about its limitations. The word does not refer to all the things the United Nations and its agencies do to try to make wars less likely, prevent them when they are imminent, or stop them after they have started. It means lightly armed troops, recruited from countries uninvolved in a conflict, furnished with blue helmets and UN flags, placed by order of the UN Security Council between the armed forces of two warring countries *with their consent,* to keep them from each others' throats pending settlement of their dispute. They are usually there for quite a while because once there is a cease-fire, the incentive to settle is sharply reduced. Peacekeeping forces dating from the 1950s and 1960s are still on Arab-Israel borders, on the island of Cyprus keeping Greek and Turkish Cypriots apart, and in Kashmir to watch Indians and Pakistanis glaring at each other over that beautiful disputed terrain.

Usually, the impetus for a UN peacekeeping operation is not an effort to prevent an imminent war. Throwing neutral troops as a third force into a no-man's-land between two governments determined to settle a dispute on the battlefield would simply ensure that the necessarily small international force would be chopped up by both sides in a preliminary bout before getting at each other in the main event. Calling in the UN's "soldiers without enemies" is normally a face-saving way for both sides to admit that making war is not getting either of them anywhere, but they are not yet ready to make love.

Short of prevention, however, peacekeeping forces have been mandated by the Security Council to do everything from passively observing agreed processes (political elections, military withdrawals) to actively attempting to quell local turmoil. In the early sixties a brigade force of some five thousand, mostly from India and Malaysia, chased the rebellious Katanga gendarmerie all over the southern part of what is now Zaire. (The presence of UN peacekeepers does not guarantee that good government will follow, as the case of Zaire amply demonstrates.) In recent years such forces have played a more passive role, although typically in perilous circumstances — as in Afghanistan after the Soviet pullout, in the Gulf to supervise the Iran-Iraq cease-fire, in Angola to ensure the departure of both Cuban and South African forces, in Namibia to police the preliminaries to independence.

What the Security Council has almost never ordered is peacekeeping where major military powers are at loggerheads. The one exception occurred in 1950, when the Soviets were boycotting the Security Council and by inadvertence enabled the United States to mount its riposte to the North Korean move across the agreed dividing line (the 38th parallel) in the form of a UN command with a Security Council mandate. Once given, that mandate could not be withdrawn because the United States could veto any proposal to change the original decision.

UN peacekeeping experience has yet to produce an integrated UN naval force. An unofficial discussion of that subject in 1989, sponsored by the UN associations of the United States and the Soviet Union, proposed "multilateral naval peacekeeping under UN auspices under some circumstances to perform limited tasks relating to the implementation of cease-fire agreements and the reopening of international waterways." The case in point was the Persian Gulf. Several proposals to reflag the fleets in the gulf with the blue-and-white UN standard were overtaken by Iraq's invasion of Kuwait. But the world reaction to that move probably reinforced the idea that peacekeepers had better be prepared to go to sea in some of the world's more contentious regional waters.

UN peacekeeping, as defined in practice if not in the Charter, is here to stay. However, if this is going to be a permanent function of the future, then the world's democratic majority needs to solve two problems: how to prepare the forces that will be needed and how to share the burden of paying for them.

Many years ago, a retired Indian general who had served as chief of staff for peacekeeping at the United Nations decided to try to fill the training gap. General Indar Rikye established as a "nongovernment" the International Peace Academy (IPA), which now works out of an office near the United Nations in New York. (He was succeeded by Olara Otunnu of Uganda, a skilled and thoughtful diplomat with long UN experience.) Over more than two decades, the IPA developed a way of thinking ("doctrine") about the soldiers-without-enemies function and organized training programs for military officers likely to find

UN peacekeeping in their horoscopes. Four Scandinavian countries, which along with Canada have been the most consistent providers of blue-helmeted peacekeepers, devise their own training programs to prepare their military for service with the United Nations.

It is high time that such efforts as these become part of a broader permanent UN peacekeeping system, funded by the world community as a whole and involving military personnel from as many countries as possible. A decade from now, there should be elements in most nations' armed forces that are trained for, and expect to serve part of their time in, UN peacekeeping.

Until recently, the Cold War made it advisable to exclude units from major military powers in peacekeeping sponsored by the United Nations, although the United States has been active in providing military airlift. Some "middle powers" (Canada, Australia) have been willing participants. For historical reasons, some countries (Germany, Japan) have opted out of this form of world community service, though they do help pay for it. In 1992, Japan for the first time authorized small contingents from its self-defense force to participate in UN peacekeeping in Cambodia. Other countries, such as Switzerland and Austria, have hung back, restrained by traditions of neutrality, while other "European neutrals" (Sweden, Finland) and "nonaligned" countries such as India and Malaysia have been generous providers of peacekeeping personnel.

With the Cold War turned off, none of the historical reasons for abstention make much sense any more. Moreover, the sizable military establishments in a good many developing countries should play important roles in world peacekeeping, for it is in the developing world that the need for UN peacekeepers mostly arises.

The other issue is, who should pay? Peacekeeping is a kind of commons, a broadly shared responsibility. Here is a prime example of the case for international taxation — not an annual debate in each national government about whether international peace is worth paying for but an automatic stream of revenues available from those activities that depend for their livelihood and survival on a world more or less at peace.

In 1992 the new secretary general, Boutros Boutros-Ghali, lost no time in pressing the UN's members to help him get organized for more and better peacekeeping. He saw the need for small numbers of troops ready for use in twenty-four hours, and asked as many members as possible to train units of one thousand troops for instantaneous peacekeeping duty.

Then he suggested that the Security Council have "peace-enforcing units" to be used in situations that go beyond peacekeeping, as for example when a cease-fire has been agreed but then breaks down. Restoring and maintaining a cease-fire, which means suppressing active hostilities between two armies' forces, would require heavier armor and special preparatory training. Peace enforcers, Boutros-Ghali made clear in his June 19, 1992, *Agenda for Peace,* would be authorized by the Security Council, would be available to the U.N. on call, would "consist of troops that have volunteered for such service," and would (as in the case of peacekeeping forces) be under the command of the secretary general.

Boutros-Ghali made clear that both peacekeeping and peace enforcement would be actions short of using the UN's ultimate punch, under Article 42 of the Charter, to "take military action to maintain or restore international peace and security." He went on to remind the UN members of their obligation, under Article 43, to get on with agreements to make forces available to the Security Council to oppose major aggression "not only on an ad hoc basis but on a permanent basis."

"Under the political circumstances that now exist for the first time since the Charter was adopted," said the UN's new secretary general as politely as he could, "the long-standing obstacles to the conclusion of such special agreements should no longer prevail." Thus "a potential aggressor would know that the [Security] Council had at its disposal a means of response." Boutros-Ghali made clear that the U.N. could not expect to take on a "major army equipped with sophisticated weapons" but would be used "in meeting any threat posed by a military force of a lesser order."

The June 1992 report was good news. It was clear evidence that another courageous and practical UN secretary general had succeeded Javier Pérez de Cuéllar and that he might prove to be closer to Dag Hammarskjöld than to Kurt Waldheim in acting as an activist neutral. Also notable was the clarity of Boutros-Ghali's thinking about the needs for, as well as the distinctions among, the three levels of UN military activity: peacekeeping, peace enforcing, and deterring major breaches of the peace.

But Boutros-Ghali's creative effort to analyze for the world's governments how the prospects for peacemaking had been transformed by the ending of the Cold War was bound to collide at first with four decades of military momentum in the UN's major governments. Two months before the secretary general's report, the U.S. State Department had warned against giving the Security Council a standing military force or trying to breathe life into the Military Staff Committee (established in the UN Charter as a big-power combined chiefs of staff but never activated in a real-life emergency).

When "Internal Affairs" Are International

The United Nations Charter, along with every first-year textbook on international law, frowns on international intervention "in matters which are essentially within the domestic jurisdiction of any state." The obsolescence of this tattered doctrine is obvious, rapid, and welcome. The real-world map is a jumble of deep mutual interpenetrations that more and more blur what used to be the political geography of the globe.

Violations of human rights have long since become a legitimate, if often discomfiting, subject of international inquiry. Peacekeeping forces are by definition now in the midst of some countries' "domestic" conflicts; sometimes, as in Cyprus, they have been there for a generation. International markets set the price for staple commodities (grains, energy) and for money, stocks, and bonds. Real or fancied international threats drive "domestic" budget decisions. Cross-border lobbyists try to influence political leaders on issues ranging from marine insurance and energy policy to carbon dioxide emissions and planned parenthood. International loans and "foreign aid" are tied to "internal" reform policies in dozens of developing countries. International trade deeply affects major "national" industries and such sensitive "domestic" issues as jobs, prices, and the survival of whole industries. The international movements of people change the ethnic mix inside countries and thus the very nature of "domestic politics." International crime, especially drug trafficking, reaches deeply into "local" communities and has brought into being a strong international network of national and local police agencies. International observers are an increasingly frequent feature of "national" and even "local" elections. The internationalization of "domestic affairs" also gives rise to wholesale changes in education and research, from preschool games to postdoctoral research.

Thus it no longer seems shocking that a growing part of "world security" is really about cross-border interventions in affairs that used to be treated as domestic. There was little talk of nonintervention as troops from the coalition in the desert, carrying out decisions of the UN Security Council, flew over Iraq's borders, pushed deep into Iraq's sovereign territory, and (after the war) set up temporary buffer zones and safe havens for Kurds and Shi'ites. The troops were making new international law the way law is usually made, case by case. There is now quite general agreement (in practice if not yet in theory) that the UN Charter principle of nonintervention has to be set aside in favor of the higher aim of making the world safe for diversity.

Two questions used to serve as litmus tests to tell whether one nation's actions inside another nation were all right:

Do the outsiders have an international mandate for their actions? That is still a dependable beacon. Looking at it from an American perspective, we did have such a mandate, from the UN Security Council, in Korea and Kuwait. In Vietnam we did not. That is one reason why we and those who joined us accomplished what we set out to do in Korea and Kuwait: push the North Koreans back across the 38th parallel and liberate Kuwait from Iraqi occupation. We failed to induce the North Vietnamese to "leave their neighbors alone," not only because we didn't know how to do it but also because popular support for this "American war" fell away. Collective security works only when it is collective.

Were the outsiders invited to intervene? This test, by contrast, has turned out to be so corruptible as to be almost useless as an ethical guide. Strong military powers can all too readily arrange to be invited. The Soviets were "invited" by local Communist puppets to stomp on uncomfortably feisty populations in Hungary (1956), Czechoslovakia (1968), and Afghanistan (1979). In the Afghan case the invitation arrived after the invasion started: a puppet had first to be installed in office. In recent U.S. history, the Nixon Administration neglected to get an invitation for its "incursion" into Cambodia (1970). President Reagan's diplomats arranged for a group of small Caribbean states to ask for the invasion of Grenada (1983). President Bush was invited into Panama (1989) by a newly elected president who took his oath of office, under American protection, just as the operation began.

From the practice of nations in recent memory, some useful fragments of international law can be derived. Here are ten candidates for tomorrow's textbooks.

1. Once you have a valid mandate to push an invader back across his own frontier, it's okay to invade the invader too. General Norman Schwartzkopf's "Hail Mary" strategy to outflank Iraq's best troops is a recent example in living color. Less current but equally choice was General MacArthur's Inchon landing in North Korea more than forty years ago.

2. It is alright to use force to deprive a rogue government of dangerous exotic weapons. It's best, though, to do this as agent for the international community. Israel bombed an Iraqi nuclear plant in 1981, when both Moscow and Washington still thought they could make friends with Saddam Hussein. The private applause was drowned out by the public tut-tutting.

3. The intervention of a peacekeeping force mandated by the UN Security Council is already an accepted way to maintain whatever accord contending armed groups can agree on. The catch here is that the peacekeepers cannot be expected to mediate the basic dispute. It is easier to drop peacekeepers between two contending groups than to create the conditions that permit them to leave.

4. Genocide and other gross violations of human rights justify international intervention. Even after the appalling lesson

of Hitler's holocaust, governments had been skittish about trying to stop other governments from mistreating their "own" people. However, the spectacle of millions of Iraqi citizens trying to escape their own government and thousands dying in the attempt drove outsiders to provide relief, grant asylum, and warn Iraq's government to stay out of sizable areas of its "own" territory.

5.   When a country's central authority loses control, it's okay for outsiders *acting together* to help cobble together a workable government. After World War II, UNRRA helped fashion government agencies in Italy, Yugoslavia, the Ukraine, and China. In the early sixties, the United Nations did something similar in the Congo (now Zaire). In 1990 the United States, China, and the Soviet Union, with the help of UN mediators, tried to put Cambodia back together. At any moment in time, there is a long list of countries that need international help to become viable states.

6.   Intervention is justified to suppress terrorists, especially when they are sponsored by national governments. International measures to frustrate criminal use of airports, banks, and the media need not be held back by squeamishness about the rights of national governments that are subverting the rights of other national governments.

7.   Rescuing hostages by force is usually acceptable. It can even be successful (Israelis at the Entebbe airport, Belgians with U.S. help in Stanleyville). It can also be botched, as when U.S. helicopters bogged down in the desert on their way to snatch hostages from the Teheran embassy.

8.   Drug traffickers and other criminals may be chased by international police teams that don't have to pay any more attention to national frontiers than the criminals do.

9.   Refugees and their repatriation or resettlement elsewhere are an international responsibility. People displaced inside their own countries are a legitimate target for humanitarian aid from abroad. The right of people to survive and settle somewhere is fast becoming a first charge on the international conscience.

10.   Coping with catastrophe, whether occasioned by natural forces (hurricanes, earthquakes, volcanoes) or human

error (Chernobyl), is clearly an international obligation regardless of the national state in which people may need emergency help.

We have already considered action under the UN Charter to frustrate aggression, intervention to deprive a rogue government of dangerous exotic weapons, and the placing of peacekeeping forces between warring groups that have agreed to cease fire. Let's look now at the other cases where the line between "domestic" and "international" has been irretrievably blurred and various forms of cross-border "intervention," some uninvited and some by local consent, are required for reasons of security and humanity alike.

Violations of Human Rights

The not-so-hidden agenda of human rights deals mostly with how governments treat their own people. In a strikingly candid speech to the UN General Assembly in March 1977, President Jimmy Carter said it without diplomatic evasion: "No member of the United Nations can claim that mistreatment of its own citizens is solely its own business." He was talking, he made clear, not only about torture of political prisoners but about "unwarranted deprivation" of the poor.

The main instrument of intervention here has been published information — careful research about individual cases by human rights organizations outside of governments (such as Amnesty International, the International Commission of Jurists, Freedom House, and the Helsinki Watch organizations in Eastern Europe and the former Soviet Union) and publicity about violations generated by governments (such as the annual reports on the state of human rights around the world mandated by the U.S. Congress and published each year by the State Department). For a quarter of a century there was a drumfire of outrage about apartheid in South Africa by a virtually unanimous UN General Assembly. Cynics thought it was wasted breath: the government of South Africa wouldn't listen. But the waves breaking on that jagged rock eventually did smooth it, changing ever so gradually the future of that troubled and still deeply divided country.

On human rights, worldwide norms are already spelled out in considerable detail — in the UN Charter (1945), the Universal Declaration of Human Rights (1948), several unratified conventions, and the Helsinki Final Act (1975). (In the last of these, a Brezhnev-led Soviet Union surprisingly agreed to incorporate, by reference, the entire text of the Universal Declaration of Human Rights, on which the USSR and its East European allies had abstained in the General Assembly twenty-seven years earlier.) Making the norms effective country by country and community by community requires the courage and persistence of dedicated nongovernments, which fortunately a number of them seem to have.

Government Breakdowns

A clear exception to the principle of nonintervention seems to exist where there is no effective government in what is still juridically a nation-state. Lebanon was a tragic modern example. The principle of nonintervention came to be meaningless. A good many countries, including Israel, Syria, Iran, and several Western nations, intervened in force; each managed to make things worse and national government less possible. The antidote in such a case would have been not to argue about intervention but to organize an *international* intervention strong enough to keep the internal peace, imaginative enough to construct a government out of Lebanon's broken parts, and well enough funded and staffed to do the kind of job that UNRRA did in devastated areas after World War II.

Cambodia, rent by four armed factions, was another such case; but there a precarious peace among the factions was belatedly negotiated at the United Nations. Other states, especially those with strongly entrenched rival factions, will face in varying degrees a breakdown of governance, inviting or requiring international action. The fragmentation of South Africa, Yugoslavia, and the former Soviet Union seems likely to require multiple interventions, from advice on elections and monetary policy to massive economic aid and peacekeeping forces, for a good many years.

In each of these cases and many more, the International Committee of the Red Cross (ICRC) can serve us here as an impressive example of activist neutrality fully and riskily engaged. Not to be confused with national Red Cross societies, the ICRC is a worldwide nongovernment agency with an all-Swiss executive staff governed by an all-Swiss self-perpetuating committee of twenty-three. It is the main instrument for carrying into action the Geneva Conventions of 1949. These famous humanitarian standards pledge governments, even when they are at war, to

- Care for friends and enemies alike
- Respect every human being, his honour, religious convictions and the special rights of the child
- Prohibit inhuman or degrading treatment, the taking of hostages, mass extermination, torture, summary executions, deportations, pillage and the wanton destruction of property
- Authorize ICRC delegates to visit prisoners of war and civilian internees, and to interview without witnesses persons in detention

Two additional protocols (1977) make clear that these principles apply to all civilians and that they are valid not only in international wars but also in civil wars.

These extraordinary aims were backed in 1991 by government contributions of only 700 million Swiss francs (about $470 million). That sum, small by the standards of government spending, buys a deep and cost-effective intervention in fifteen or twenty of the world's hottest spots at any given time.

By the nature of its mandate, the ICRC is deeply immersed in the "domestic affairs" of sovereign states, usually at moments in their history when emotions about sovereignty and self-determination run high. Yet the gutsy Swiss seem unimpressed with theories of nonintervention and undeterred by doubts about interference. Theirs is a ticklish role at best. ICRC "delegates," ready to plunge into the midst of conflict anywhere to help the world's most defenseless people, exhibit every day a very high standard of practical morality, with no time for moralizing about it because there's so much work to be done in so many dangerous places. It's hard to think of another domain in which less than half a billion dollars buys so much human goodness reinforced by so much wisdom and courage.

Terrorism, Hostages, and Drugs

Terrorism is the threatening or mistreatment or murder of innocent bystanders for purposes of extortion — whether the ransom sought is private money or public action (such as the release of particular prisoners). State-sponsored terrorism is not new; Genghis Khan and Adolf Hitler spring to mind. But the use of semi-independent nongovernments as "contractors" (how else describe the relations between the hostage-taking Hezbollah in Lebanon and the government of Iran?) is terrorism with a difference.

Except in the amplifier provided by the mass media, terrorism is not big-time. During the decade from 1980 to 1989, 6,500 international terrorist incidents occurred worldwide, leaving about 5,000 people dead and 11,500 wounded. The number of such incidents actually fell in 1989 by more than a third from 1988's total of 855 attacks. Even so, in 1989 the citizens and property of more than seventy-four countries were attacked by international terrorists in more than sixty countries. Among those murdered were Rene Muawad, the president of Lebanon; Alfred Herrhausen, West Germany's leading banker; and Colonel William Higgins, one of the U.S. hostages who had been held in Beirut.

The total number of incidents was down not only for one-time reasons (the Afghan government curtailed its terrorist campaign in Pakistan after the Soviet troops were withdrawn, the Palestine Liberation Organization reduced its support to terrorist groups affiliated with it, there was dissension in the Abu Nidal organization) but also because of greater cooperation among national police forces, more physical security at airports and border crossings, and stiffer prison terms for those that were caught.

Defining state-sponsored terrorism for the purpose of achieving a near-universal agreement to outlaw it should not be an impossible task; even some of the current state sponsors are reluctant to admit engaging in terrorism. Piracy and the slave trade have presented civilization with analogous puzzles and have been almost entirely abolished. But such an international agreement would also require the major powers to curb their miscalled "intelligence capabilities," as the U.S. Congress did (after several embarrassments) in outlawing assassination. The "enforcement" of norms in this arena, as with human rights, is primarily the searchlight of exposure, leading to government-to-government persuasion.

It will be increasingly important not to permit an outlaw government, by taking hostages, to "change the subject from its behavior to our yellow ribbons," as Iraq tried to do after its takeover of Kuwait, by detaining thousands of foreign residents. The dilemma is excruciating for the political leaders of the nations of which the detainees are citizens. Yet no government can even pretend to protect all its citizens — especially those who stay in a country or region after their governments warn them to get out, as was the case with some of the hostages in Lebanon.

At any given moment, for example, about 1 percent of the U.S. population are traveling, living, or working abroad. They (we, since I travel a lot) are inherently at risk. If our government is to be paralyzed each time one or a hundred of us are snatched (as it was during the Iran hostage crisis of 1989–1990), the future is handed over to the gangsters.

The evidence from the Iraq crisis of 1990 and 1991 was that governments were learning this lesson and tried hard not to treat the hostages as the centerpiece of the story. (The same could not be said of some of the best-known TV commentators, who were almost as anxious as Saddam Hussein to be seen fraternizing with hostages.) For a time, while state terrorists absorb the lesson too, hostages and their families will be even more in the front trenches of the war on terrorism than they already are. In a longer view, if governments demonstrate that they cannot be swayed by the plight of a few of their citizens abroad, hostages should seem less valuable and all residents and travelers outside their own countries correspondingly safer. Let's keep our yellow ribbons in the sewing drawer.

When it comes to the private entrepreneurs among terrorists, we have to look for the key "valves" in the system. They are not hard to find. Nearly every terrorist scenario includes three elements: luring the mass media to give wide publicity to the terrorist act, its rationale, and the demands for ransom; getting an airplane and landing at one or more airports; and relying on one or many veiled bank accounts.

Let's examine these elements in reverse order. Banks are everywhere subject to national regulations and international sanctions. For any substantial bank to protect a person who kidnaps or murders innocent bystanders is a grotesque perversion of the protection bankers themselves are accorded by public policy. Without the cooperation of banks, terrorists (and drug traders) would find it much harder to hide the proceeds of illegal transactions. No banker or banking regulator can even pretend to be neutral on this subject. The secrecy of numbered bank accounts and safe havens for money laundering are too often accessories to crime.

Access to airports is under government control even in the most wide-open democracies. Not all terrorists intend to go somewhere else; but if those who do knew ahead of time that they wouldn't be able to land anywhere, it could make a big difference. When Fidel Castro decided to remand to Cuban dungeons hijackers landing in Havana, there was a sharp decrease in hijackings on the East Coast of the United States.

Terrorists understand very well the power they derive from the spread of information. The prime terrorist technique is to hold bystanders hostage or to kill them for the delectation of the mass media. If the major media paid no attention, the terrorists would have much less to work with.

Freedom-of-the-press traditions constrain what governments can do to prevent terrorists from manipulating the media. But the traditions do not prevent media executives from developing their own codes of ethics in a serious effort to avoid becoming coconspirators whenever a terrorist wants to do something outrageous enough to be noticed.

In the United States, the major commercial television networks have an informal understanding that they will not point cameras at crazies who run out on the playing field during a televised football game. The norm is almost ridiculously trivial; but it has been effective in curbing such incidents. If the most-watched media can thus restrain themselves on a triviality, is collective restraint on matters of life and death too much to expect?

The objection will be that all the world's media would never go for such self-policing. But the people most terrorists most want to reach are not watching *all* the world's television networks, more likely fewer than a dozen of them. They listen to the radio newscasts of only a few networks. They read the newspaper dispatches of only a handful of international news services. Is leadership from the leaders in international com-munication — responding to their own ethical standards, not to any government's — out of the question?

The drug epidemic does require a major international effort led by governments. Instead of the fruitless debate among those who prefer to work on the demand for drugs, the produc-tion of drugs, or the marketing of drugs (all three are required for a full-court press), what is needed is an international deter-mination to solve the problem, a norm around which govern-ments and nongovernments of many kinds can mobilize a major (burden-shared) investment in relevant activity.

Education and treatment are obviously an important part of the mix of remedies. So far, the international communities of educators and social agencies have not made drugs a priority issue; and (as Bloomfield puts it) "demand, particularly in the U.S., simulates the 'image of the market' in a perverse echo of other global market-driven transformations we applaud."

The combination of drug interdiction and enforcement is likewise a much more important and more international task than has yet been tackled. To take it seriously will require an international police effort on a scale without precedent. And once again, the "valve" called the international community of bankers is ready to hand, if not yet thoroughly engaged.

Refugees and Displaced Persons

In 1992 there were more *international* refugees in the world (eigh-teen million plus) than there were right after the horrors and holocausts of the Second World War (about sixteen million). At least as many more millions of "displaced persons," pushed from their homes by turbulence in their own countries but lacking the status of international refugees, are wandering homeless or sequestered in camps, uncomfortably similar to the concentration camps of yore, in and around Lebanon, Cambodia, Ethiopia, Mozambique, the Sudan, and other places where turmoil and terror are the daily standard of life.

The world of the Cold War was divided between two kinds of national governments. Some worried about their people moving out. The others worried about too many people moving in. When police states went out of fashion, more people had freedom to travel. Then the democracies began to close the doors and bar the windows, leaving more people in limbo than ever before.

For nearly half a century, to be granted asylum and treated as a "refugee," a person was supposed to have "a well-founded fear of persecution" back home. Long before the Cold War began to dissipate, a succession of activist UN high commissioners for refugees kept stretching that narrow rule to cover more and more people escaping not only from oppression but from civil conflict, racial discrimination, ecological disaster, and just plain poverty.

The widening definition of who has a right to be helped reflects multiple changes in the people-movement problem:

- *from* a primarily European problem forty years ago *to* a worldwide hemorrhaging of people from their homes to somewhere else
- *from* a temporary displacement that resettlement would fix *to* a permanent condition in which the numbers of refugees and migrants keep growing but their geography and ethnic origins keep changing
- *from* a concept of international refugees *to* a parallel concern for people displaced inside their own countries
- *from* a focus on political persecution *to* the more generous idea that no matter what people are escaping from, they have basic human needs to be met and basic rights to be protected

- *from* the idea that the movement of people is primarily a matter for national states to handle *to* a growing conviction that displacement, destitution, and distress of people anywhere requires humanitarian actions by the human family as a whole

The new world disorder—the discrediting of communism, the evaporation of the Cold War, the multiple outbreaks of ethnic violence—added large numbers to the population in limbo. It also planted the problem once again squarely in Europe. For some East Europeans, the new freedom meant "voting with their feet"—and heading west. Resentment in Western Europe of this intra-European migration then fell out on refugees elsewhere who wanted to resettle in Europe. Already worried about the free flow of people that was in prospect for residents of their single market, most Europeans were still willing to help refugees elsewhere—so long as they didn't move to Europe.

That's why Sadako Ogata of Japan, in her first year as the High Commissioner for Refugees, was saying in 1991 that the new answer for most refugees was simply to go home—wherever *home* was not a synonym for persecution. *Developmental migration* came to be the buzzword in Geneva. That meant helping countries such as Mexico become societies so vibrant and successful that they would lure their citizens (and flight capital, too) to come back where they "belonged." The trouble was, many refugees did not agree. Democracy and economic opportunity are magnetic. Those who enjoy them will find it necessary to share them—in societies that will become more multicultural whether they like it or not.

Whatever the temporary prospects for individual refugees—repatriation or resettlement, soon or late—the refugee problem is clearly now a permanent one. We need to get organized to treat it as such.

Until the 1980s the UN High Commissioner for Refugees had an outstanding record of imaginative and competent efforts to cope. A series of high commissioners was effective in mobilizing support for transient camps and providing some refugees with temporary international identity papers. That office has had the help of a wide variety of private voluntary agencies from many countries. Those agencies have filled with first-rate talent many gaps resulting from the indifference and cultural reluctance of some governments and the stingy financing of most.

For a while in the 1980s the High Commissioner's Office became much less effective and was plagued by scandals and criticism that reduced its support from governments. But its previous record and its potential under new leadership qualified it in the early 1990s to become the core of a major UN agency but maintaining, I would hope, something like its present status as a unitary international executive with an advisory committee from governments rather than the orthodox committee-of-sovereigns-with-a-staff.

Essentially, the office should have two functions. One is the temporary care (health, feeding, education, protection) of people in limbo, people who cannot go home and cannot yet be resettled. For this function, it should be generously funded, and it should use the funds to develop even further the capacity of private voluntary groups to help share in this temporary care; they will in turn add some funds they are able to raise from nongovernment sources.

The other function is to develop and create what Bloomfield calls "a uniform legal status for refugees, stateless persons, and displaced persons" who cannot be repatriated and should not be sent home against their will. Such a status would require broad consent from governments, which would have to accept the high commissioner's much more numerous "international passports" in lieu of the usual national credentials.

The term *displaced person* is a slippery one, for it includes not only people outside their native countries who have not established themselves as bona fide refugees (by convincing some authority that they would be persecuted or in danger if they were to go home) but also very large numbers of people who are destitute *in their own countries* as a consequence of civil or ethnic conflicts and other forms of social and political disorder. The newly strengthened refugee agency should also be mandated to arrange with national and local authorities relief and rehabilitation efforts to save as many of those people as possible. If the problem gets much worse, a new dimension of international effort may be needed along the lines of UNRRA, which, from 1944 to 1947, saved many millions of people displaced in their own countries by World War II.

Coping with Catastrophe

That there will be disasters of various kinds, made by people through inadvertence or by nature according to laws we imperfectly understand, is predictable. That these disasters will engage worldwide humanitarian concern is also certain. What is uncertain — what kind of disaster and where and when and how serious — requires a permanent efficient international system of immediate disaster relief.

Three kinds of emergency planning are needed. One is getting international agreement ahead of time to act, not just mourn aloud. Another is arranging for funds and airlift and pre-positioning supplies and equipment near the most likely trouble spots. (That should have been, but was not, done in anticipation of a big refugee exodus from Iraq in 1991.) The third is ensuring a supply of people trained and ready at overnight notice to take charge in life-or-death crises without knowing when, where, and with what they are going to have to cope. That is as important to the United Nations as it is to every hospital emergency room.

In the past, international operations on a huge scale have been successful in repairing damage wrought by human foibles combined with natural forces. To help defend China against the Japanese in what later became World War II, the Chinese diverted the Yellow River from its normal riverbed. For a decade it wandered across North China, depositing millions of tons of sand in great fertile valleys. UNRRA's largest single project anywhere was to rebuild the Yellow River dikes and put that great silty flow back into its normal channel — an earth-moving task equivalent to building the Panama Canal, thus tying it for second place (behind the Great Wall) among the greatest construction jobs in history. Later the United Nations took on the mind-boggling task of cleaning up the Suez Canal, clogged as an aftermath of the Suez crisis. These precedents suggest that it is not inherently impossible for very large international operations to be mounted — provided that those countries with the resources and know-how and management skills are willing to pool them in common cause.

In recent years we have had a taste of disasters brought about by human error. The explosion of Union Carbide's Bhopal plant in India, though it didn't require a fully international response, became a metaphor in the chemical industry for what could happen anytime anywhere ("Bhopal wasn't our plant, but it might as well have been," said one chemical company executive) and might require disaster relief on a very large scale.

The Chernobyl calamity not only induced the Soviets to seek the help of the UN's International Atomic Energy Agency, which assembled some of the world's best scientific talent without regard to ideology to advise how to handle radiation accidentally spewed into the atmosphere. (According to Mikhail Gorbachev, Chernobyl also converted the Kremlin to a lively and constructive interest in environmental protection.)

Natural disasters, such as hurricanes, earthquakes, and volcanic eruptions, are at least as probable as those contrived by people. Earthquakes in Mexico City and the Gulan area in Iran and floods in Bangladesh, brought forth an outpouring of materials and technical assistance from around the world. But again, the emergency operations were adhockery at best.

Flood, famine, and pestilence were also considered works of nature in Biblical times, but we know now that their human impacts are as much the product of social systems, discrimination against the poor, and human miscalculation, as they are the workings of mysterious forces beyond our control. There is evidence that the early-1970s drought in the Sahel was only the last straw in pushing many African peasants over the precipice of poverty. Says Andrew Maskry, an expert on disaster mitigation: "Vulnerability to any kind of hazard is essentially determined by poverty."

Whatever the trigger for catastrophe at a given time in a given place, disaster relief requires, quite as much as peacekeeping does, ready forces and facilities in place and the resources and executive energy to deploy them in a big hurry. Needed are a central planning staff, advance consensus on the rapid provision of people and supplies, the skills to learn and quickly analyze what has happened and what it takes to help, and the leadership to pull together the requisite mix of resources. Providing some of the forces and facilities is a constructive way to employ armed forces not currently engaged in hostilities, which is most of the world's military personnel and equipment. U.S. forces are regularly used for humanitarian duty, as they were in 1992 after Hurricane Andrew in Florida and Hurricane Iniki in Hawaii. (General John Vessey, former chair of the U.S. Joint Chiefs of Staff, says there are typically five humanitarian operations assigned to the U.S. armed forces at any time.) Under international guidance, some national troops might even train together for sudden disaster relief duty, another "soldiers without enemies" role.

There is a UN agency for disaster relief; the experience with it, according to Bloomfield, is "dismal." Perhaps, he suggests, "the best model is not an intergovernmental bureaucracy but a chosen nongovernmental instrument based on professional experience and excellence. The examples that come to mind might be an expanded and subsidized International Committee of the Red Cross or *Médecins Sans Frontières*," a highly effective French voluntary agency that operates all over the world.

As in so many of the issues cited here, what is essential is a wide consensus ahead of time to take the function seriously. That means pledging public funds to support the planning, pre-positioning some supplies and equipment, getting promises of rapid airlift as necessary, and above all, knowing ahead of time who will be immediately available to manage large sudden operations in unknown places at indeterminate times.

eight

WORLD ECONOMY
Managing with Nobody in Charge

[T]he ideas of economists and political philosophers, both when they are right and when they are wrong, are more powerful than is commonly understood. Indeed the world is ruled by little else. Practical men, who believe themselves to be quite exempt from any intellectual influences, are usually the slaves of some defunct economist. Madmen in authority, who hear voices in the air, are distilling their frenzy from some academic scribbler of a few years back. I am sure that the power of vested interests is vastly exaggerated compared with the gradual encroachment of ideas.

—John Maynard Keynes, The General Theory of
Employment, Interest and Money

DON'T LOOK NOW, but the "invisible hand" is palsied.

Most of the star performers in the postwar world economy chose a market path to prosperity. In the Atlantic and Pacific democracies, deregulation was the story of the 1980s. The brightest meteors—South Korea, Taiwan, Singapore, and a lengthening list of export-led copycats—bet on systems in which open markets, while different from each other, were a priceless ingredient. That wager paid off handsomely. The apostates of central planning in Eastern Europe and the former Soviet Union and even its apostles in Beijing then started gingerly to let many *perestroikas* bloom.

Yet just when so many nations seemed to be adapting market economics to their domestic travails, world markets were spinning in unruly, ungovernable, unpredictable gyrations. Watching stocks, bonds, commodity futures, and the U.S. dollar these past few years, even a devoted disciple of Adam Smith would have to conclude that the "invisible hand" has taken to playing with a yo-yo.

136

From "Places" to "Networks"

What's going on here? The diagnosis is now plain. The information revolution has stormed the ramparts of the nation-state, and most of our favorite economic theories, capitalist as well as Marxist, have been trampled in the rush. Peter Drucker, the oracle of business management, wrote years ago that information had become "the central capital, the cost center, and the crucial resource of the economy." He was writing about the United States. His prescient words now apply almost as well to what the French economist Albert Bressand, compressing the two words for rhetorical effect, calls the *worldeconomy.*

Data networks of extraordinary speed and complexity already link commodity traders, airline ticket agents, air traffic controllers, weather forecasters, public health officials, currency speculators, music lovers, modern librarians, and multinational executives with each other. Criminals and the police forces that chase them both depend heavily on electronic networking. Grain merchants have an intelligence system that (on subjects in which they share a vital interest, such as the internal politics of Argentina) probably overmatches the combined capacities of British intelligence and the CIA.

It no longer matters so much where you are if you are electronically plugged into what the buyers and sellers you care about are doing, wherever they are. The notion of a "New York market," a "Tokyo market," a "London market," or a "Zurich market," already sounds quaint. It evaporated before our eyes on Black Monday 1987, as information about prices and pessimism ricocheted around the globe. There is no longer much reason, save tradition and personal convenience, for the New York Stock Exchange to be in New York. It could probably work just as well and with a good deal less overhead if it were put in South Dakota, alongside Citicorp's credit card operations, or in Fort Lauderdale, Florida, where American Express conducts a worldwide business by computer-assisted communications. Even time zones seem dated. If you are buying and selling money, precious metals, commodities, bonds, or shares in big companies, you (or your surrogates) have to be awake twenty-four hours a day, or you will be overtaken by those who are.

It is not yet true of culture, but it is certainly true of economics, that modern civilization is built less and less around communities of place and more and more around communities of people. All the really important markets are world markets. Daniel Bell, the premier philosopher of the information society, foresaw long ago "a change in the nature of markets from 'places' to 'networks.'" That change has come.

The Confidence Game

The almost instantaneous transport of data and its rapid processing into usable information have not only blurred the frontiers between nations. They have also blurred the line between investment and speculation, detached both from the slower-moving world of production and trading goods and services, and torn the exchange of national currencies loose from the moorings of public responsibility.

What made world business an increasingly single market was not primarily trade, aid, or alliances — even the alliance that was so successful it dissolved its Eastern rival in Europe. What happened was that with the help of fast computers and reliable telecommunications, capital (because it is a form of information) could flow so much faster and more freely than things.

Money exchange between countries is needed to pay for things shipped right now and for trade *futures* (promises to buy things that aren't available yet). Money is also sent across frontiers to buy things that don't move, like automobile plants in Europe, forests in Brazil, rubber plantations in Indonesia, golf courses in Hawaii, and Rockefeller Center in New York. Large amounts of money, contributing greatly to bank-created credit inflation, are devoted to the even larger chance to make money by buying money itself and money futures too. The communities of people who arrange investments and move money around — bankers, credit agencies, foreign exchange markets, futures traders, and all those whose business it is to guess about future financial flows — have thus been enabled by information technology to create an explosive growth in their own activity, sustained by a credit inflation out of all proportion to the trade in things that money flows used to reflect.

Money exchanges that buy and sell numbers (once bits of paper, now electronic bytes) amounted in 1989 to $420 billion. This was thirty-four times the $12.4 billion paid for goods and services (what we call *trade*). The comparable numbers for 1980 were $94 billion and $7.6 billion. Thus in the decade of the 1980s, money used to finance trade expanded by only 63 percent, while foreign exchange transactions grew by 447 percent. The world economy keeps knitting itself more tightly together; but within it, the exchange of money favors a much tighter weave.

The numbers are numbing and not in themselves very revealing. Better to think with a metaphor. It is as if a bright light nearby were shining on the "real" world economy, projecting a huge shadow play on a faraway wall: a complex plot full of fast breaks and arthritic adjustments as people make quick judgments about future values of present realities, compounded by guesswork about the future value of each national currency in its relation to all the others. None of the actors has a clear idea of the script for the next scene; each lender sells the debt he is owed to another, usually bigger, lender (usually for less than its face value, reflecting an agreed guess about when or whether the debtor will ever pay up).

The whole shadowy pyramid is sustained by confidence, the confidence of the alcoholic who assures his friends he can handle his next drink and the one after that. But a confidence game is always vulnerable to a breakdown of trust. Any loss of confidence in the creditworthiness of the debtors can turn the pyramid on its head, as each actor in the shadow play scurries to leave the confidence game just before everyone else does.

No one knows just how big the shadow can become; that depends on the lenders of last resort. The ultimate suckers in this shadowy game of musical chairs used to be governments, especially the U.S. government. ("Governments aren't like companies, they can't go bankrupt." This tenet of the banker's belief system has been badly frayed by recent experience.) But just when U.S. banks realized that getting most of their profits from impoverished countries, high-risk junk bonds, and overvalued real estate was not the way to stay in business, the Reagan-era budget and trade deficits and savings and loan crisis removed what everyone else in the confidence game had been secretly counting on: the capacity and willingness of the United States of America to pick up the check when the binge was over.

The consequence is that no national government now controls the value of "its own" money. Banks and other governments create dollars as required, lots of them, without so much as a curtsy to Washington, D.C. The international monetary system, already out of national control but not yet under international control, is chronically at risk of a nervous breakdown.

In the first half of the postwar period, the monetary system had a measure of stability; that is, companies and countries knew what their money would be worth in other countries because exchange rates among all currencies were fixed by international agreement (the Bretton Woods agreement, administered by the International Monetary Fund). Once the United States got off that train in 1973 and prompted the other major currencies to do so too, currencies started to "float" in their comparative values. From then on, what each major country's money was worth (compared to other nations' money) depended on how well it managed its own economy: nursed its growth rate, avoided too much inflation, recovered handily from recessions.

Meanwhile, *market* does increasingly mean *international*. The earlier, more successful deals (among fewer countries) to dismantle obstacles to commerce, under the General Agreement on Tariffs and Trade (GATT), helped the volume of trade across frontiers to grow by as much as 500 percent between 1950 and 1975, while the increase in global output was growing about 220 percent. And that meant "national" economies were increasingly beyond the reach of presidents and prime ministers, parliaments and congresses, or even the formerly powerful central bankers.

Since nobody was in charge of the system, more and more of the policy-making had to be done by negotiations between governments. Trade experts at GATT in Geneva hammered out international codes and rules, trying to make national policies compatible with the continued growth of international trade. Central bankers intervened in the money markets to prop up their own and the others' currencies. Finance ministers lectured each other about the dangers of inflation. And the heads of the seven biggest industrial democracies (Britain, Canada, France, the Federal Republic of Germany, Italy, Japan, and the United States) gathered in summit meetings to pretend that they were steering the global barge. Meanwhile the barge, loose from its moorings, was drifting with the currents created by millions of buyers and sellers in largely unregulated worldwide markets for things, services, information, and money.

Openness Is Good Business

Many people in government and business, feeling that a "world market" is too unstable and too unpredictable, are tempted to blame the market's openness — and invent complex ways of closing it by erecting Maginot Lines to protect their own national parts of it. So the first rung on the ladder of understanding is that *openness is a technological imperative in the global knowledge society.*

An impressive passion for market economics has nearly everywhere been part of what bubbled up along with aspirations for democracy in politics and government. Both *democracy* and *market* were more metaphor than policy analysis, of course; but the instinct of dissidents and protesters, in one communist country after another, to glue them together in their rhetoric was sound.

The connection between *market* and *democracy* is basic. Market divides and distributes economic power as democracy does political power. Markets may lead to concentrations of economic power (producers' or labor monopolies), which can be dangerous or inefficient or both. And democracy, if narrowly defined as majority rule, may also lead to oppressive concentrations of political power. So incantations of *market* and *democracy* are not good enough, either for the new experimenters (Eastern Europe) or for those market democracies that are also still experimenting, even if they have been around for a while.

What is needed are constitutional rules that define the limits of power of political majorities and of economic power centers (whether "public" or "private" or "mixed"). Only on the basis of well-understood norms — a social contract, if you will —

can a durable and widely acceptable balance be achieved between liberty and equality, or efficiency and fairness, in both political and economic realms. The most critical constitutional principles are those that define the boundary between the realm of the state, where decisions are made by majority rule tempered by minority rights, and that of civil society, where decisions are made by countless interactions, such as buying and selling agreements, voting arrangements, and myriad other forms of cooperation and competition in the private nonprofit sector.

This boundary between the state and civil society cannot be defined by cookie-cutter ideologies: for example, that fairness will be assured by having government employees decide just how what is produced will be distributed, or that efficiency will be guaranteed if private entrepreneurs are just left alone. Defining and redefining the frontier, which is the essential problem of governance, requires concrete, case-by-case analysis of the trade-offs involved in assigning a particular decision to a public authority or a private market.

The best economic outcomes seem to be the product of mixed systems. The worst are those that rigidly divide the distributive decisions from decisions about production. These include "social democracy" dogmas designed to bring about a continuous wrestling match between a private sector (responsible for productive efficiency) and a public sector (responsible for deciding who gets how much of what is produced), or "free market" dogmas that depend for fairness on trickle-down assumptions and for efficiency on leaving concentrations of economic power alone.

The most durable political arrangements try to balance liberty and equality in thousands of concrete instances, without assuming that either should ever "win it all." A French aphorism is apropos: *"Entre le fort et le faible, c'est la liberté qui opprime et la loi qui affranchi."* (Between the strong and the weak, it is liberty that oppresses and law that liberates.)

Part of the connection between democracy and market is that people governed by consent want to do business (shop, invest, work, watch television) across borders that are as open as possible. The other part is that a democracy's economy (the goods and services that are traded, the information that is shared) is necessarily and inevitably more open to the rest of the world, and the rest of the world will be more open to it. That ensures a growing role for global companies, already the most dynamic actors in international affairs. It also seems bound to accelerate the leakage of economic power from national governments to international regulators and cooperation systems, to international nongovernments (global companies and also powerful associations of professionals, such as the international communities of scientists, lawyers, and economists), and also to subnational authorities and enterprises (in the United States, the states already are taking the initiative on issues that used to be preempted by the federal government). Again a Daniel Bell dictum is validated: "the nation-state is becoming too small for the big problems of life, and too big for the small problems of life. In short, there is a mismatch of scale."

The most successful industries (including agriculture) are now *high-tech,* a shorthand way of describing processes with unusually high ratios of brainwork, thus fewer but better jobs. Information is also, and increasingly, a marketable commodity, a product in itself. The result is to change the very nature of comparative advantage — now less a matter of the price of physical resources and the cost of labor and more a function of unpriceable imagination, innovation, and time (how far you are ahead of competitors from whom trade secrets cannot be kept for long, if at all).

Comparative advantage is better ideas, more promptly acted upon, better devised for more rapid manufacture, more vigorously marketed, adapted faster by learning from real-life customers, with the resulting knowledge applied as even better ideas, more ingenious inventions, more flexible human systems — a continuous spiral of enterprise in which no one is ever dependably ahead for long.

It is most obvious at the high-tech end of the scale that time is the priceless ingredient of comparative advantage. In the old days what counted most was being the first to discover a gold mine or an oil well. Because knowledge is so perishable, what counts nowadays is to be the first (or at least earlier than most) to develop new ideas, new skills, new processes. What made the United States a large and successful economy was never the capacity of Americans to do even better what they used to do well (like manufacturing muzzle-loading muskets or oversized Chryslers). It was their propensity, in each generation, to do what had never been done before in world history: to design the Model T Ford, fly a heavier-than-air machine, split the atom, splice genes, develop the modern computer and then marry it to electronic communications. It is the prizes for being first, or at least well ahead of the pack, that have spurred the development of supercomputers with their high speeds and mass storage.

Information, the raw material for producing knowledge, cannot be bottled up for long; it leaks. No company or country can achieve a monopoly of data, or information storage and retrieval capacity, or specialized knowledge, let alone integrative wisdom and flashes of intuition. Even the United States, which stayed ahead for quite a while, did it by providing an opportunity culture for a continuous stream of imaginative immigrants (the Einsteins, Fermis, Von Neumanns, and so many others) and by exchanging science and technology with enthusiasm in a global information commons from which the Americans got at least as much as they gave.

The best of the high-tech industrialists, especially those selling information technology, seem convinced that their competitiveness depends on their being (as John Rollwagen, chairman of Cray Research, puts it) a "sponge" for inventions, innovations, and applications elsewhere, "learning at least as much from our customers as they do from us." More than half of Cray's customers are outside the United States. Rollwagen speaks of "the product as receiver"; he thinks of a supercomputer sale not as the end of a marketing process but as the beginning of even more active learning.

If a company or a country keeps its ideas secret, whether from a misguided desire to hang onto "trade secrets" or a misguided belief that a nation can stay ahead by monopolizing information, it will attract that much less knowledge from others.

And it's the new knowledge the old products attract that determines whether companies and countries will be able to do in future what has never been done before. In a rapidly changing information environment, what a company or a country can derive from openness usually outweighs, sometimes by a wide margin, the value it can preserve by keeping secret what it already knows at the expense of what it might yet learn.

Such an idea was, of course, anathema to the old Soviet ideology. In 1988 I heard a Soviet official proudly tell an Aspen Institute audience that one million personal computers were planned to be built in the USSR the following year, half of them destined for Soviet schools. By 1989 the United States was spending about 10 percent of its gross national product on information technology; thirty-nine million PCs were scattered around the country, seventeen million of them with modems imbedded or attached.

Soviet leaders simply missed the boat by not moving, in their whole society, to the second industrial revolution, spurred by the pervasive use of computers linked to telecommunications. In recent years, something like half the increase in world production has been due to information technology. But the idea that value added might be primarily based on human creativity was too dangerous a thought to let loose outside the technological elite that was spending close to a quarter of the USSR's national income (more than even the West's hardest-line Kremlinologists were estimating) on a huge defense program and a world-class series of space shots.

The economies of Western Europe, Japan, and North America moved way ahead because they developed the capacity to produce, acquire, and disseminate knowledge, especially new knowledge. In the maturation of information technologies, the contrast is especially instructive. In the industrial democracies and especially in the United States, computers and electronic communications (and their interaction) have been dynamically developed in the civilian sector, permeating every aspect of people's life and work. Military systems have been able to feed off this civilian research, invention, and innovation (partly but not mostly funded by government contracts). Such technologies were not at all a mystery to some Soviet scientists and engineers, as they demonstrated for the world to see beginning with *Sputnik I* in 1957. But in the Soviet Union, their development took place primarily inside a secretive government's military and space centers, and the trickle-down effect on the rest of the Soviet economy was deliberately and fatally sluggish.

As long as the Soviet Union and Eastern European governments were trying to make command economies work, to the growing disenchantment of their own people, they were almost a negligible factor in the worldeconomy. Almost nobody elsewhere yearned for their inconvertible rubles, their tired civilian technologies, their inefficient agriculture, their dishonest central planning, their corrupt and repressive politics.

The new, fragmented republics, market democracies in prospect but not yet in being, then started to relate to the worldeconomy, with shocking misery as a first step. In global perspective, however, they are likely to provide for the rest of this century less dynamism than drag. They will doubtless need large unrequited infusions of grants, loans, investment, and technical aid from the information economies of Western Europe, North America, and East Asia.

China, too, will still for a time be marginal to the worldeconomy — that is, until several years after its new leaders decide (if they do) to climb aboard the two-horse sleigh of political democracy and market economics. Even in world politics China's relevance — except on regional matters such as Cambodia, will be more related to its weaknesses than its strengths. Yet one-fifth of the world's population will sooner or later be a major factor in world development. And by an accident of history China is already a major partner in UN politics with its veto vote in the Security Council.

It will be important to identify issues in which the Chinese can be full partners — such as reducing the emission of atmospheric gases, which contribute to climate-warming, or inhibiting the spread of nuclear, chemical, and biological weapons — and then undertake global projects in which China, as well as Russia and other legatees of history's great civilizations, can play major roles in bringing them to life.

The Dwindling Relevance of Geography

During the forty years from 1949 to 1989, the two great and growing stockpiles of unusable weapons seemed so overwhelmingly
important that changing economic power relations did not get
the attention they deserved. When the bipolar world so abruptly
disappeared, three great centers of economic strength stood out
in sharp relief. Many scholars and analysts, pundits and political leaders — people whose mind-sets predispose them to harden
their thinking in tidy categories — leapt to the conclusion that
the world of the 1990s and beyond would be organized around
the three geographic regions dominated by the world's economic
locomotives.

The most obvious evidence of this mind-set was the slide
toward three trade blocs: the European Community's "single
market," a North American "free trade" zone, and Japan and
the reincarnation of its prewar "coprosperity sphere" in East Asia.
In this scenario, pity the developing nation that wouldn't attach
itself to one of the three trading empires.

In the early 1990s the organizers of these blocs were engaging in an elaborate "let's pretend" game: a claim that cliquey
in-groups are somehow not harmful to freer trade, faster growth,
and fairer outcomes. It was a charade: trade blocs were on a
collision course with the prosperity-producing growth of global
trade. They have "raised fears, and rightly so," said Jacques La
Rosiere, governor of the Bank of France, in 1991, "that these
blocs-in-formation will close themselves off from external partners."

Japan had to take a special share of the credit, or blame,
for the regional-bloc trend. Its ambitious penetration of international markets had combined with Japan's inscrutable domestic barriers to produce defensive reactions in Europe and North
America. These in turn fed Japanese feelings that the rest of
the world was ganging up on them, which it was. A classic trade
war was in prospect if each of the three blocs really got organized
to defend its ramparts from the other two.

The three blocs were coming into being because the alternative was working so badly. That alternative was freer trade
for all countries at once, by worldwide decisions arrived at in

suffocatingly tedious negotiations arranged in Geneva by GATT (the General Agreement on Tariffs and Trade).

The Geneva negotiations from 1985 to 1992 set a new standard for long delays, stubborn diplomacy (notably between France and the United States on farm subsidies), and sluggish progress in negotiations that didn't nearly keep pace with technological change, the integration of the worldeconomy, or the emergence of information rather than things as the world's dominant resource. The failure of GATT requires a better mechanism for achieving freer trade worldwide, not a retreat into trade blocs defined by geography.

But the idea that geography is the key to power, that your potential depends on your location, dies hard. *Geopolitics* was the idea that a nation's clout depends largely on geography: how defendable its frontiers, how fertile its soils, how rich its bedrock in mineral deposits, how plentiful its fresh water, how extensive its coastline. Cities often developed because they were seaports or on critical inland waterways, or (earlier) on important overland caravan routes or (later) on important railway lines.

The importance of countries often seemed based on the natural resources they had discovered (or conquered) and developed on "their" territory: the spices of the Orient, the rubber and tin of Southeast Asia, the coal and iron of Central Europe, the diamonds (and later uranium) of South Africa, the fruits of Central America, the petroleum reserves of Indonesia and Mexico and Venezuela and North Africa and North America and the North Sea and the Persian (or Arabian) Gulf, the soils that produced those "amber waves of grain" in the Ukraine and the Great Plains. These crucial resources left an indelible mark on the peoples that happened to find them in their backyards. But it was the brains of people who found and exploited them — often, like colonists in earlier centuries and corporations in our own time, coming from great distances to do so — that made them resources at all.

That's why, nowadays, it's the countries with the biggest flows of information we call *developed*. We know that anybody can extract knowledge from the bath of information that nearly drowns us all. You don't have to find it inside your own frontiers, you don't have to grow it in your own soil, you don't have to fabricate it in your own factories or put it together in your own assembly plants. You do have to "get it all together" in your own brain, and then combine your insight and imagination with other human brainwork in networks, companies, or alliances.

The passing of remoteness, in a world of speedy computers, responsive space satellites, and global telecommunications, is one of the least heralded and most important macrotrends of this extraordinary time of our lives. The dwindling relevance of geographic regionalism bears witness.

In the late forties and early fifties, the founding fathers of the postwar system (only one founding mother: Eleanor Roosevelt) thought that one way to avoid global paralysis — by everybody being in on everything — would be to build strong regional organizations, disaggregating world order by continents. Except for the European Community, however, geographic nearness turned out to be a precarious principle of international cooperation.

In security matters courage is quite commonly proportional to distance from the problem. In merchandise trade the iterns with the most value added, such as microchips, are bought from low-cost suppliers wherever they happen to be. In the sharing of facts and ideas by modern information technology, geography is almost wholly irrelevant.

Outside of Western Europe, only in Southeast Asia has a geography-based organization, the Association of Southeast Asian Nations, shown a spark of life. Those in Eastern Europe, Latin America, Africa, South Asia, and the Arab League in the Mideast never became major players in international affairs; some are notably overstaffed and underemployed; one, the Communists' COMECON, has disappeared altogether. By contrast, networks that link like-minded people wherever located — such as the oil cartel, drug traffickers, the international community of scientists, Islamic fundamentalists, and the rich nations' club called OECD — have proved more cohesive, more durable, and more influential in world affairs.

In this perspective, geography-based trading blocs, even

very big ones, are revealed as a throwback to the era before the
sharing of information began to edge the exchange of things out
of the center-stage spotlight. Like the dinosaurs of old, they may
last quite a while, requiring brainier but smaller creatures to
be nimble enough to avoid being squashed underfoot.

Yet it seems overwhelmingly probable that an international public sector regulating both trade and money will now
have to be built to match the private markets for commodities,
manufactures, capital investment, and money. None of these
are much constrained by geography, and all of them are global
in their reach. This economic probability is reinforced by a political imperative. The main trading economies are, by no coincidence, the world's leading democracies. It's in their mutual
interest to enhance the economic environment for expanding
political democracy worldwide. In this larger context, for three
groups of democracies to circle each other warily like three tom-
cats in the presence of a desirable pussycat in heat — with the
likely result that by fighting each other none will get his heart's
desire — doesn't make sense.

Needed: A Global Public Sector

International economic relations are certainly not a *free market*
in its classic meaning, of which history records no real-life examples. Nor are they *planned* in the centralized, socialist sense,
of which there are no successful examples. So traditional theories about free markets and centrally planned economies are
equally rusty tools for thinking about the new state of affairs.
The worldeconomy is too large and complicated for canonical
measures of planning and control, yet too important to be au-
tonomous, freewheeling, unfettered by considerations of stability
and fairness.

Just the same, three things can be said for sure on the
evidence of four decades past. The fewer the obstacles to trade,
the more trade there will be. The more trade there is, the more
wealth is created. And the more predictable is the value of money
needed to do business, the more business (as differentiated from
speculation) will get done. What the evidence doesn't show is

that more trade and more stable money spread the increment of wealth around more fairly.

Jan Pronk, the Netherlands' thoughtful longtime minister for development cooperation, suggests we look no farther than the three "value systems" that have worked in such countries as his own — a mixture of public and private enterprise, a practical concern for fairness, a polity of pluralistic participation — for clues to the puzzle of international cooperation in the world-economy: "We need a global mixed economy including a strong and clear international framework of powerful public institutions, a kind of global public sector, enhancing the wealth and welfare-creating capacities of the global private sector. We need an internationalization of the concept of the welfare state with international transfers to correct gross inequities. We need an international pluralistic democracy within which Third World countries can participate effectively in international decision-making."

An uncentralized management system for the worldeconomy requires a mix of two levels of activity, and a clear-headed distinction between the two:

- Collective standard setting by international public authorities, with the participation of those whose cooperation in following the agreed standards is essential. The aim is to establish norms designed to assure fairness, encourage incentives for innovation, and maximize the predictability of the value of money.
- Uncentralized market-driven international business activity, within the framework of agreed norms and standards, for the actual exchange of goods and services, for the sharing of information and mutual learning, and for the clearing of financial transactions.

The political hang-ups in the world's key democracies are serious. Governments can fall or rise, political careers can be ruined or made, by the way they are handled. But none of them is nearly as intractable as, say, absolute poverty, or defusing the population bomb, or the cultural and religious rivalries in several world regions, or even finding, soon enough, alternatives to fossil fuels that can meet the world's needs for energy.

Let's suppose for a moment that the United States and Canada, Japan, and the European Community can develop the morale, the capacity for self-renewal, and the political leadership to do what they say they want to do: develop an open system of world trade, maintain steady economic growth, manage predictable changes in the value of money, protect the global environment, and make a special effort to eliminate the worst aspects of poverty worldwide. That's an agenda well within the scientific, technological, and financial capacity of the world's democratic states. What needs to be done to work out the details and make these things happen? The rest of this chapter speaks to Pronk's call for a global public sector. His other two value systems, fairness and pluralism, are the subjects of Chapters Ten and Eleven.

On trade and on money, two major initiatives are needed. I will state them quite bluntly.

Trade

In order to achieve sustainable economic growth, the leading democracies should promise each other to remove national barriers on all major commodities and products by a date certain, say, ten years from the time of the agreement.

The way to accomplish this is not to negotiate detailed concessions or product-by-product reciprocity. The seven-year "Uruguay round" of GATT trade talks ran out the string on that kind of negotiation. The outcome of the trade talks in Geneva from 1985 to 1992 would (as estimated by the *Economist*) "increase the joint income of North America, Europe, and Asia-Pacific by less than $100 billion a year. If instead those three regions reduced their tariff and non-tariff barriers by 50%, the total gain would be close to $740 billion"—nearly three-quarters of a trillion dollars.

A truly open world market would certainly push the national-income benefits of trade liberalization well above a trillion dollars. The mutual reduction of farm subsidies to zero (the

United States has already espoused this idea) would alone remove a "deadweight loss" of $72 billion (at 1988 prices) from the countries that make up the OECD, the rich countries' research facility. The *Economist* estimates that this would lift a burden three times that great from the consumers of farm products, who are everybody; indeed, "individual countries would all gain from liberalising their farm policies unilaterally." The removal of farm subsidies would also leave more room for exports of farm products from developing countries, perhaps as much as $30 billion a year, which might make the development aid bill look suddenly much more manageable.

Setting such far-reaching goals for international trade (exchange of goods and services) and sharing (of technology and other information) will require something much more effective than the UN pattern: a large committee (in the 1990 GATT negotiation, sixteen committees) with a technical staff. This is one auspicious role for the kind of extranational institution described in Chapter Five. Here is the way it might work.

• The starting point would have to be a goal-setting political act by the main trading countries, such as the ten-year mutual promise just suggested. (This would be comparable to the action of the governments forming the European Community when they set the end of 1992 as the target for establishing the single market.)

• The new institution would be established by a treaty that reserves to the extranational body the function of proposing standards and timetables for the liberalization of trade and sharing to meet the goals set by governments; arranging for and chairing needed negotiations on thorny points of disagreement (which would typically be on proposed changes in domestic policies), and monitoring progress against the goals, standards, and timetables.

• The institution's central organ would be a body of executive commissioners appointed for a term of years by governments (or groups of governments) but removable only by all participating governments acting together. The commissioners would act by consensus under rules of procedure they themselves would develop.

- The commissioners would establish machinery to over-
see and monitor international markets. For this purpose they
would be authorized to engage nongovernments without direct
financial interest in the markets involved.

- In setting standards and timetables, the commissioners
would need the discretion to bring into public consultation major
nongovernments such as global companies, international banks,
environmental advocates, other special interests (labor, agriculture, communications media), and professional groups such as
those representing science, engineering, and political economy.

- The governments signing the treaty should have the
right to veto (but not to edit) policy actions proposed to be taken
by the commissioners. Governments would act by consensus
or by some form of weighted voting that reflects both the differing stakes of different states in the worldeconomy and the need
for fairness to the smaller states adhering to the treaty.

Money

Not long after the stock market crash of October 19, 1987, I
sat in on a postmortem with some of the movers and shakers
of world finance. They didn't know where to move, but they
were shaking. The one thing that was clear to everyone in that
plush meeting room in New York's World Trade Center was
that the markets for everything important are now global. (As
a nice case in point, Wells Fargo Bank was then suing Citibank
about a loan of Eurodollars deposited in Manila.)

No one had a solution, and most were fuzzy about the
diagnosis; financial managers are, as scared of malpractice ac-
cusations as physicians are and with even more reason. But they
did agree on three things: the problem is international. It be-
gins and ends with the unpredictability of the value of money.
And, these free marketeers thought, there is an urgent need for
regulation of international financial markets. One of them
summed up the consensus: "We need rules of the game that permit the main actors to have safe sex cheaply."

In monetary affairs as in trade, the first need is for a public sector able to formulate norms and set standards, not to clear
transactions but to ensure fairness in an uncentralized market.

To make some of the "law that liberates," there is already a committee-of-sovereigns-within-a-staff, the International Monetary Fund. But there is a strong case for bringing together this time the process of making public rules both for the liberalization of trade and the control of the money supply.

Separating trade policy (which now includes banking, insurance, and foreign investment) from monetary policy no longer makes sense, if it ever did. The gulf between the two — different people from different national ministries, served by different international staffs, meeting in different cities — confirms and intensifies the detachment of money flows from the underlying flows of goods, services, capital investment, and information. To the extent that money flows exceed what is needed for buyers and sellers to seal their bargains in the "real" international economy, the money market serves as a gigantic computerized parimutuel system for betting on the future values of different national currencies as they relate to one another from day to day. That part of the money market seems to enrich the already rich and lacks what the U.S. Supreme Court, in distinguishing between art and obscenity, called redeeming social value.

To make international money markets more predictable for traders and investors and less vulnerable to wide and sudden swings that benefit mostly the most wide awake speculators, the money supply should be monitored as if it were part of the same subject as trade and investment. And that argues for rules of the game to be developed within broad government-agreed guidelines, by the same extranational commissioners as were just described in the discussion of trade.

Any suggestion to do something fundamental about the way money is handled on world markets sets many teeth on edge. Those who make a good living betting on exchange rate instability would naturally like to leave things as they are. But there are also those who hanker after the kind of stability the old Bretton Woods fixed-rate system did in fact provide for its time, from the mid forties to 1973, when President Nixon led the parade to "floating" rates because the U.S. economy was no longer so dominant that the U.S. dollar could safely be used as everybody else's international medium of exchange, measure of value, and money in reserve. The flows in international financial markets

had become so large and there were so many important players
in the game that it was fanciful to think that some central authority could fix exchange rates and keep them that way. The
"end of Bretton Woods" in 1973 was just a way of acknowledg-
ing that fact of economic life.

The system after 1973 became equally unstable. This was
not because the central bankers fell down on their jobs (to keep
things on as even a keel as possible) but because the United
States — whose dollar remained, for lack of anything better, the
world's key currency — kept shoveling large uncertainties into the
system: running big budget and trade deficits and in consequence
borrowing inordinate amounts of money from the rest of the world.
(That wouldn't have worked, of course, if the United States hadn't
continued to be one of the world's most attractive safe havens for
money escaping from dangers and instabilities elsewhere.)

The cure for this kind of instability is not fruitlessly to
try to fix exchange rates but to achieve international agreements
that require more discipline in internal fiscal and monetary policies. For the financially weaker countries that come to the International Monetary Fund for help, the IMF still plays this
Dutch uncle role. Moreover, the IMF's tough advice has to be
taken seriously, or its tellers don't open their windows to the
delinquents. But nobody can tell the more powerful countries
what to do if they don't want to do it. At summit meetings of
the Group of Seven, no amount of lecturing from abroad has
yet stiffened the spines of U.S. presidents or bought any votes
in Congress for budget discipline.

Most U.S. experts and political leaders are not yet ready
to take that kind of discipline from an international community. But if we cannot generate the morale and consensus in-
ternally, the pressure is going to have to come from abroad.
Getting their fiscal and monetary house in order is now the single greatest contribution Americans can make to put in place
a worldeconomy that works for producers, investors, and consumers. It's even more important to a world of peaceful change
than desert-trained soldiers, high-tech fighter bombers, and
nuclear weapons in invulnerable submarines, though they too
are a joyless requirement in a turbulent world.

Where does this argument lead? Straight toward much tighter cooperation among national governments and central banks, especially among the major industrial democracies, simply because they do most of the world's trading and earn and spend most of the world's money. Committee meetings of bankers or heads of government haven't been a match for the problem. Yet it is also impractical to fuse the world's currencies into a single currency and have a world central bank to manage it.

In 1988 the editors of the *Economist* speculated about the likelihood of a world currency. They even suggested a name for the new money, the *Phoenix,* and thought that something of the sort would be in place by 2018.

The IMF does already issue Special Drawing Rights (SDRs), a kind of international money that can be held only by central banks. The value of SDRs fluctuates only mildly because it is tied to a basket of major currencies (notably Japanese yen, German marks, and U.S. dollars) and is thus somewhat protected from the sudden weakening or strengthening of a particular currency. Building on this idea, experts keep coming up with different ways of moving toward a truly international currency — that is, money agreed to be acceptable anywhere for buying and selling or for holding in reserves. The notion is that such a world currency unit should be convertible into any nation's money, or even used as it is by consumers anywhere in the way that credit cards already are used (though today's credit cards are still denominated in dollars, yen, marks, francs, pounds, lire, or whatever). The main reason for moving in this direction would be to increase the predictability of the international business environment. Predictability of money values is the other name for good health in a market system.

If the European Community (EC) had succeeded in breaking down the cultural resistance to a single European currency and established a European central bank, that might well have been a first step toward a world currency unit with a world central bank to match. But in 1992 the European Community acted out a drama that helps explain why money cannot be integrated until there is a political community unified enough to make a single currency work. Before we try to prescribe remedies for the world's monetary confusion, it is important to understand the cautionary tale from Europe.

For more than a generation, there had been at least one fixed point in world politics: the complex but stable transatlantic bargain between Western Europe and North America. Two kinds of political chemistry brought the "Atlantic idea" to life. One was the obvious need for solidarity to face the Soviet Union and its allies-under-duress. The other was the enticing dream of French economist and diplomat Jean Monnet: that a federal Europe could be fashioned by functional economic steps, one at a time. After that, the federalists hoped to go beyond trade and money to a common European defense and an integrated European presence in world affairs.

By 1992 this technocratic strategy for European unification had put in place a prosperity-producing customs union, a wide free-trade bloc, and (to begin on January 1, 1993) a "single market" for goods and services, capital and labor. Money markets had also been closely linked in the Exchange Rate Mechanism (ERM) by which the German Bundesbank, which controlled Europe's strongest and most stable currency, made monetary policy and established interest rates for its members.

The next step was to have been European Monetary Union (EMU), a European central bank issuing a single European currency. EMU was the centerpiece of the Treaty of Maastricht, but that treaty was narrowly rejected by a popular vote in Denmark early in 1992, then only narrowly approved in a French referendum later that year.

In these popular votes, the squashing together of Europe's currencies was the main issue. Rightly so. EMU posed, for the first time, a clear choice between technical cooperation among sovereign states and a formal federalism, on a subject — the value of money — that is central to the exercise of sovereignty.

When push came to shove in 1992, only five countries in the EC could be classed as having "hard" currencies: Germany (despite the enormous cost of absorbing its eastern third), the "Benelux" trio (Belgium, The Netherlands, Luxembourg), and, less dependably, France. Their government leaders saw the stability and strength of their money as the key ingredient in their strategies for economic growth. They mostly resisted expanding their economies in Keynesian or Reaganesque ways, by which a government spends more than it takes in and prints new money to cover the resulting deficit.

The other Europeans had "soft" currencies; they lived with high inflation and high interest rates. They got away with it because they attracted large inflows of capital from investors who liked those high interest rates. The outside investors were not naive. They knew that the British pound, the Italian lira, and the Spanish peseta were overvalued; indeed, it was their investments that made "prosperity despite inflation" possible for the British, Italians, and Spaniards. But investors were willing to take the risk of devaluation because Europe's softer currencies seemed credibly linked to the German mark. That assumption was torpedoed in the autumn of 1992 when Britain and Italy pulled out of the Exchange Rate Mechanism, cutting the exchange value of their currencies by unilateral decisions.

This series of setbacks to monetary union raised the same question in every country of the European Community: who would gain from a single European currency run by a European central bank?

Not the soft currency countries. Their interest rates would go down as the price of money inside the club converged toward equality among the members. That would chase away the imported capital that had propped up their prosperity. If the weaker countries stayed out, they would have to keep devaluing their currencies to offset their higher inflation rates and higher costs of labor compared to the more prudently managed economies inside the single-currency club. Some of them wouldn't qualify for admission anyway. The Maastricht Treaty limited a member country's internal debt to 60 percent of its gross national product. The Italian government's debt load in 1992 was more than 100% of Italy's GNP.

France would thus be the only major European partner tightly linked through a single currency to a normally less inflationary Germany. With no franc to manipulate, the French government would lose the option of devaluing it. If France kept losing control of its labor costs, its economy would lose more jobs, adding to its already high rate of unemployment (more than 10 percent). Foreseeing such an outcome in their own case, British negotiators opted out of the money provisions of the Maastricht Treaty even before they signed it in December 1991.

Then would a single European currency be good for Germany, the "fat boy in the canoe"? The German central bank already had a clear leadership role, with other European currencies linked to the deutsche mark. A "European" central bank could not be nearly so German-dominated. Most of its governors would be more responsive to the politics of expansion than German bankers, whose nightmares are flashbacks to the runaway currency inflations of the early 1920s and the late 1940s.

A single currency would thus give each country, the strong as well as the weak, less control of its destiny than it had in 1992. That's why a monetary union was not in Europe's horoscope in this century. The European Twelve will not graduate, any time soon, from a customs-union-and-free-trade-area to a federal government that encompasses money, defense, and "foreign policy." The dream of Jean Monnet, to build "Europe" in economic increments, has gone about as far as it can go.

The next steps in the construction of "Europe" are much more likely now to be "building out" than "building deep." More than a dozen other European nations are yearning for some form of membership. By the year 2000, the European Community will look less like a tight federal union than like the world's largest common market.

The single currency idea embodied in the EMU rested on a dubious premise: that it would require a supranational central bank to achieve *sound money*—a money managed with priority for price stability and avoidance of violent economic ups and downs. In practice, sound money so defined is much more likely to be protected by a system in which national monies exist side by side in competition with each other—competing for the stability of their purchasing power, or, in other words, their relative acceptability as a means of payment and a measure of value. This presupposes that a *lead currency*—at least one of the competing currencies used by one of the larger and wealthier members of the club—is managed soundly and rather consistently over a long period of time. In Europe, the German mark has in fact played this role, which explains the relative success of Europe's Exchange Rate Mechanism during the decade of the eighties.

Let us now widen the focus to the world. Three currencies—the German mark, the Japanese yen, and the U.S. dollar—perform the lead currency function, each serving for a dozen or more trading countries and many developing nations as a means of exchange, a measure of value, and a reasonably safe haven for storing reserves. The deutsche mark was threatened when West Germany had to finance reunification with its eastern third. The yen's stability was eroded by the ambitious overexpansion of the big Japanese banks and by corruption and uncertainty in Japanese politics. Stability of the dollar has of course been greatly eroded by the government's heavy deficit spending during the 1980s and early 1990s—though damaging flights from the U.S. dollar have been limited by the comparative safety of the American political system and the sheer size and resiliency of the American economy.

For the foreseeable future, a worldwide sound money system can only be fashioned by continuous negotiations among the world's three dominant economies: Japan, Europe (monetary management by Germany), and the United States. How and where these negotiations are carried on doesn't matter nearly as much as how credibly "sound" is the monetary management of the leading economies. And of the three global partners in this emerging money *entente,* what matters most of all will be the success of the Americans in getting their budget and trade deficits back under control.

Keep the peace. Make world markets work efficiently and fairly. Achieve and maintain the soundness of the world's key currencies. It's an ambitious agenda for "postwar planning without having the war first." But it's still not enough. Even a coherent strategy for peaceful change won't work if the world's poorer peoples, left out of the worldeconomy, challenge world security with increasingly powerful weapons and help make the global environment uninhabitable in the twenty-first century. Then all the rich countries' peacekeeping and wealth creation, all the promotion of growth, stability, and environmental protection, would deserve the sour comment of Jean Girardoux: "It is the privilege of the great to watch catastrophe from a terrace."

The antidote to this unpleasant prospect is an unprecedented international venture to achieve growth with fairness in those large parts of Asia, Africa, and Latin America where poverty is still more important to most people than either market economics or political democracy. Where there's a will there's a way. Read on.

nine

WORLD DEVELOPMENT
Promoting Growth with Fairness

Those who make peaceful revolution impossible will make violent revolution inevitable.

—*John F. Kennedy, 1962*

For two millennia, affluent Christians have been comforting themselves with Jesus' dictum that "ye have the poor always with you" (Matthew 26:11). Followers of other faiths have doubtless been able to find equivalent fragments of scripture to justify a near-universal complacency about the persistence of poverty.

In recent decades we have been saved by a secular religion, the growth ethic, from guilt or passion about the poverty of a billion fellow members of the human race. If the world can produce more and more wealth, we told ourselves, the poor will rise with the economic tide. It didn't happen. Each year the number of people below the poverty line (wherever that line is drawn) has grown.

The Underlying Crisis

Development, the conscious promotion of economic growth with social fairness, has not for two decades been central to policy-making in the capitals of the world's knowledge-rich countries. They have increasingly been preoccupied with their own development: West Europeans with their economic integration, Americans with challenges to their competitiveness, Canadians with their recurring constitutional crisis, Japanese with their tension between global economic success and internal cultural cohesion, Australia and New Zealand with reconciling their European past with their Asian future.

163

The donors and lenders also increasingly became disen-
chanted with their own inability to make sure what they do in
faraway societies results in enriching the poor instead of the already prosperous. And in the early 1990s, the struggling new
former communist republics elbowed their way to the front of
the foreign aid queue.

Even in the developing countries, development was often
overshadowed by regional wars and rumors of wars, arms races
with increasingly dangerous conventional weapons, and such
other concerns as the drug trade, epidemic disease, climate var-
iation, and natural disasters.

The underlying crisis of inequity is now destined to become a dominant issue in world politics, however. Each year
after 1984, the developing countries made to the industrial countries a *net negative transfer* (that is, repayment on old loans was
more than new loans received). In 1988, for example, the "poor"
countries thus transferred to the "rich" countries more than $50
billion. At the same time direct investment by the rich in the
poor dwindled: in the five years between 1982 and 1987, it was
halved from $25 to $13 billion. Also during the eighties, flight
capital, or money invested abroad by rich individuals and organizations, was a sizable fraction of the debt their own nations
incurred. By 1991 the load of developing-country debt–$1.3 tril-
lion, mostly unrepayable in foreign exchange — was a thunder-
cloud threatening stormy weather for the international monetary system. A "lost decade" indeed.

Meanwhile, the poverty cycle spiraled down. The number of poor increased as a geometric function of population
growth. There were 1.5 billion people alive on Earth in 1900.
By 1990 we were more than 5 billion, projected by the UN (using
its median estimate) to keep growing to 6.2 billion in 2000 and
8.5 billion in 2025. The World Health Organization guessed
in 1990 that 1.3 billion people, 20 percent of the global population, were "seriously sick or malnourished." Forty thousand children died every day, said James Grant, executive director of
the UN Children's Fund (UNICEF); twenty-five thousand of
them were dying of preventable causes, eight thousand of these
from not having been vaccinated. His *State of the World's Chil-*

dren 1989 estimated that it would cost $5 per child per year to eradicate the simple diseases from which most of these children die. That $5 was not available; but a trillion dollars ($200 for every person on the planet) was spent in 1988 on the means of warfare. Alan Durning, in a 1989 *Worldwatch* paper, provided the catchiest capsule on wealth and poverty: "The world today has 157 billionaires, perhaps 2 million millionaires, but 100 million people around the globe are homeless, living on sidewalks, garbage dumps, and under bridges. . . . It has half a billion who eat too much, and an equal number who eat scarcely enough to stay alive."

In these circumstances what the world's comparatively affluent minority, and most of the political leaders in the poor countries, might regard as norms of civilized behavior were bound to be at risk. Terrorist acts, rationalized by resentment of unfairness, exploitation, and perceived threats to cultural identity, are now commonplace. The dikes built to contain these resentments — especially bilateral "foreign aid" and private investment and multilateral loans and grants — are now quite generally acknowledged to be too little and too late. Indeed, these international measures often skewed the distribution of wealth inside countries, helping those who knew how to take advantage of them and disadvantaging the rest. Moreover, if you consider the equity effect of the four great sci-tech revolutions of our time — explosive power, biotechnology, information technology, and human-made change in the global environment — you find that they have, so far, widened the rich-poor gap both between and within countries.

The gradual realization that nuclear weapons are not militarily usable has helped unleash wars "smaller" than Armageddon. But these wars are fought with weapons destructive enough and with motives bitter enough to kill and maim millions of people, waste much of the Third World's foreign exchange earnings, and perpetuate violations of basic human rights.

It is, so far, overwhelmingly the most advanced countries that are capitalizing on the new potentials of biotechnology, including genetic engineering. It is not a conspiracy, and no one really intends the general outcome; but on balance, biotechnology is helping the rich get richer and the poor get poorer. Unless affirmative action is taken to find opportunities to apply biotechnology to growth with fairness, the promising new potentials will be part of the problem and not of the solution.

The new information technologies, born of the marriage of computers and telecommunications in the 1980s, likewise have been used first by the already powerful and affluent to increase their power and affluence. It was partly that trend line that apparently persuaded Mikhail Gorbachev and his advisers that unless the Soviet Union executed a rapid U-turn it would fall hopelessly behind the industrial democracies. Some newly industrializing countries also realized that educating their own people to retrieve and use the rich flow of information floating around the world would help overcome both domestic poverty and third-class international citizenship.

The growing awareness of global change produced by human activities on earth also risks perpetuating the disadvantages of the disadvantaged, as the already affluent decide to ban industrial pollution and discourage the use of fossil fuels just when governments and entrepreneurs in developing countries are learning how to industrialize and thereby increase their fuel consumption.

None of these outcomes was foreordained. The inner logic of science and technology does not require injustice and inequity. The reality that the biggest explosions have no place in military strategy can be good news for regional peacekeeping and peacemaking. Most of the resources of a *bioworld* — solar radiation and biomass — are concentrated in the so-called poor countries; it is education for biotechnology that is missing. In a world society where information is becoming the dominant resource, as such societies as South Korea, Taiwan, and Singapore (and, earlier, Japan) have shown, the poor can get rich by brainwork. Nor is development incompatible with environmental sensitivity, but may indeed depend on it.

The summons for our generation is to organize a shift in direction in the face of four decades of inertia and half-measures called foreign aid and overseas development assistance. The beginning of the new wisdom is to face squarely three facts:

1. Growth-with-fairness is mostly a function of decisions inside the political economies of nations both rich and poor.
2. While governments have to show the way, most growth-with-fairness will be the result of effort and enterprise by nongovernments, from small farmers to local companies.
3. Staring at a mountain of debt which won't ever be repaid in foreign exchange is no way to jump-start growth-with-fairness in developing countries.

Internal Affairs Are International Affairs

If poverty is above all a matter of "domestic" arrangements that discriminate structurally and systematically against the poor, then doing something about poverty is going to require hard decisions inside both the less and the more advanced members of the family of nations. In Asia, Africa, and Latin America this means decisions about land tenure and rural reconstruction, upgrading educational systems and widening access to them, creating more opportunities for women, training for new technical skills and modern management attitudes, and developing "basic needs" strategies. It means maximizing incentives for productivity, attracting private investment, choking corruption, protecting human rights, and widening the chance for all kinds of people to participate in making decisions that affect their own destiny.

In some societies this prescription may require no less than a revolution of some kind, as turned out to be necessary in Eastern Europe. Those in charge, even in poor countries, are usually not poor themselves, especially if they have been in office for a while. They are more likely to see economic growth than social fairness as clearly in their interest.

The internal politics of the developing nations need to be faced frankly and discussed out loud in international planning for growth-with-fairness worldwide.

But . . . the political leaders and scholars in developing countries will say they need help from elsewhere in bringing about these miracles, not just aid but new kinds of hard decisions on matters treated as domestic politics inside the industrial countries. They want the richer nations to control their budget deficits and trade surpluses, keep the cost of money low, ensure access to their big markets, reduce the protection of their farm products, get their scientists and engineers to work harder on new technologies usable in and for developing countries, make foreign investment more attractive, transfer more resources as development aid, contribute generously to international funds and banks, and open wide their educational opportunities for young people from the developing world. These leaders and scholars also want the developed nations to manage their locomotive economies so as not to export inflation or generate recession, give developing countries longer grace periods for complying with new environmental rules, regulate what their multinational companies do abroad, and persuade their banks to give overseas debtors a break. The least developed countries will also need a special ration of hope: the early margin or surplus that allows wise development policies to be accepted and adopted by their own people.

Here too we are talking about revolution of a kind: sudden changes in traditional thought patterns and workways. Each of these areas for decision (public or private and very often both) is sensitive, politically charged, and commonly treated as the province of domestic politics. The decision makers are not only political executives and civil servants and legislators and courts. They are also labor leaders wanting to protect their members' jobs, business executives wanting to protect profit margins, banks wanting to stay in business, farm lobbies wanting to protect high prices, environmentalists wanting to protect nature, consumers wanting to protect their purchasing power. These and other special-interest groups, especially if they band together, are quite capable of bringing government to a halt, even bringing governments down, just as huge crowds in a central city's public square can and, these days, quite often do.

The internal politics of the industrial nations need to be faced frankly and discussed out loud in international planning for growth-with-fairness worldwide.

But . . . the political leaders and scholars in the industrial countries will say they need help to accomplish these miracles. They want help in providing assurance to their legislators, bureaucrats, bankers, corporate executives, special-interest lobbies, and especially their voters that all this effort will actually do something effective about poverty in each developing country that is in on the bargain. It is partly their uncertainty on this score, based on a quarter-century of disappointing experience, that has eroded public support for foreign aid, especially among the largest traditional contributors and investors. And this brings us back, full circle, to the internal politics of the developing nations.

There is a basis here for macrobargains; that is, for arrangements that provide international assurances to each participating nation about the internal policies, reforms, and even restructuring in other nations that will make positive-sum international relations possible. The needed bargains are not once-and-for-all decisions. They require a continuing partnership as an essential outcome of the bargaining.

Existing systems of development assistance are typically too narrow in their purposes to tackle directly the fairness issues inside developing countries, too constrained by their basic mandates to engage the governments of developing countries in candid bargaining about the domestic obstacles to growth-with-fairness. Besides, their mandates typically exclude any bargaining at all about domestic policies of the countries that are rich enough not to need their help.

The International Monetary Fund, for example, sends missions from its Washington headquarters to developing countries to intervene in domestic debates about economic policy on the side of the ministries of finance, advocating tough controls on inflation and conditioning its financial aid on budget balancing and other prudent fiscal and monetary policies that its U.S. neighbors a few blocks away have trouble making decisions about themselves. The purpose of such IMF recommendations is usually to squeeze demand, with equilibrium, not fairness, as the primary goal. Their consequence is often to pass the cost of economic reform along to the poorest of the poor, who are in no condition to complain. The IMF's logic may be persuasive to the central city elite and their advisers who have been educated in Western graduate schools, but its policies too often fail to deal with the politics of fairness or the economics of poverty.

The World Bank makes loans, often very large ones, for "projects." Its mandate requires it to make sure that the government it is dealing with can credibly promise to repay the loan (which comes from money the World Bank itself must borrow on the open market). The bank does invest in public infrastructure such as roads and dams and even education and family planning and environmental protection, but its obligation to act as a bank makes it timid in bargaining with its borrowers about such sensitive issues as their plans for meeting their citizens' basic human needs. The bank also has to act as a bank even when its judgment proves faulty. In Africa, according to one observer, "50% of World Bank–financed rural development schemes to 1986 have failed. However, the debt remains, at 100% of face value."

Other aid agencies, national and international, public and private, mostly play it safe by investing in specific projects that can be defended as useful in themselves, without trying to address larger questions about a society's structural discrimination against its own poor. The same is generally true of private investors; they worry about political stability, but economic unfairness is likely to be lower on their anxiety scale.

What's lacking is a policy marketplace for making bargains that reach into domestic decisions on which a healthy international development effort will crucially depend. The one-way conditionality of the present system creates mutual resentment and resistance that get in the way of doing something about poverty. In that policy marketplace, the private sector companies and agencies will have to play a much larger role in the future than they have in the past.

The international private sector that impinges on growth-with-fairness is an enormous mosaic of great complexity. Global companies have their headquarters in national jurisdictions that provide their executives with passports and try to collect taxes from them. But meanwhile the executives move resources around the world to take maximum advantage of changing skills, supplies, transport, and fluctuations in money values in daily search of the profits without which they would be out of business. Governments do well to keep up with what they are doing, let alone regulate their transactions.

Many charitable foundations focus part of their wealth on development. Sometimes a foundation funds an imaginative idea that makes a big difference. That happened when the Rockefeller Foundation, later joined by the Ford Foundation, the World Bank, and others, started what became the global network of agricultural research institutes that focuses on soils, plants, and animals of special importance in the developing world.

Environmentalists come together to mobilize opinion and pressure the World Bank. Geophysicists measure in common the globe they share. Atmospheric scientists exchange models of the global climate and consult across national frontiers about global climate and Antarctic ozone. Microbiologists convene to consider a code of ethics for microbiology. Publishers gather to sell books and complain about unenforceable copyrights. Local police agencies assemble to internationalize the tracking of criminals. Drug traffickers consult across borders about new ways of evading their local police. And fanatics coordinate their next targets for terror.

As we have seen in our glimpse of "what works and why," one solid prediction can be made about international conflict and cooperation: governments are losing their grip; nongovernments are coming on strong. Therefore, in the policy-making on norms and standards, the development tax, and other matters affecting nongovernments, it will be especially important to bring into consultation representatives of the main nongovernmental actors in the world economy. This suggestion does not stem from an ideological stance about the importance of private enterprise. The reasons for involving nongovernments are pragmatic.

For one thing, nongovernments and especially private investors can do so much to make growth-with-fairness work or cause it to fail. It is in the nature of human cooperation that private actors expected to translate broad public policies into practical actions had better be consulted ahead of time. If they are not, the private will not reflect the public policy. By the same token, public officials and democratic publics on both sides of the global development bargain need to be assured that the boards and managers of large transnational business firms and international nonprofits will be acting in ways that are consistent not only with their own narrower purposes but also with doing something about poverty.

Debt Can Be Opportunity

By the early 1990s everyone knew, but those involved still couldn't bring themselves to admit, that most of the $1.3 trillion debt of the developing countries is unrepayable now or later in convertible foreign exchange. The wonder is that the biggest debtors, including the Latin American Big 3 (Brazil, Argentina, Mexico), hadn't long since declared the emperor unclothed, formed a "debtors' OPEC," and tried to bargain collectively about what they were going to repay. Instead, they were trying, one by one, to negotiate their way out, with Mexico as the bellwether and Citibank, the biggest holder of bad loans, as the lead horse among the banks. The U.S. government, which had its own money problems, was urging the banks to paddle their own leaky canoes.

Meanwhile the street value of Third World external debt sank to something less than a third of its book value. And the relations between rich and poor countries focused more and more on debt service rather than development.

How did the best and brightest of the banking profession get their borrowers and themselves in such a mess? The story starts with the great oil-dollar spill of the 1970s. First the Arabs, then all the main oil exporters got together and hiked the price of crude oil, in stages, fourfold. (That was what made the Alaska pipeline, which had a fourfold cost overrun during the same period, look like such a brilliant piece of strategic planning.) The oil was still just as cheap to pump as it had been before, so the petromonarchs profited hugely; ditto the merchants who did their bidding. The newly rich had to put all this money somewhere, and the big banks of Europe and North America scrambled to oblige. But then the banks had to find big borrowers who needed dollars so badly they would pay more for them than the banks were paying the depositors.

In biblical times all this was called usury and was commonly regarded as a Bad Thing. But we moderns think that it has served civilization well, enabling most of us to live beyond our means. The system does work, actually, if no one gets too greedy. However, the slosh of petrodollars was too great a temptation. All the players got greedy at once.

The eager bankers found their big borrowers in the Third World: ambitious political leaders protected by ordnance-hungry armies, encouraged to borrow and keep borrowing by those who got to spend the money. Prominent among the spenders were local friends of the political leaders, local bankers and business executives who saw the borrowing as good for business and all manner of middlepeople. Some of these came from abroad to help manage the bonanza. In another time and place they would have been called carpetbaggers; nowadays they are called consultants.

The collusion was mostly not conscious, but all of the above — depositors, banks, borrowers, spenders — shared a philosophy in common. They saw in the flood of foreign exchange much short-run wealth creation for themselves and didn't think the long-run consequences were really their problem. So the debt piled up.

For a while, the pileup was obscured by the peculiar way banks kept their books. If a bank was overextended with dubious loans, it could lend the borrower even more money, compassionately helping a poor nation pay the interest on a hopeless loan. That transaction was then double-counted as good news on the bank's books: another loan had been made to a valued client; and interest on the bad loan was paid, making it a good loan after all. Great satirists like Lewis Carroll and Jonathan Swift would have enjoyed high finance in the 1980s.

By the early nineties it was more than obvious: somehow the debt burden would have to be lifted so that developing countries large and small could generate the economic enterprise, political energy, social fairness, and financial resources to mount a real war on poverty worldwide.

The banks were taking, perforce, a share of the hit; it was their careless judgment about risk and repayment that, more than anything else, built the maze in which they lost their way. Governments, which means taxpayers, also have to be part of the solution. But, said more and more analysts, bankers, and political leaders, can't the bailout be something besides a reward for short-run thinking?

Some good ideas came out of trying to answer that sensible question. One was to swap debt for equity, that is, to use debt to "buy" local productive enterprise in the debtor country (Mexico, say, or Brazil) and ensure its effective management. Other swaps were also negotiated: creating institutes for biotechnological research, setting up university fellowships, exchanging debt for agreements to protect rain forests and otherwise enhance the global environment.

What these ideas have in common is that debt that is supposed to be repaid in dollars is paid instead in local currency *to accomplish something in the debtor country that is internationally recognized to be valuable.* A rough historical precedent might be the local-currency *counterpart funds* established forty years ago in each Western European country to match the transatlantic dollar transfusions from the Marshall Plan. These local funds, under the joint supervision of each European country and a U.S. mission residing there, were applied to all sorts of useful development projects that might otherwise have lacked the local political support to be funded.

There is a political pitfall, and it's a big one. Even a weak government will balk at ceding any part of its national patrimony to foreign governments or corporations. So each swap has to be a cooperative enterprise, with the developing country as a full partner. For example, Brazil's constitution declares parts of its most fragile forests to be its "national patrimony." But in a "debt-for-nature swap," a consortium of creditor nations could join with Brazil in declaring some forestlands a "global treasure." What would otherwise have been hard-money debt would then be converted into investments by Brazil in its own currency. The resulting fund (supplemented by technical help and new investment from abroad) would then be devoted to protection of Brazilian forests of international concern. Management of such a fund would have to be a joint arrangement between Brazil and an international agency. But the "global treasure" concept rquires no cession of sovereignty on the part of Brazil.

Before this kind of common sense can prevail, though, we are going to have to stop thinking of "the debt problem" as something to be bargained out between the two parties most responsible for the mess: the debtor governments and the international bankers. The challenge is to broaden the conversation, widen the purposes to be served by each settlement, opening up opportunities to convert debt into investment, repayments into development, and the problem into an opportunity.

Measuring Basic Needs

The centerpiece of an international bargain to do something about poverty would have to be a broad consensus on what members of the United Nations and the International Labor Organization have already, on paper, agreed: that everyone is entitled to a minimum life and literacy by virtue of having been born into the human family and that this "poverty line" (already a familiar concept in every advanced country) is properly a matter of international concern and cooperation. It would not be a much longer step to seek international agreement that the meeting of basic needs worldwide should be regarded as a first charge on world resources.

It is not necessary to seek international agreement on quantitative measures of basic needs. These will vary according to geography, climate, culture, tradition, social priorities, individual and family preferences, individual life cycles, national stages of development, and time. Yet it is essential that the meeting of basic needs be internationally measurable. And this means a new development push will have to use some better yardstick for growth-with-fairness than gross national product (GNP), that grotesquely blunt instrument for measuring a nation's strength or weakness, success or failure.

The GNP has been around for half a century, so its two fatal flaws are no secret. Until the early 1990s, however, it had no serious competitors in the marketplace for social yardsticks. One of its flaws is that GNP measures only the part of each country's economy that is paid for with money, and clean money at that. Many full-time parents and homemakers have long complained that economists discount to zero the value of their full-time jobs. Criminals, smugglers, and people who barter their services ("you fix my roof and I'll repair your plumbing") don't

complain out loud; the tax collector might be listening. The
GNP's other flaw is that it doesn't discriminate between useful
and harmful goods and services. Nourishing food and harmful
drugs both have positive signs.

The blunt instrument loses all its shape when economists
measure the wealth of a whole population by calculating its per
capita GNP. The average obscures all the really interesting
questions about the distribution of wealth, such as education,
health, life, and death. Charles Yost, a gentle but hardheaded
diplomat who served as U.S. ambassador to the United Nations, put it crisply: "GNP is a peculiarly undiscriminating indicator. . . . Like Oscar Wilde's definition of a cynic, it knows
the price of everything and the value of nothing. It is true to
its name—it is gross."

A better tool now comes to hand. In the late 1980s the
UN Development Program and the Swedish government entrusted to Mahbub ul-Haq, a brilliant political economist who
had been Pakistan's minister of finance, the task of construct-
ing a new index to judge and compare, country by country,
what economic growth is doing to and for people. In 1990 the
human development index (HDI) was born.

The HDI, focusing on outcomes, fused together three indicators: life expectancy, literacy, and "real" income (adjusted
for purchasing power). The result was illuminating. Saudi Arabia, with all that oil and a small population, ranked high on
the per capita GNP scale; the HDI judged the Saudi performance as remarkably modest, behind the Philippines and just
ahead of the Dominican Republic. Costa Rica, with no army
and a durable democracy, ranked about even with the Soviet
Union and ahead of South Korea and Singapore. Japan, whose
per capita GNP was below that of Switzerland, the United States,
Norway, and the United Arab Emirates, climbed to the top of
the HDI by virtue of long life and high literacy. (The United
States ranked seventh in the world, ahead of France and Britain but behind Canada and Sweden.)

The 1990 report that accompanied the index also calculated the ratio of each country's armed forces to its schoolteach-
ers. Ethiopia and Iraq led this race with more than four times

as many soldiers as teachers. But Brazil, even during a generation of military rule, stressed schools as well as weapons: it had only twenty-four soldiers for every one hundred teachers.

Refinements to this UN index in 1991 were bold and imaginative:

• Knowledge beyond literacy was given more weight, by factoring in years of schooling and the output of graduate schools.

• An additional index of how women are doing concluded that "gender discrimination is a worldwide problem." With a "gender-sensitive" index, the United States dropped from seventh to tenth in the world sweepstakes. Japan dropped from first to seventeenth. In Japan, the share of national income that females earn was still only 26 percent.

• Nearly $50 billion a year was wasted in developing countries, the UN's 1991 report said; it ought to be captured for development. Much of this could come from just freezing (not even reducing) military spending, which alone absorbed 5.5 percent of GNP in Asia, Africa, and Latin America.

• "Halting capital flight" is also imperative: "In Mexico and Argentina, an amount equal to at least 50 percent of the money borrowed in the past fifteen years has flown out again."

• "Combatting corruption" would also save huge amounts. "In Pakistan," says the report authored by the former Pakistani minister, "the illegitimate private gain from one's own public position is unofficially estimated at 4% of GNP. Estimates of corruption are even higher for many other countries."

• The boldest refinement to the 1991 report was the addition of a human freedom index. Using forty indicators from travel to torture, the UN team brazenly ranked eighty-eight countries. Sweden headed the 1991 freedom parade, Iraq unsurprisingly brought up the rear. (The United States was tied for thirteenth with Australia, just ahead of Britain and Japan.) "A sustained investment in people," says the report, unleashes "creative energies" and loosens "the authoritarian grip of their leaders." Before the Year of Democracy, 1989, no UN panel would have dared to publish such an index, let alone draw such policy conclusions.

The human development index won't elbow gross national product off stage. But the new goal it highlights — aggregate human progress, not just aggregate economic product — gives those who aren't poor a powerful tool to help reshape a better future for those who are.

"Doing Something About Poverty"

No matter how well each developing country manages to mix public and private enterprise and how skillfully it uses initiatives, subsidies, and incentives to maximize both economic growth and social fairness, it is clear that the developing world (roughly, Asia, Africa, and Latin America plus islands in the Pacific and the Caribbean) will need major inputs of public grants and loans and private investment from Europe, Japan, and North America to achieve the kinds and rates of growth that will make fairness an attainable goal. A strategy of "doing something about poverty" will require an assured source of incentive funds for development. Those funds should be raised by an international development tax, raised in one or more of the ways outlined in Chapter Five.

How much will be needed and from which transnational activities it should be derived will be matters for hard bargaining among governments and international nongovernments. Before you ask how such a process could be organized and how the proceeds will be allocated, bear with me while I sketch the other task that the world community will somehow need to undertake in order to mount a serious growth-with-fairness effort worldwide.

If the world's governments and nongovernments are going to turn to and help developing nations grow fast enough and healthily enough to lift the poor and poorest above the poverty line, then two actions will have to be taken and in the following order. First, each developing country that expects the rest of the world to help will have to frame and present to the world its own economic and social strategy, including its own definition of basic human needs and an explanation of how (with outside help) its growing economy can be managed so as to meet and sustain them. Second, those strategies will have to be reviewed and judged internationally to certify to the outside contributors (international banks and funds, governments, and private donors, lenders, and investors) that aid from abroad will actually "do something about poverty."

In the nature of politics, "face," national sovereignty, and human relations, such a review and certification process cannot be one in which the richer nations sit in judgment on the poorer ones. One way to avoid this—startling only at first glance—would be for an international certifying agency to organize a review process in which the countries needing outside help would review each other's national development and basic needs strategies.

There is a successful precedent for such a process. When the Marshall Plan was launched, its U.S. administrators decided they did not want to be in the position of sitting in judgment on each European country's recovery plans. Yet they had to be able to assure the U.S. Congress and the American people that those plans, individually and together, were well calculated to serve the purpose of the Marshall Plan, to foster European recovery. The United States therefore threw to the Europeans (grouped at that time in the Organization for European Economic Cooperation, the OEEC) the task of dividing by country the billions of dollars authorized for transatlantic aid.

As an official of the Marshall Plan agency in Washington, I had a chance to witness in Paris some of the resulting "country reviews," in which each national plan was examined by all the other European beneficiaries of the U.S. aid. The national plans were prepared with high professional competence and subjected to polite but searching criticism by equally professional analysts from other countries. The Americans sat in only as observers. I recall, for example, that when the Italians were in the witness chair, they were confronted with evidence that their national plan would have the effect of discriminating against the Mezzogiorno (the relatively poorer southern half of Italy). When in their turn the French explained their fiscal needs, the delegates from other European countries asked why the *Chemins de Fer Français* piled up such a whopping deficit each year. "The rest of us seem to be able to run our national railways without losing nearly so much money," said a critic from one of the other countries, in flawless French. "Why should Marshall Plan aid go to France to fill up that unnecessary hole in your national accounts?"

As the Europeans delved deeply and mutually into the domestic economic, social, budgetary, and monetary policies of each OEEC country, no one cried foul and invoked the principle of noninterference in internal affairs. This was because the process was fair, it was conducted among peers, and something vitally important ($5 billion the first year, nearly $14 billion of transatlantic aid over four years) was at stake. National sovereignty was by no means set aside. What happened was that the several sovereignties were pooled in a common recovery effort from which all the Western Europeans emerged winners, in one of the twentieth century's greatest triumphs of international cooperation. (The idea of review by peers might well be replicated in the work of the European Bank for Reconstruction and Development, set up to help Eastern Europe's transition from "planned" to "market" economies.)

As with extranational institutions, arguing from a European analogy is perilous. It is easy to think of a dozen ways in which the development puzzle in present-day North-South relations is different from the problem of European recovery forty years ago. In world development, the effort now required is incomparably larger; it will take much longer; the needs are much more diverse; the developing countries in two hemispheres and three continents don't have nearly as much political like-mindedness to glue them together as did the smaller number of Western Europeans, on half of a small continent.

The central idea is nevertheless suggestive. The developing countries might be able to do as a group (or more likely as several groups, according to geography or development status or even political congeniality) what they cannot do individually: make sure that the coming global effort to overcome the worst aspects of poverty worldwide is in fact pointed squarely at that goal and that the net contributors to the process can depend on it.

A Real Development Community

Is the world community capable of organizing so complex and far-reaching an effort as I have here described? Of course it is. At the end of World War II, the United Nations established a large operating organization, the United Nations Relief and Rehabilitation Administration, to help some of the most devastated countries (including Italy, Greece, Yugoslavia, the Ukraine, and China) and sixteen million refugees besides. The problem is not scale and complexity but political will and consent.

Before the Soviet Union's about-face in the late eighties, which made possible the mostly peaceful revolutions of 1989 in Eastern Europe and the tamping down of East-West wars by proxy on three other continents, it was hard to imagine a world stage on which a serious worldwide growth-with-fairness effort could be mounted. Now that postwar planning can actually be done without having the war first, such an undertaking is not only conceivable but imperative.

What it takes to get the job done is patently beyond the capacity of the usual committee-of-sovereigns-within-a-staff. The kind of organization required was described in a general way in Chapter Five. Such an organization must ultimately be responsible to its own council of governments (as UNRRA was) but driven by a strong and self-confident executive leadership, obliged to analyze problems and initiatives from an international point of view, capable of dealing with government ministers as peers, confident enough to operate in the open, flexible enough to bring into consultation other public international agencies and private international nongovernments.

I hesitate to label it with a name in capital letters; but I think of it as a *development community.* It should be a major new international institution mandated to promote growth-with-fairness in very practical ways, with resources it would be authorized to raise on its own authority (the way many provincial and local governments do). Many of the existing international organizations with their specialized mandates and special constraints can supplement, but none of them can coordinate and

energize, a worldwide effort to "do something about poverty."
A new start requires a new start.

The new agency can, and I believe should, be established
within the framework of the United Nations Charter; its purpose would be precisely, as the Charter's Preamble says, "to promote social progress and better standards of life in larger freedom," and "to employ international machinery for the promotion
of the economic and social advancement of all peoples."

It could be established within the Charter but outside the
UN as an organization. The World Bank and International
Monetary Fund were set up by the Bretton Woods agreement
with their own governing boards but are affiliated, somewhat
tenuously in practice, with the United Nations. Yet their fundamental purposes and principles are those described in the
Charter. So it would be best for the new, serious effort to "do
something about poverty" worldwide to be legitimated by the
General Assembly of the United Nations — not another rhetorical development decade and not another specialized agency
either, but a new kind of agency built on the extranational principle already described.

The new agency would have its hands full. It would be
mandated to do the following:

* Establish norms and standards for its own operations and
  for the guidance of its members, including the generic definition of *basic human needs* on which each developing country
  would be free to embroider in its own way.
* Raise a sizable development fund through international taxes
  on transnational activities and transactions. Governments
  would agree to facilitate as necessary the levying and collection of the development tax. (Another possible source of
  regular revenues would be the sale of bonds guaranteed by
  governments. But taxing activities that benefit from a peaceful world would avoid annual head scratching by national
  legislatures that are chronically in budget trouble.)
* Call for national development strategies designed to assure
  growth-with-fairness.
* Arrange an international process for reviewing these strate-

gies and monitoring progress against goals established by
the member countries themselves.

- Report in the open to donors, lenders, investors, and the
United Nations (presumably through its Economic and Social Council) on how each country, whether net recipient
or net provider of resources for development, is measuring
up to the central purpose of growth-with-fairness.
- Arrange for bargaining among member countries (both developing and advanced) on domestic policies that interfere
with cooperation to achieve growth-with-fairness worldwide.
- Serve as a catalytic agent in arranging debt swaps. Since
most of the developing-country debt overhang cannot be
repaid in foreign exchange, it makes sense to write it off as
a part of bargains whereby chunks of it are used as local
currency to conserve rain forests, generate new development-
related research (for example, in biotechnology), or attract
new private investors to purchase equities in productive local
enterprises.
- Allocate the revenues it raises for development, following
the guidance available from the reviews of growth-with-
fairness strategies. These tax revenues would not be subject to year-by-year government decisions. They could be
allocated directly to governments or applied through contracts with other development agencies such as the World
Bank, the World Health Organization, or the UN Children's
Fund or even contracted out for specified development tasks
to qualified nongovernments.

The formulation of norms and standards for growth-with-
fairness would be arranged by the collective executive in wide
public consultation with governments and nongovernments.
They would be approved as a basis for the rest of the new organization's work. They would be of such wide public and political interest that they should probably be debated in the UN
General Assembly as well; but any action by the General Assembly on a matter of substance could only be advisory to the
UN's member governments.

In the international review of growth-with-fairness strategies and in arranging the bargaining about domestic obstacles to international cooperation in promoting growth-with-fairness, everyone need not get involved. But worldwide arguments about development are too likely to bog down in political name-calling, as they did in the misnamed "North-South dialogue" of the mid 1970s. The collective executive of the new development community could arrange and chair dialogues among smaller groups of advanced and developing countries on concrete issues of special interest to them and form groups of manageable size to conduct the mutual reviews of national growth-with-fairness strategies.

Many years ago, when I was in the foreign aid business in Washington, I complained that we were "tackling twenty-year problems with five-year plans manned by two-year personnel and funded by one-year appropriations." That is still an uncomfortably accurate description of the world development enterprise.

At this open moment in world politics, we have a chance to tackle anew, worldwide, with all the resources of science, technology, and the human spirit, the ancient but now solvable puzzle of poverty. Compared to the costs of war, the task cannot be rated as expensive.

ten

A GLOBAL COMMONS
Trusteeship for the World Environment

*The first man who, having enclosed a piece of ground, bethought himself
of saying This is mine, and found people simple enough to believe him,
was the real founder of civil society. From how many crimes, wars and
murders, from how many horrors and misfortunes might not any one have
saved mankind, by pulling up the stakes, or filling up the ditch, and crying
to his fellows, "Beware of listening to this imposter; you are undone if you
once forget that the fruits of the earth belong to us all, and the earth itself
to nobody."*

—Jean-Jacques Rousseau, The Social Contract

VERY LARGE CROWDS of educated people waving placards cannot be ignored. That's the lesson dictators and democratic leaders
alike have been learning in recent years—many by finding themselves suddenly unemployed. Beyond a certain size (enough to
overflow a big-city plaza) protesting crowds cannot be subdued
even by force.

The fusion of education with frustration is obviously explosive. Polish steelworkers, Indian villagers, South African
blacks, Mexican campesinos, Romanian miners, Korean auto-
workers, Moscow "liberals," and Americans for and against abortion rights have all known how to create media events that mor-
tify, in order to modify, established authority.

But the biggest crowd so far—two hundred million people in 140 countries, possibly the largest grass-roots demonstration in history—came out on Earth Day 1990. Stay-at-homes
could judge as trivial the televised images of local recycling (easier to photograph than the global atmosphere), jibe at the litter
demonstrators left behind for someone else to clean up, and

185

wince at the spectacle, here and there, of half-naked young people with painted faces having fun in the sun.

Some conservatives, fearful for economic growth, worried aloud that green might be the color of recession. Some
liberals reacted as columnist William Raspberry did: "I don't
think I, or people like me, are the true enemies of the Earth,"
he complained in a comment on Earth Day. The polluters, he
thought, are the other guys: big corporate villains that spill oil,
produce the "industry-spawned pall" in the people's clean air,
build autos with engines that spew exhaust fumes. A polluter
was not, in his vocabulary, a consumer who uses petroleum,
buys industrial products, or drives a car.

Earth Day might 'do actual harm," Raspberry warned,
by persuading folks that "everything will be fine if we clean up
our individual acts." Yet it is the acts of individuals that produce
the pervasive threat to the global environment.

The Big Mind Change

The poor and the rich, we are cooperating to destroy — in different but mutually reinforcing ways — the environment we share.
The problem is precisely the behavior of innocent voters unwilling to tax pollution, innocent peasants cutting down trees,
innocent couples having more babies than they can raise to be
healthy and productive, innocent citizens thinking that government regulation and corporate responsibility are not matters for
"people like us."

We are dealing now with a new class of problems: they
are global, and they are also behavioral. Global, because answers will be found only by widening our worldview, changing
our minds about the scale and dimension of what we face. Behavioral, because answers require literally hundreds of millions
of people, not just roomsful of experts and political leaders, to
do something or stop doing something.

The world community, to the limited extent that it is yet
a community, has had some practice in tackling environmental
issues of global scale where the facts aren't all in but timely action is needed by millions of people. Smallpox, for example,

was eradicated by vaccinating untold hordes of children and lots of adults too. Putting in place a world network of agricultural research stations, getting international consensus on the security of civil aviation, and cleaning up the Mediterranean and other regional seas, didn't require nearly so many people to participate personally, in the manner of smallpox vaccinations. But they did require acquiescence in behavioral change by very large numbers of people. These acts required getting used to funny-tasting rice, submitting to the indignities of airport searches, modifying waste disposal practices.

In another way, the Earth-wide threats that bring out the big crowds are without precedent. We are accustomed to acting to protect the environment after it's already clear that something bad is happening — that is, after we can smell the smog, diagnose the radiation poisoning, see the fish turn belly-up in our favorite lake, measure the pockmarks acid rain makes on our ancestors' gravestones, watch the defoliation of a nearby forest, or analyze the chemicals that have seeped from a landfill into our drinking water.

But when it comes to protecting the ozone layer that protects us from skin cancer or heeding the global warming forecast for the twenty-first century, nothing certifiably bad has actually happened yet. Scientists are still debating whether the great summer drought of 1988, which got the attention of political leaders and the media, was direct evidence that the forecast warming had already begun. How does a consensus for policies affecting millions of people get built around the calculations of experts?

The answer lies in exploiting to the full the information technologies that enable all of us, reading the lips of scientists through the popular media, to understand how and why we are destroying so much without really meaning to destroy anything: the genetic diversity of tropical forests, the purity of lakes and streams and inland seas and even the oceans, the quality of the air we breathe, and the balance of atmospheric gases that keep the planet habitable. As a direct consequence of information technologies, the international scientific community has discovered a common interest in *global change,* a merciful shorthand for what scientists call *biosphere-geosphere interaction.*

On some big mind changes, a majority of the scientific community often trails public opinion, pooh-poohing the dangers of technological progress and complaining that more research is needed before anything definitive can be said. On such issues as nuclear power, toxic waste, and three decades of arms buildup, the scientists dissenting from prevailing government/industry definitions of *progress* were a minority, though sometimes a vociferous one, among their own colleagues.

Global change is a notable exception. It was U.S. scientists, soon followed by a growing chorus of expert opinion from around the world, who blew the whistle on worldwide environmental destruction.

Scientists receive their accolades and rise in their chosen professions through excellence and imagination on the frontiers of their own comparatively narrow specialties. But global change has induced a kind of culture shock, pushing impressive numbers of first-rate scientists to reach out for broader insights that can come only from colleagues in cognate fields. John A. Eddy of the National Center for Atmospheric Research writes of an "ecumenical movement in the biological and earth sciences," which brings together disciplines that have been focusing separately on the atmosphere, the oceans, agriculture, geology, geophysics, and outer space. (Students of society — economists, political scientists, social psychologists — are hurrying to catch up.)

"Advances in understanding," says Eddy, "will inevitably drive bounded areas of study onto the terrain of adjacent fields." He cites the "mutual and beneficial encroachment of studies of climate, by meteorologists, and of vegetation and primary productivity, by plant ecologists. The movement has recently been spurred by findings of variations in the quantity of carbon dioxide entrapped in Greenland ice, demonstrating the critical role of biotic processes in global changes of the past. It has been driven as well by progress in modeling global climate and regional ecology, promoting feelings that we are now within reach of the ultimate goal of coupled, numerical models of the whole earth system." But today's supercomputers are still far from matching Earth's unimaginable complexity; the scientists who have complicated their inquiries by combining several disciplines will keep pushing for enormous increases in computational speed and storage.

In the mid 1980s the greenhouse effect began to attract broad public notice. In international discussions of the global environment, it came to stand as a metaphor for a fundamentally new state of affairs. Before the end of the 1980s, no less an authority than Frank Press, president of the U.S. National Academy of Sciences, was describing the historic watershed out loud: "humankind has become a more important agent of environmental change than nature."

Scientists were saying that the warming of the globe could, within the lifetime of today's young people, make dust bowls out of some of the world's traditional grain-producing breadbaskets, expand the volume of water in the seas, melt some polar ice, and produce an irreversible rising of the world's oceans. Futurist James Dator called my attention to a large blue poster displayed in Australia, depicting the famous "sails" of the Sydney Opera House, the only things visible above the risen water. The words on the poster: *If you act as though it matters and it doesn't matter, then it doesn't matter. But if you act as though it doesn't matter and it matters, then it matters.*

When in 1988 the Canadian government assembled in Toronto three hundred experts, advocates, and officials from forty-eight countries, they certainly thought the greenhouse effect mattered, so much so that Prime Minister Gro Harlem Brundtland of Norway, who had just chaired a World Commission on Environment and Development, said it shouldn't be called a greenhouse but a heat trap. The mood at the meeting was already alarmist and activist. "Humanity is conducting an enormous, unsanctioned, globally pervasive experiment whose ultimate consequences could be second only to a global nuclear war," said the Toronto conference statement, paraphrasing a comment first made years before by scientist Roger Revelle. Four years later, at the huge Earth Summit in Rio de Janeiro, both alarm and activism were greatly enhanced.

Global warming already looms as the biggest environmental issue on the political horizon. It has become such an issue because information technologies—collecting data by satellite sensing, modeling the atmosphere with the most powerful computers, sharing analyses worldwide by electronic telecommunications — produced raw materials for knowledge, wisdom, and guesswork that were only possible starting in the 1980s, when supercomputers were developed and married to telecommunications.

We will need, then, to treat the global environment not as a series of separable puzzles in corporate strategy or national policy but as parts of an integrated commons, with hundreds of millions of people responsible for its health because its health is the key to their own.

Earth, Sea, and Sky

Four enormous environments, still mostly unexplored, are already treated in international law and custom as parts of a global commons. The oceans, outer space, the atmosphere, and Antarctica are geophysically and biochemically related to one another, but each has its own history of human relations.

Oceans

Oceans have the longest human history. Because they were accessible to a few courageous seafarers but a dangerous mystery to most land dwellers, the oceans have long been an unregulated highway for those with the technological prowess to travel it.

The most recent Law of the Sea Treaty, completed in the eighties, declares the deep ocean and its seabed to be "the common heritage of mankind." The phrase came with good credentials: the Holy See had spoken in 1978 of the "universally accepted" principle that the seas are "the common heritage of mankind," though the pope's thinkers neglected to explain from Whom mankind received the inheritance.

As useful marine resources were discovered and perceived to be scarce, nations have tried to make up rules for their exploitation. The difficulty of regulation increases with distance from the shoreline (offshore oil, seabed minerals) and mobility of the resource (fish). One of the resulting absurdities was an unenforceable edict by the U.S. Congress that salmon spawned in western U.S. rivers carry their American citizenship with them as they travel the wide Pacific Ocean.

Under the treaty, large chunks of ocean space out to two hundred miles from the world's shorelines are reserved as *exclusive economic zones*. But even in these zones, the resources are to be managed by the states that happen to be nearby as a kind of trust for the generality of humankind. The only part of the treaty still in limbo would have set up an international "enterprise" to regulate the use of seabed minerals; the United States and a few other countries refused to sign the whole treaty with that provision in it. Not long after that, however, the White House in Washington announced that all the rest of the treaty could be regarded as "customary international law." This may have set a record for a mutation from custom to law.

Outer Space

The Outer Space Treaty, with its parallel "common province" concept, assumes that human exploration outward from Earth will be unique, establishing a kind of monopoly in which human decisions will be definitive.

Some such decisions have been made. Nuclear weapons deployed in orbit and antiballistic missiles (ABMs) have been banned by treaty. In the 1980s, research by both U.S. and Soviet governments on space-based military operations made the earlier demilitarization of outer space a fragile concept. Beyond discouraging military applications, other human decisions are urgently needed: to deal with space debris, to allocate fairly the most popular orbits. The best low Earth orbits are a finite resource, and at geosynchronous orbit there is already a "parking problem."

The Atmosphere

Weather and climate (*climate* is long-term weather) have not been claimed as the exclusive province of any nation. Clouds, winds, and storms, unlike human artifacts such as aircraft and balloons, move through "national air space" without picking up any of the attributes of national sovereignty. The World Weather Watch

was put together without provoking a single claim that the
weather belongs to anyone.

Atmospheric pollution is obviously everybody's business.
The Environmental Modification Treaty blocks "hostile" changing of the atmosphere. Some short-term weather can be modified at human command, but even where that has been done
for many years (for example, Israel's cloud seeding in the eastern
Mediterranean, which enhances rainfall not only in Israel but
also in Syria and Jordan), it has not yet produced international
conflict.

Antarctica

Antarctica was established as a special kind of commons when
in 1959 a dozen nations (most of which had laid claim to pie-
shaped slices of the empty continent) signed the Antarctic Treaty;
a few others have since joined the still exclusive club.

Any nation with the technical capacity can conduct scientific research, or just explore, anywhere on the icy continent.
Military operations are not allowed and nuclear weapons are
banned. You don't need a visa to visit Antarctica, but you do
need plenty of help to get there and survive.

The treaty came up for review in 1991. None of the original members defected or tried to press their former territorial
claims. Some outsiders wanted to hedge against the discovery
of valuable minerals under the ice or just offshore, but that
seemed such a far-out contingency that agreement was reached
to ban commercial minerals exploration for fifty years.

These four huge environments are for practical purposes indivisi-
ble: they are bounded by each other, affect each other's behavior,
must take each other into account. No person, corporation, or
nation can establish exclusive ownership of the oceans, outer
space, the global atmosphere, or the continent of Antarctica.

It is in fact possible for a person, corporation, or nation
to try to control some of the resources these commons environments may contain — not information, which is bound to leak,
but fish, krill, oil, hard minerals, energy vents, upwelling cold

water, induced rain, gravity-free manufacturing, solar energy, hydrogen, and other humanly useful elements. But to establish and hang onto rights to use or abuse the commons depends, like any consensus decision, on the acquiescence of those who care and the apathy of those who don't.

Rio: A New Beginning

Many of those who care about the global environment and some who do not—altogether thirty thousand people, including the top political leaders of 178 countries—gathered in Rio de Janeiro the first two weeks of June 1992 to argue about who should be doing what about world-scale hazards and wonder how to induce them to do it. An 800-page document emerged, agreed to by the consensus of exhaustion. Much of it illustrated the quip about diplomatic discourse by Dean Acheson, the sharp-tongued intellectual who was President Harry Truman's secretary of state: "One can always get an agreed paper by increasing the vagueness and generality of its statements."

But the Rio declaration departed from the diplomatic norm in one important way: while ringing alarm bells about global pollution, it zeroed in on poverty as a major pollutant and called for "eradicating poverty." Big environmental dangers come both from profligate use of resources by the rich and from the way the poor lay waste to forests, soils, and cities as they scrabble for subsistence. Because the bill for eradicating poverty wasn't attached, everyone agreed.

Elsewhere the massive document declared that "the polluter should bear the cost of pollution." This important idea was hidden in a thicket of reservations, described as "an approach," adopted "in principle," "without distorting international trade and investment." The government delegates, peering through the hedges, perceived no irrevocable commitments and agreed.

The Rio declaration came out, predictably if not passionately, for women, youth, indigenous peoples, and the oppressed; for technology transfer to developing countries; for the spread of "appropriate information," an acceptably fuzzy phrase; for economic growth and an "open international system"; for "liability and compensation for the victims of pollution"; for timely notification of adverse effects on others; for peaceful resolution of disputes; for interdependence and "global partnership," and above all for "sustainable development." Everyone agreed. Why not? No one was committed to do anything dangerously or expensively specific.

Obscured by the negotiated ambiguity, however, was a fresh face of the old collision between rich and poor, North and South. At Rio, the South wanted help in dealing with its environmental troubles. Even though this looked to many critics like old-fashioned foreign aid in green garb, most of the richer countries agreed to ante into the new game. Japan promised to raise its contributions for "sustainable development" from $800 million to $1.4 billion a year through 1996; Europe pledged $4 billion; Germany alone promised more than $6 billion. The United States, which had insisted on removing explicit promises of aid from agreed documents and explicit promises of performance from the draft treaty on global warming, held its pledges to figures with far fewer zeros, such as $25 million to help countries analyze how to reduce greenhouse gas emissions and $150 million to help protect the world's forests.

The American tactic, embarrassing to U.S. environmentalists and America's industrial allies, infuriating to the majority of developing nations, was to stress its national bragging rights and avoid international leadership. Some American claims about its national performance were certainly impressive: emissions of lead down 97 percent, carbon monoxide down 41 percent, atmospheric particulates down 59 percent. But the United States resisted international agreement on explicit targets or timetables about the future. It watered down the draft climate convention. It also refused to sign a draft treaty aimed at slowing the rate at which the diversity of living species is dwindling.

Sensitive to its own abortion debate in a presidential election year, the United States also vetoed language that would link population growth and environmental damage. The Acheson principle came into play again: all 178 countries agreed to have "appropriate demographic policies." The chairman of the Rio meeting, "Tommy" Koh of Singapore, who moved the huge meeting along with a quick gavel and a lively sense of humor, was heard to remark, "This will teach the United Nations not to hold a conference in an American election year."

But such a worldwide gathering of nations is not to be judged by specific actions with immediate effect. Despite the years of advance preparation, the Rio conference was bound to produce more of a beginning than a conclusion. "This is a launching pad, not a quick fix," said Maurice Strong, who had organized the preparations and served as executive secretary at Rio.

The responsibility of nations and of their citizens for the health of the global environment is a clear enough global consensus now. This was, for example, the first time forest management had been put firmly on the international political agenda. It will take much scientific analysis, countless national and international consultations, many treaties and rules and regulations, and above all widespread knowledge conveyed by near-universal education to translate general responsibilities into specific behaviors — by governments and corporations and individuals — in every part of this endangered globe.

More than five billion human beings are now Nature's prime change agent. "Every person on Earth is part of the cause, which makes it difficult to organize an effective response. But every person on Earth also tends to suffer the consequences, which makes an effective response essential and ought to make it possible to find one — once the global pattern is widely recognized." So wrote Senator Al Gore, who headed the U.S. congressional delegation at Rio, in a book published early in 1992. A month after he returned from Rio, Gore was selected by the Democratic party to run for vice president of the United States. The global environment had just been moved to center stage, and Gore was selected partly because he had worked hard to understand what that would mean to the United States and to the world.

The rhetorical consensus was impressive. But the Rio outcome was flawed in its assumption, so common to UN agreements, that the only real actors in international affairs are states. Most of the world's past pollution has been caused, and most future environmental actions will be taken, by nongovernments, from individual peasants to large business firms. Many of the firms, if not the peasants, were in Rio on the fringes of the conversation; Maurice Strong had tried hard to create access channels for them. But the net result was essentially a tract about what national governments should consider in making environmental policy. In the next round, corporations, their executives and their governing boards, had better be brought early and often into the conversation; they are the people who can do the most to carry out the talkers' intentions.

The focus on states was troublesome in other ways as well. Monitoring and environmental assessment were treated as something states should do. But in the twenty-first century, won't keeping track of the global environment be quintessentially a task for *global* concepts, technologies, and institutions? Moreover, the global commons does not belong to states. In consequence, except for the debates about the atmosphere, this largest part of the world's environment languished on the outer edge of officials' attention at Rio.

One other comment may be worth making before we leave the Earth Summit. Abstract phrases are useful if they lead to practical actions and pragmatic cooperation. But does "sustainable development" lead to "the eradication of poverty"? Sustainable is becoming a status quo word, a too-easy argument for no growth in the name of environmental protection.

Our purpose in the global environment should be not just to keep it from further degradation at human command, not just to protect it from ourselves. Certainly we have to protect ourselves and each other from letting the global commons become humanity's littered backyard, its waste-disposal dump. But the present "tragedy of the commons" is that we are not yet using what it freely provides. The marvels of space satellites and information technology have not yet been used to narrow the gap between rich and poor; they mostly enable the affluent to work more efficiently with, or against, each other.

We are wasting most of the sun's beneficent rays by not converting them into usable energy. We are neglecting the power still locked in the temperature difference between the tropical sea surface and the ocean deeps. We are not yet stretching our biotechnological talent to use for development the resources that could make poor countries rich — their own dense biomass and solar radiation.

The idea of sustainability bids us conserve whatever environment we have left. That's not nearly a dynamic enough idea to generate a worldwide push for growth-with-fairness.

The Management of Global Behavior

The problem is not management of the global commons. It is the management of human behavior in the commons. *Eco* serves as prefix to both *economics* and *ecology*. The road ahead is littered with ethical choices, to reconcile what's efficient with what's prudent and fair.

• What claim do future generations have on today's decision makers? The traditional way to take our grandchildren into account is to "discount" them. But shouldn't today's products be priced at their full social cost, including what we're borrowing from those very grandchildren? Should today's poor be favored over tomorrow's descendants of the affluent? Who, in decisions made today, can act as ombudsman for the yet to be born?

• Rates of consumption are another name for rates of pollution. Can we stop subsidizing inefficiency (as in energy), surpluses (as in food), and toxic waste? China expects to double its gross product in a few years, using soft coal and emitting carbon dioxide that will warm up the world the rest of humanity shares with the Chinese. Would it make sense, as a measure of global environmental protection, for the rest of us to help China make 750,000 boilers fuel efficient?

• "We the people" will number 6.3 billion by the year 2000. That's already built into our horoscope. Whether world population can be stabilized at 8 billion or 11 billion or 14 billion is the biggest single question about the global environment. Who should be doing what about this? Why isn't it being done?

(In a dramatic failure of market economics, private sector

companies have mostly stopped trying to sell contraceptives around the world for fear of litigation and trouble with their own governments. The ironic consequence is a sharp increase in the use of abortion as a means of birth control.)

• If the global commons environments are not to be further polluted by human choice, who sets the outer bounds of human behavior in the commons? Only those with the technical prowess to despoil Antarctica, foul the oceans, damage the ozone layer, spew out global-warming gases, and sprinkle debris in outer space? Or some agreed surrogate for the "everybody" that owns the commons?

Let's say it again: global change is now being produced by what hundreds of millions of individuals and couples are doing. Its pace and direction will only be changed by what hundreds of millions of individuals and couples do or stop doing.

Since the new genre of problems depends on such wide participation, reaches into so many technical and professional fields, and touches so many economic interests and political sensitivities, it is not to be expected that any one system of governance would work. One thing will surely not happen: the adoption of an overarching constitution for this class of problems. The global commons will be governed pluralistically or not at all.

The global commons may best be thought of as a *system,* not as a place or a space. So we need to identify what Maurice Strong calls the "boundary conditions" and "linkages" in the global system. Once the appropriate limits of human activity are widely understood, there is plenty of room for a pluralism of choices and a plethora of ideologies, as long as it is clear what human activities impinge on those boundary conditions and therefore who should be doing what, or stop doing what, to stay safely within them. The Rio conference was unable to push the logic quite that far, to establish the boundary conditions that had better not be transgressed.

The two-tier principle of organization clearly applies here. The commons systems, and the dangers of degradation and conflict that arise from them, require the establishment of universal norms, standards, rules of the road. Their conservation and use can then be handled by public, private, and mixed enterprise, within the framework of the agreed upon norms and standards, a framework that the operating people have had a consultative role in framing.

Who can fashion the rules of such a game? It has to be a club that credibly speaks for "all mankind," the plural owners of the global commons. The club that takes on such a responsibility has to be of manageable size, yet it must also represent the people who can do something about the problems that beset the commons, that is, those who pollute global air and water, chop down tropical forests, leave debris orbiting in outer space, and litter the icy wasteland of Antarctica. If they don't agree on what's to be done, it won't get done. The important thing is not to debate blame but to organize remedies.

There is an unemployed piece of international machinery that might well be put to useful work protecting and supervising our common heritage. It is the United Nations Trusteeship Council, a major UN Charter organ (parallel to the General Assembly and the Security Council) that the success of decolonization has now left without a function.

Experts on the United Nations will object that it would be too complicated to wrench the Trusteeship Council loose from its stagnant moorings and steer it toward the turbulent waves of the global commons. Certainly its original purpose (policymaking for territories held under mandate, or "detached from enemy states as a result of the Second World War," or otherwise unable to govern themselves) was as different from policymaking for the global commons as the 1940s were from what the 1990s are. For a start, however, the name is just right: some body acting for humankind should act as trustee for our four great surrounding environments.

The Trusteeship Council itself could probably not take on such a task; its original members were supposed to be a balanced mix of countries administering trust territories and an equal number of those that did not. A change in that rigid membership formula would mean amending the UN Charter, which could open that valuable document to pollution of those eloquent purposes in the Preamble and Chapter I. But the now dormant council could readily form a special trusteeship commission on the global commons, consisting of those countries most able to protect and preserve "the common heritage of mankind" — not only the traditional "great powers" but great nations such as Brazil with a special stake in the commons plus some rotating members, as in the UN Security Council.

Such a first-tier commission should not "manage" anything. Its task would be to negotiate norms, standards, and guidelines for exploring and exploiting the global commons and to keep the health of the commons environments under open and continuous review. The commission's role could only be advisory; it should operate by consensus, not by voting. It should make room in its work for major nongovernments (corporations, environmental groups, human rights enthusiasts, scientific academies, and other professional associations) that could bring to the Trusteeship Commission the fruits of technical and policy analysis and the assurance that having been consulted about norms and standards, they would be more disposed to be guided by them in their own day-to-day actions.

The new commission would not duplicate, it would use in its own continuing analyses, the monitoring functions of other international agencies — for example, the ambitious global environmental monitoring service (GEMS) already organized by the United Nations Environment Program. It might, however, add to them a UN satellite capability (also suggested, in Chapter Seven, as an element of a new world security system).

The Trusteeship Commission's mandate for the human uses of the global commons could be lifted directly from the UN Charter guidance (in Article 76) to the original Trusteeship Council: "to further international peace and security; to promote . . . political, economic, social and educational advancement . . . ; to encourage respect for human rights and for fundamental freedoms for all without distinction as to race, sex, language, or religion, and to encourage recognition of the interdependence of the peoples of the world; to ensure equal treatment in social, economic, and commercial matters for all Members of the United Nations and their nationals."

While not itself engaging in operations, the Trusteeship Commission might be empowered to ask other international agencies, nongovernments, or individuals to serve as centers of initiative on particular problems in the commons, as UNEP did so well on both the Mediterranean cleanup and the Ozone Treaty.

The Antarctic Treaty is a special case. There a comparatively few countries have worked successfully together for more than three decades by continuously consulting with each other, without setting up an international organization as such. But peoples outside the Antarctic club have a right to know that what the insiders learn does not deprive the outsiders of whatever benefits may result from the scientists' free access to the world's last unexplored continent. The Trusteeship Commission on the Global Commons could serve as a forum in which the Antarctic Treaty nations could consult in the open about what is being learned from work in the Antarctic, without the commission trying to second-guess national programs of scientific inquiry or regulations agreed among the treaty signatories.

Within the policy frame established by such a norms-and-standards commission, there are roles aplenty for many different kinds of nongovernments and indeed for domestic public and private groups not usually considered as participants in international relations, particularly in heightening awareness and educating whole populations about needed changes in individual and group behavior as it affects the global commons.

Practitioners of world-scale policy analysis are to be found in some think tanks, universities, environmental agencies, medical and health associations, and research laboratories. They can help design the norms and standards and help explain them to those who are supposed to be guided by them. There is a role for "relay stations" to disseminate authoritative insights about how to use the commons without degrading it. There is a role for business leaders in regulating their own ecobehavior and explaining to their stockholders and customers why that is so necessary. There is, of course, a role for the communications media in generating public interest and projecting relevant metaphors.

Perhaps most important of all, there is a role for educators in making sure that children in all cultures grow up with, and their parents develop, a feel for the new global/behavioral

issues and relate them constructively to their own cultural identities and traditions. Education about the global commons from
preschool through adult learning should be aimed at patterns
of behavior and value systems consistent with a sharing environment. Not only the schools but the media, political leaders, and
nongovernments of many kinds will all have to be teachers about
human conduct compatible with life in a shared commons.

The Remedy Is Us

The vast, distant, mysterious commons — outer space, the atmosphere, the oceans, Antarctica — has contracted a degenera-
tive but not irreversible disease. The impulsive actions of human beings now clearly outweigh the slower evolution of Nature
in the global scheme of things. The diagnosis is increasingly
clear, and the remedy is us.

In the global commons we are moving by fits and starts
toward a remarkably commonsensical idea: it's unwise to export to the commons the laws and customs and practices that
have proved so useful on dry land.

The framework for international politics, security, trade,
finance, and the movement of peoples is solidly based on who
owns what. In such a framework, land and human artifacts are
exchanged. The places where deals are negotiated and bargains
are struck we call *exchanges*. Even people — hostages, spies, prisoners of war — are exchanged as if they were properties belonging to someone. But the global commons is, by its nature, a
sharing system. The four environments that make up the global
commons cannot, by their nature, be bought or sold, given or
received, yielded up, seized, or appropriated. They have to be
shared. And for sharing environments we do not yet have either
a solid body of law or a settled theory of political economy.

That's why conflict and competition, the laws of war and
the rugged traditions of market economics, are not very useful
for thinking about the global commons. It's why, in protecting
the iciest and wettest parts of our surround, in cleaning up the
air we breathe and using with prudence the sunlight that sustains life, concepts such as commonwealth and community are
coming into vogue.

Should we impose our values on a mostly vacant commons? It's true that whenever we touch it, we tweak in unknowable ways what millions of years have wrought. The wilderness approach, driven by a paralyzing sense of our own ignorance, would say, "Don't touch," "*Ne touchez pas,*" "*Verboten.*" Lao-tzu's cautionary question of twenty-five hundred years ago is still worth pondering: "Do you think you can take over the universe and improve it?"

As a practical matter the commons will not be left alone. So the problem is to organize world consensus, place by place and case by case, in ways that balance our appetite for adventure and our civilizing mission with a healthy respect for the foul-up factor in every human enterprise.

eleven

THE CLUB OF DEMOCRACIES
A Coalition of the Willing

*Democracy . . . is a charming form of government, full of variety and
disorder, dispensing a sort of equality to equals and unequals alike.*

—*Plato,* The Republic

We have glimpsed how the electronic conquest of remoteness,
the sheer speed and complexity of global telecommunications
enhanced by fast data processing, has transformed local markets into worldwide networks, widened local conflict into world
security issues, transmuted local poverty into a world development problem, and enabled us to see how the behavior of individuals cumulates into global environmental threats.

Each of these in turn requires a broadening of our ways of
thinking, widened concepts of management and governance. Yet
for the foreseeable future, world affairs will be dominated by a
comparatively few postindustrial states, fewer than a dozen if the
European Community is counted as one, a couple of dozen on
issues that tempt European states to make their mark separately.

Three of the leading clusters of advanced information societies are already closely associated as the nucleus of an emerging, open-ended club of democracies. The parts of Europe outside the European Community and a good many of the larger
or more successful developing countries will qualify soon or late
as influential states governed by consent and will join the club
whether the more established democracies like it or not.

This expanding fellowship, acting in shifting patterns of
cooperation and competition, will primarily decide over the next
generation what the formal organs of the United Nations will
be empowered to do; what its members will do together them-

selves, within the UN Charter but outside its procedures; how stability and fairness are to be reconciled in peacekeeping and peacemaking, in economic growth and social development, in using and protecting the global commons — in sum, whether and how they will work together worldwide for better standards of life in larger freedom.

The Politics of Coalescence

When Iraq's ruler provoked a midsummer's bad dream in 1990, he set the stage also for the most far-reaching test of the toughest section of the United Nations Charter. He further demonstrated that if World War II's victorious Allies (who called themselves the United Nations even during the war) had not already established the UN Security Council, it would have had to be invented in the final decade of the twentieth century.

For control of exotic weapons and the management of other global policy-making, we have seen a need for two-tier systems of setting universal or nearly universal norms, then trying to make sure the behavior of citizens, leaders, national governments, and international organizations is consistent with the world standards. The crisis in the desert illustrated just such a pattern.

For the setting of norms, it is not necessary for people or governments to agree on why they are agreeing. In the Iraq case, some were outraged by the reversion to colonial conquest in this postcolonial era. Some wanted to protect their supplies of oil and keep its price down. Others had special fish to fry: the Soviets were working on détente with the West, the Turks wanted to qualify as good Europeans, the Iranians wanted to make sure the Gulf was as Persian as possible, the oil-rich sheikhs wanted to hang onto their crowns as well as their riches. All the Arab leaders wanted more Arab unity, but most of them didn't fancy Saddam Hussein as the Saladin of the 1990s.

What they all needed in pursuing their differing aims was a principle around which to coalesce and an instrument of coalescence. For an unarguable principle, they hardly needed to go beyond the first purpose in Chapter I, Article 1 of the UN Charter:

"To maintain international peace and security, and to that end: to take effective collective measures for the prevention and removal of threats to the peace, and for the suppression of acts of aggression or other breaches of the peace, and to bring about by peaceful means, and in conformity with the principles of justice and international law, adjustment or settlement of international disputes or situations which might lead to a breach of the peace."

The instrument of coalescence was likewise ready-made: the disused and dusty peace-and-security provisions of the Charter. The successive resolutions of the Security Council condemned the invasion and annexation of Kuwait hours after they occurred, decreed mandatory economic sanctions, told Iraq to let all foreign nationals depart, and authorized states to mount first a naval and then air traffic blockade to enforce economic sanctions against Iraq. These were the quickest and toughest actions to deal with aggression in the forty-five years after the UN Charter was adopted at San Francisco.

They legitimated the deployments of those (led by the United States and Britain) whose immediate instinct was to act. They provided the political cover for those who needed it (the Soviet Union, Turkey, Iran, the twelve Arab nations led by Egypt's Hosni Mubarak). They helped shame into cooperation those who at first wanted to stay friends with Iraq no matter what. They were designed also to impress the miscreant with his isolation. Moreover, they posed some interesting questions, testing for the first time the boundaries of the Charter's no-nonsense Chapter VII, which converts the world's debating society into a global enforcer.

Once sanctions have been declared by the Security Council, is it legal for a group of nations to do what it thinks is needed to make them effective? Yes. The Charter's Article 51 endorses "the inherent right of individual or collective self-defense if an armed attack occurs against a Member of the United Nations." A "coalition of the willing" can act to make the UN's decree effective. The naval armada that assembled in the Persian Gulf in 1990 was just such a coalition. When the Security Council voted to make sure the sanctions were enforced, that didn't make the armada a UN force but a coalition formed to carry into action a UN purpose. And, said U.S. Ambassador Thomas Pickering, the authority granted "is sufficiently broad to use armed force . . . depending upon the circumstances which might require it." The Charter specifically mentions *blockade*. Even during the Cuba missile crisis of 1962, lawyers tiptoed around the *B*-word (calling their first belligerent actions a *quarantine* instead) because under international law a blockade is an act of war. But of course Chapter VII is an act of war to deal with an outlaw.

Assembling a mighty coalition to face Iraq was agreed without dissent in the Security Council. But that was not exactly what the drafters of the Charter thought would happen next. They assumed that if Chapter VII sanctions were found not to be working, the Security Council (under Article 42) would itself take on the enforcement job, using air, sea, or land forces contributed by UN members. The effect would have been to make the armada, air forces, and ground troops a UN force. A UN commander would have been appointed; he would have reported to the Security Council through the Military Staff Committee, a body frozen in amber for forty-five years by the Cold War.

In some future case, a UN military operation may turn out to be needed. But in 1990 the Security Council made a fragment of new law, whereby a coalition of the willing undertakes to enforce a widely endorsed standard of international behavior. That may be a very important precedent. It says that once there is near-universal agreement in the United Nations on what needs to be done, the world organization itself does not necessarily have to mount what might prove to be a complex and expensive undertaking. The operation may be more suited to the skills or the political cohesion of a smaller group, such as regional powers in Southeast Asia or the Western Hemisphere, the European Community in its area, or regardless of geography, an ad hoc consortium of those concerned enough to act together to enforce the Charter norms and willing to contribute the men and women, skills, machines, money, and imagination needed to carry into practical effect the expressed will of the world community.

The Art of Consultation

What keeps such a coalition together is a broadly common purpose reinforced by unremitting consultation. That is what made
NATO work during its forty years as history's most successful
peacetime alliance. Consultation was often fragile; the United
States, and from time to time other allies, would too often
promise consultation and deliver at best advance notice of national decisions already taken. This was especially the case on
matters outside the immediate purview of the North Atlantic
Treaty.

In October 1962, Dean Acheson was sent to Paris by
President Kennedy to talk to President Charles de Gaulle of
France about the Cuba missiles and what the United States proposed to do about them. De Gaulle's first question, so the story
goes, went to the heart of the alliance relationship: "Are you
informing me or consulting me?" Acheson, who knew better than
to pretend, replied that this was advance notice, not consultation. *Le Général,* having made his point, smiled. "In that case,"
he said, "I will tell you that I agree with your decision."

For those who have the responsibility to decide and the
urge to act, unremitting consultation is a very hard lesson to
remember. In the 1980s the United States lost the habit of consultation even with its best friends, let alone with its adversaries
(which is sometimes equally important). A *New York Times*
roundup of such incidents recalled that the Reagan administration withdrew U.S. Marines from Lebanon without telling
the British, French, and Italians, who had also put units there
to show their solidarity. White House efforts to sell arms to Iran
and finance the Nicaraguan contras with the proceeds were kept
secret not only from Congress but from allies with their own
stakes in those regions. "Alone and with scant warning" the U.S.
Navy attacked Iranian oil rigs in the Persian Gulf. The early
years of the Bush administration showed a similar pattern: it
invaded Panama without telling Latin American neighbors,
peeved its European allies by closing the U.S. Embassy in Afghanistan without notice, and offended some Asians by suddenly
withdrawing support for the opposition parties in Cambodia.

The first people to learn that the United States intended to interdict Iraqi commerce at sea—well before the UN blockade was agreed on—were listeners to a TV interview with the secretary of state on a Sunday morning talk show.

As the task of dealing with Iraq became a large, long-drawn-out worldwide enterprise, however, President Bush and his closest advisers got plenty of practice in unremitting consultation. By telephone and personal visits, in around-the-clock diplomacy at UN headquarters in New York and the NATO and European centers in Brussels, they talked with (and listened to) dozens of national leaders, opening long-dormant channels of communication (for example with Syria), campaigning for fair shares of sacrifice, dramatizing the Soviet Union's turn toward cooperation in matters of global concern.

Writing about American local communities, public philosopher John Gardner described consultative politics in world affairs as well: "The play of conflicting interests in a framework of shared purposes is the drama of a free society. It is a robust exercise and a noisy one, not for the faint-hearted or the tidy-minded. . . . Wholeness incorporating diversity is the transcendent goal of our time."

World Politics Is Local Politics

What coalitions of the willing will form, for what shared purposes, how robustly and how noisily, is not primarily a function of the "foreign policies" of the major players, the postindustrial nations that make up the core and power the drivewheel of the club of democracies. What determines whether and how they will work together on any given issue is their capacity and willingness to govern themselves in ways compatible with a world political economy that delivers needed change without violence— with nobody in general charge. None of them are yet doing that.

The United States

In the United States, the interconnected deficits in the national budget and balance of trade, the "selling of America" to foreign investors, and the heavy borrowings from European and Japanese banks have all been economic symptoms of democracy's deadlock. The American people, the patients in this badly run clinic, are uncomfortable and angry at the doctors and expecting to be taken soon to the emergency room.

Paradoxically, the big economy of this great capitalist nation so short of capital has been so strong and resilient that despite its $4 trillion national debt (swollen from $900 billion during the eighties), its swing from world's largest creditor to world's largest debtor, its decline in competitiveness in some highly visible sectors such as automobiles and semiconductors, its low low rate of savings (5 percent compared to Japan's 18 percent), its deficiencies in schooling, its urban poverty, its drug scene, its racial tensions, its porous southern border, its high-cost health care, its crumbling bridges and potholed roads, its environmental troubles, its buildup of toxic wastes — despite all these well-advertised delinquencies, in the 1980s the U.S. growth rate was mildly positive (2 to 3 percent). Similarly, its unemployment and inflation rates (around 5 percent) were low by world if not by German and Japanese standards, its gross product set a world record at more than $4 trillion, and its military spending (some $300 billion a year, more than 7 percent of GNP) was the main prop of the successful NATO alliance. Moreover, the United States remained the most desired destination for refugees and emigrants from elsewhere. (The comedian Jack Paar, no foreign policy expert, said it: "Immigration is the sincerest form of flattery.")

At first the impact of U.S. budget and trade deficits was felt more abroad than at home, which made it hard for U.S. leaders to treat it as a national crisis rather than a political football. (Hubert Humphrey, the genial and perceptive senator from Minnesota, summed up before he died in 1978 the U.S. budget debates of the early 1990s: "To err is human. To blame it on someone else is politics.") Modest economic growth without unacceptable inflation or joblessness didn't seem so bad to most Americans, even if it was made possible only by massive borrowing that weakened the dollar on the world's exchanges and required a reluctant receptivity to large flows of foreign investment without precedent since foreigners funded and immigrants built the transcontinental railroads in the nineteenth century.

The net result? A still-strong nation, still able to be the first among equals in a crisis (as in the Iraq crisis of 1990 and 1991), but bedeviled by domestic troubles that restrain it from leading with the purse in the style of the Marshall Plan four decades ago.

Canada

Neither Americans nor Canadians like to think of Canada as a U.S. satellite, but when it comes to economic policy, these two countries, each other's biggest trading partners, are more one country than two. Canada, like the United States, accepts immigrants without major complaint; it handles some social issues (such as health care) better and some issues of political cohesion (such as Quebec) less well. On world issues it has often been out ahead of its big southern neighbor, as on recognizing Communist China, managing foreign aid, and contributing to UN peacekeeping. But as a factor in the world economy, Canada is necessarily a close partner of the United States, adding to its strengths but unable to compensate for its weaknesses.

Japan and the Pacific

Japan was experiencing in the early 1990s the political agony of its spectacular economic success. That success was the wonder of the world. It was produced not just by discipline and hard work but by a remarkable capacity to achieve national consensus in working toward broad national goals, by inventive manufacturing research and development, by unique business management systems, by a rate of personal savings matched in the industrial world only (surprisingly?) by Italians and a rate of capital investment to match (Japan was actually spending more on plant and equipment than was the United States with an economy nearly twice Japan's size), and by a huge balance-of-payments surplus that had made Japan rather quickly the largest aid giver to the developing world.

The agonies were almost equally manifest. One-party government, fraying at the edges and riddled with corruption in high places, remained in office only because no viable alternative had yet developed. The high per capita money income, not far from that in the United States, masked a much lower real income, skyrocketing prices for real estate, pollution in the air and along the coastlines, congestion on the highways, and crowding in unaffordable urban housing. Japan's long-term demographic shift was an obvious threat to continued dynamism: by the year 2020, people over sixty-five were expected to be 24 percent of a plateauing total population.

Collisions on trade policy and investment practices were already in the early 1990s souring relations with Japan's closest ally, the United States. Collisions were imminent between Japan's consensus desire to maintain racial purity and all sorts of major-power obligations at home and abroad. These ranged from the need to absorb many more refugees and the put-down of Koreans living in Japan to the imperatives of doing global business in an interdependent, multiethnic world. The underlying dilemma seemed to be the contrast between a Japanese reluctance to take the lead and the assumption in the rest of the world that Japan's wealth required it to step forward and help shape peaceful change in the new world disorder.

There are worse problems than being rich and expected to do more. But the dilemma will not disappear. Japan's economy will likely continue to develop at the cutting edge of the global knowledge society. So Japan's financial and technological strength will enhance its global interdependence.

Solutions are probably to be found in a more open trading system than comes naturally to so homogeneous a society and in mounting ambitious international ventures, especially in the developing world, disproportionately funded by Japan and its investors. But then many Japanese will have to learn the lesson Americans took so long to learn: the capacity to pay is not the same as knowing it all. No nation however affluent has a monopoly of the huge amount of brain work, imagination, and initiative the management of peaceful change is going to require.

In the Pacific area, some of the world's most dynamic peoples have chalked up the outstanding successes in growth-with-fairness. The Pacific Ocean laps the world's first and second national postindustrial societies, most of the world's food-exporting capacity, and most of the economies (South Korea, Taiwan, Hong Kong, Singapore) that in the seventies and eighties graduated from "less developed" status and earned the nickname *tigers*. With the important (and probably temporary) exception of China, markets are winning over Marx.

There are still big pockets of poverty. But in a generation of time, there need be no poor countries in East Asia and the Pacific if war can be avoided and if the Americans, who did so much to make this upbeat prospect possible, have the patience to stay the course.

The Pacific future is, of course, still full of uncertainties. Will China, once the Long March veterans fade away, still regard economic dynamism as too politically dangerous? Will Mainland China lure the other two "Chinas" — Hong Kong and Taiwan — into its embrace, or will their magnetism pull the Middle Kingdom's southern provinces away?

Will Russia return those marginal islands to Japan and thus, paradoxically, act more as a Pacific power? Will Russia's Asian peoples get tired of waiting for Moscow and take their future into their own hands?

Will reality come to resemble the Japanese metaphor of a formation of flying geese, with Japan as the lead goose and other East Asians taking their places in line according to how well their economies are doing?

Or will a larger Pacific grouping emerge, along the lines of the Asia Pacific Economic Cooperation (APEC), joining the United States and Japan with the Pacific's unusual endowment of middle powers (the Republic of Korea and the other East Asian tigers plus Canada, Mexico, Australia, and New Zealand) in a partnership that makes Japan's impressive and growing strength seem safe to its neighbors, as Germany's became more acceptable in an increasingly integrated Europe? APEC is already open-ended, with room for China when its people gain the right to govern themselves and for Asian Russia when it gets its act together.

In the twenty-first century, sharing an ocean may be at least as good a basis for cooperation as sharing a landmass. In the twentieth century, the North Atlantic became a thick web of connections: mutual security, trade and investment, cultural exchange, the liberal movement of people and ideas. A similar destiny is in store for the Pacific Basin in the century to come.

Europe

Europe is well on its way to being the world's largest market and potentially its largest economic power as well. Politically it is not yet "Europe" and may never be more integrated than David Calleo's description: "a never-ending and rather dialectical process . . . a confederation of states with a collective bureaucratic structure attached. . . . [N]ot," he adds, "such a bad way to govern a continental economy."

After forty years of trying out the dream of Jean Monnet, the European nations remain culturally and politically strong even as they pool their sovereignty in carefully circumscribed ways to achieve economic union. On the other hand, the economic moves have been impressive. In the early 1980s, Europeans and their transatlantic friends were shaking their heads about Eurosclerosis, and their high costs of labor and capital gave them good quantitative reasons for Europessimism. By the early 1990s, with the 1992 single-market target for goods, services, and labor taken very seriously, the surge of morale and vitality and enterprise and ambition was extraordinary. It attracted Japanese and U.S. investment and corporate joint ventures in many high-tech fields. Measured by intrastate trade, Europe was already highly integrated: in 1988, trade among European Community countries accounted for 20 to 25 percent of their combined gross domestic product (GDP), approaching the ratios (25 to 35 percent) for the trade with each other of major states in the United States.

Germany, even with its poorer Eastern cousins back in the fold, was the strongest economy but, as Kurt Biedenkopf put it, still "an economy in search of a nation." In fact if not in law, the German Bundesbank became central banker for the

continent. The role of the other nations' central bankers in helping the Germans make their decisions was far from clear. Pollution of Europe's lovely rivers and its urban aid had gotten out
of hand and brought "Greens" into politics. And as in Japan,
future demographic trends in an aging continent were troubling
for the longer run: in 1990 German retirees were one-third as
numerous as the active work force, in 2030 they would be two-
thirds unless much larger immigrations from elsewhere changed
the ethnic face of Germany and its European neighbors.

So in the early 1990s Europe's troubles were palpable, and
not all the portents were fair. For the immediate future, Eurodes-
tiny looked bright, and the European Community's new dynamism was fast pulling both neutrals and ex-communist states into
its economic orbit. Yet developing a European foreign policy
was troublesome. In dealing with such issues as Iraq's aggression and the breakup of Yugoslavia, Europe remained a determined diversity of cultures well short of a common worldview.

Even faced with a mortal threat to its energy supply line
from the Mideast, the still fragile community at first had trouble shifting gears from its preoccupation with economic integration to a posture of political solidarity. In France, even with
a Socialist government, the Gaullist hesitance to be seen following a U.S. lead died hard. In August 1990 a poll showed
65 percent of the French people applauding the quick U.S. reaction to the Iraq crisis, while 61 percent agreed with their own
government's reluctance about the UN sanctions. A columnist
in *Le Figaro* was caustic: "Either there are 126 percent of French
people, or some of them think France no longer can play the
slightest role in matters of planetary importance." In a matter
of weeks the taking of hostages and Iraq's invasion of diplomatic
properties left no middle ground. France joined with the United
Kingdom and others in sending ground forces to the desert.

There soon arose an even more ticklish policy puzzle closer
to home, when Croatia and Slovenia declared their independence and bloody civil war broke out on the European Community's border. Germany and Italy wanted to recognize Yugoslavia's breakaway states. Other Europeans such as Spain and
the United Kingdom had their own ethnic separatists to worry

about. At first, to avoid a split, the European Community tried to mediate between Serbs and Croats and achieved only a series of fractured cease-fires. Then, again to avoid a split, the community agreed that its members could start dealing with the neighboring fragments as full-fledged states.

The Treaty of Maastricht, signed early in 1992, set up formal machinery to develop European foreign policy. Indeed, the shifts in the world's political economy (Japan's relative rise, the evaporation of the Soviet Union, the relative decline of the United States, the democratic trends in Eastern Europe, and the reunification of Germany as part of Western Europe) now made it possible for "Europe" to function in some degree as a global power in politics and security.

Yet even though Western Europe was fast becoming a single economy, it was still far from becoming an all-purpose "Europe." "We have lost the habit of urging solutions to global problems," said Georges Berthoin of France and the Trilateral Commission. My favorite American observer in Europe happens to be also my Paris-based brother, a former Citibank vice president. "Political union," he wrote, "presupposes a sense of belonging to a community of destiny, a community of nations possessed of a will to play collectively the role of a great power in the defense of and projection of the distinguishing values of European civilization. Without that political will and ideological ambition, a European unit would remain a technical artifact, useful as such but 'without soul and without roots,' as Charles de Gaulle once said."

NATO's Global Lessons

The Cold War was Eurocentered, deep-frozen in nuclear confrontation and political divergence. The early stages of its wind-down were also focused on Europe: gluing Germany back together with safety for its neighbors, helping Eastern Europeans deal with the economic consequences of their political choices, getting on with economic integration, trying to figure out if there was a future for NATO.

The North Atlantic Alliance would have to be in business at least for a few more years, to deal with the dangerous residues of the Cold War, the old issues that were now providentially ripe for resolution. The huge concentrations of men and matériel, anomalous, alarming, and even absurd in a Europe at peace, needed to be scaled down, and in a hurry. This was the central task. NATO had to get on with it and deserved to celebrate, not agonize about, its success in doing what it had come to do.

There is already a much looser forum for larger issues in which the Soviet Union and the United States/Canada were rightfully or necessarily involved, a forum that might engage the energies of the new East European democracies and the European neutrals. (Was there anything left for Sweden, Finland, Austria, and Switzerland to be neutral about?)

This is the security-with-human-rights framework of the Commission on Security and Cooperation in Europe (CSCE), established with thirty-five nations (including Canada and the United States) by the Helsinki Final Act in 1975, with an expansion in numbers though not in territory when the Soviet Union broke apart. Under the CSCE umbrella useful work has already been done to develop confidence-building measures in Europe (advance notification of troop movements, that sort of thing) and keep governments' feet to the fire on their human rights abuses. Even during the Cold War it was the "Helsinki process" that established most clearly that how governments treat their own citizens is everybody else's business too.

So for Europe-centered issues, there is plenty of machinery lying around. The European Community will be at the center of things, not only with a single market but, admirers of European civilization will hope, with an increasingly coherent European worldview as well.

Yet Europe's destiny is no longer in Europe. It is now so bound up with the future of the globe — with world security, the world economy, world development, the global environment — that there is no such thing as a "European" solution to the questions that matter. The rearrangement of power in world politics profoundly alters Europe's potential role in the wider world. The puzzle is whether European economic integration will gradually produce also a new kind of world power, a collective projection of European civilization.

In these new circumstances, "What's the future of NATO?" became a question with less and less content. What can we learn from the NATO experience about organizing a wider club of democracies? That is the question.

NATO was needed (1) to confront an ambitious and expansionist Soviet Union, (2) to enable German recovery to be both successful and safe, and (3) to provide the security surround for European prosperity. There is now a worldwide analog to each of these needs.

1.   The dogmatic determination of authoritarian regimes to dominate their neighbors and deprive their own people of inalienable rights was never a Communist monopoly. Moldy rhetoric and freshly dangerous weapons will continue to fuel similar ambitions elsewhere. They will need to be isolated and contained.

2.   Along with Germany, another ex-enemy, Japan, needs to be able to develop its impressive talents in a framework of democracy, reassurance, and cooperation. The two nations need to become, as Berthoin puts it, "full co-sponsors of the system that helped them get where they now are." Germany (its dominant Western part) has had forty years of practice in this role. But Japan has been the odd man out, and not only geographically, in the "West." In some ways so have Australia and New Zealand, linked to the West by culture and ANZUS, a troubled alliance with the United States. And there is a growing group of economically successful and increasingly democratic states, in Asia but also in Latin America, that are earning their own place as viable democracies.

3.   The puzzles of poverty and development, now solvable without a single new scientific discovery, need a world security system within which growth with fairness and cultural diversity can proceed in freedom from fear, as Europe's economic recovery flourished behind the sword and shield of NATO.

An open-ended club of democracies is already in formation as the best kind of living monument to the democracy movements of recent years. It is a consultative grouping of those willing and able to act together, in different guises with differing leadership for different problems, on issues requiring an unusual degree of international cooperation to get anything done.

The club of democracies was the core of resistance to Iraqi aggression in the Gulf. Its economic core is seen in the periodic summits of the Group of Seven on trade and money issues. It is the guts of the UN peacekeeping function, the determined majority in the UN Security Council, the main source of support for the World Bank and International Monetary Fund, and the moving force behind such disparate events as the treaties to protect the global ozone shield and the 1990 children's summit at the United Nations.

The club of democracies is not a new organization complete with secretariat and a permanent headquarters somewhere. It is a confederation of the concerned, a center of initiative, a habit of consultation.

It coordinates government policies where governments are the main actors. It will increasingly have to bring nongovernments into consultation where they too are major actors, as they obviously are on the world economy, on international development, on the global environment.

If you bring together the nations that are now governed by consent and add those that are trying in their fashion to get that way, you have the bulk of the world's economic output, communication lines, science and technology, financial resources, and military power. This strength needs to be mobilized to help develop norms to be established in universal forums (the United Nations and its specialized and affiliated agencies and from time to time special meetings like the path-breaking UN conferences on the human environment held at Stockholm in 1972 and Rio in 1992) and to make those norms effective by acting together to promote and defend them.

Those who have a stake in a thoroughly democratic world have the resources, if they work together, to make change peaceful and prosperous and thereby help democracy itself to flourish in its own diverse patterns. Their magnetism, their willingness to help each other and the United Nations in keeping the peace, frustrating aggression, feeding economic growth, and promoting fairness and human rights, should attract to the club of democracies many peoples still burdened by tyranny and terror, even if they first have to jettison their domestic tyrants and neutralize their domestic terrorists. The Poles, Hungarians, Czechs and Slovaks, the Russians and Ukrainians and Kazhaks and others, by showing the rest of the world how to do just that, have already made the down payment on their ticket of admission to the club of democracies.

Sometimes national governments and other organizations participating in the club of democracies will lend their power and their people to the United Nations as such or to regional organizations for undertakings beyond the normal means or competence of those organizations or not necessarily of vital interest to all the nations governed by consent of their people. Examples might be the rapid mobilization of a UN peacekeeping force, a worldwide attack on AIDS coordinated by the World Health Organization, an ambitious regional program of economic cooperation for development, a global effort to invent and market biotechnologies especially helpful to tropical countries or island communities.

Getting everybody in on everything is too often an excuse for doing nothing. Organizing to get things done is best done when it's clear what needs to be done and when those with the capacity to act are disposed to act. In functions and regions where those two conditions don't prevail, having a permanent "organization" awaiting consensus and contributions may actually be an obstacle to developing the consensus and attracting the contributions.

On many issues there is nearly universal agreement that something should be done: isolating a regional conflict until it can be settled, outlawing chemical and biological weapons, monitoring the global environment, stabilizing interest rates, developing alternative energy sources, and so on and on. But not every country can or will want to contribute, and the two-tier principle applies: after the policy is made, at least some of those who did the talking need also to club together to do something about it.

The U.S. Role: Leadership of Equals

The club of democracies will have to energize the world system, cope with the complexities of international governance, in a world with no dominant imperial superpowers. Who leads, and how, when no nation or race or creed or "system" is in overall charge? (Remember that democracy is not a system: it is the idea that no one person or group gets to say, with authority, what democracy is.)

In the 1990s at least, the accidents of twentieth-century history narrow down to one the nation that can take the lead in building a club of democracies that can spin off "coalitions of the willing" in support of the UN Charter's purposes. Because that nation is the United States and because I am an American who might be thought to have a *parti pris,* I should explain that I come reluctantly to this view. I have spent sizable chunks of my life consulting with non-Americans to try to produce a result that is genuinely international, and educating young people (Americans and students from around the world) to be predisposed to cooperate with each other, to practice consultative leadership in consent-based systems.

Looking at the past half-century as objectively as I can, I have to conclude that during this time, the United States has been the only nation-state with a truly global reach, not just in military and space spectaculars but in science, technology, economic strength, culture, declarative values (human rights), and ideology (constitutional democracy). It is also fair, I believe, to conclude from the postwar record that the American people never really wanted to be in charge of world order. If there was a consistent American mind-set during this time, it was that others should "get off our backs," take up their responsibilities, "make their own beds" — in current parlance, that the burdens of leadership should be shared.

This was a mind-set without precedent in earlier empires, perhaps because it was the first time imperial policy had been made by a whole people rather than a comparatively few leaders. Whatever the reason, the evidence is clear in the postwar American enthusiasm, backed by U.S. public aid and private investment, for the recovery and unification of Western Europe, including a strong but democratic Germany; for the creation of a strong but democratic Japan; for the chance that colonial peoples have to pick their own political leaders; for the help that some developing countries (especially in East Asia and the Western Hemisphere) received to achieve self-reliance; for the promotion of private enterprise; and for the imagination and initiative needed to create and support the United Nations and its specialized and affiliated agencies — and to enable them to keep on working when even the most powerful nations found themselves unable or unwilling to work in harness.

It is true that during the 1980s Washington tried to pull the rug from under some of these American-sponsored programs (such as the UN's work on population, first proposed by President Kennedy in the early 1960s) and indeed from under the United Nations system itself by not paying assessed dues that are a treaty obligation. During this "lost decade" the United States also accelerated its own relative decline in the world economy by running unprecedented deficits in both its national budget and its international balance of trade and slowing its growth rate to a gentle walk.

Nevertheless, the net effect of both "liberal" and "conservative" U.S. policies between the late 1940s and the early 1990s was to build up the strength and self-reliance of the other industrial democracies and especially to speed the recovery of West Germany and enmesh it in the integration of Western Europe, to revive the capacity of Japan's hardworking people to astonish the world with their productivity, and to jump-start the economic surge of some developing countries.

As of 1992 the United States, combined in a free-trade area with Canada, was still the world's largest economy. But the former locomotive of the global economy and guide star of its monetary system had enormously increased its dependence on others for energy, for markets, for low-wage labor, and for borrowed money. The world order puzzle had become much more diffuse, the capacities to act spread out and scattered around.

World order had consisted largely of initiatives born in Washington and backed by U.S. willingness to pay what they would cost, the other nations following suit because they lacked the resources or the power or the will to generate alternatives. This old-style leadership has lost its magic and mislaid its checkbook to be replaced by what, pragmatically, works: leadership constrained by genuine consultation, initiatives burdened by burden sharing, the pluralistic management of uncentralized systems.

World leadership used to mean paying the piper and calling the tune. Now the irony is that those best able to pay are precluded by their history from playing a major military role. Those with the largest armed forces (China, Russia, and some of its neighbors) aspire to no more than regional influence. Those who have the most advanced military technology (the Americans) are financially weak and politically uncertain. The dubious relevance of nuclear weapons, which used to distinguish superpowers from all other nations, argues for a new pattern in which there are no superpowers, only powers more or less ready to take the lead when a lead needs to be taken.

By this logic, whether some Americans like it or not, the United States is still the only available chair of the executive committee for a club of democracies that calls the shots for world order, prosperity, and development. In consequence both the American electorate and the political leaders they elect are having to climb a steep learning curve about the new game of post–Cold War politics. For the United States must lead by imagination, consultation, and persuasion, not just imagination backed by the power of the purse, Marshall Plan style. It's a difficult style to master; much will depend on the quality of its mastery.

U.S. power may have dwindled, relatively. That was the unannounced and perhaps unconscious purpose of a half-century of American foreign policy. But power is a multiplication table: the capacity to act times the willingness to act. Those who have written off the United States of America as a has-been may be surprised by the story of international governance as it now develops.

GENESIS OF THE BOOK

THIS BOOK IS THE PRODUCT of two intersecting lines of thought. I came to write it because I happened to be standing in puzzlement at the intersection.

Two Converging Ideas

Two decades ago I was introduced by John McHale to what he called *The Changing Information Environment,* the title of his seminal book first published in 1975. The work of Daniel Bell, Fritz Machlup, Graham Molitor, Marc Porat, and others helped me get a fix on the idea of information as a resource, a resource so different from physical resources in its abundance and accessibility, so much harder to hide and to hoard. The evidence seemed persuasive that information (processed into knowledge, sparking intuition, integrated into wisdom) was becoming the dominant resource in the more developed countries and potentially worldwide.

This notion was intriguing partly because it so flatly contradicted the then prevailing conventional wisdom, reflected in *The Limits to Growth* and other jeremiads suggesting that the world was in imminent danger of running out of resources. It has now become evident that the relevant shortages will be not mostly of things but of ideas, imagination, willpower, and leadership.

225

I had for many years been interested in leadership, both practicing it as a public executive and reflecting about it as a writer. So I naturally started speculating, reading, and writing about how this information revolution would affect the roles and functions of executive leaders. My thinking about this produced a couple of dozen articles, many lectures and seminars, a new kind of leadership education (at the University of Minnesota's Hubert H. Humphrey Institute of Public Affairs), and a book, *The Knowledge Executive: Leadership in an Information Society* (New York: Dutton, 1985, republished in paper in 1989).

The other broad avenue leading to this crossroads of ideas is my long-time interest in international organizations and their capacity to act — especially where nation-states acting alone are finding it harder and harder to cope. Here again I have mixed practice and theory in my own work life, starting early as a UN relief and rehabilitation administrator; spending the 1960s as assistant secretary of state for international organization affairs and then as U.S. ambassador to NATO; and during six years (1974 to 1980) as director of the Aspen Institute's Program in International Affairs, pulling together experts from governments and international organizations to explore what we called a "planetary bargain" focused on rich-poor, North-South issues. This work led to much writing and speaking and to two books published by the Aspen Institute: *The Third Try at World Order* (1977) and *Humangrowth: An Essay on Growth, Values and the Quality of Life* (1978), written with Thomas W. Wilson, Jr.

When I moved to Minnesota to develop the University of Minnesota's Hubert H. Humphrey Institute of Public Affairs, becoming its first dean, I tried to maintain a global perspective, teaching a course titled "The Management of Peace" and organizing The Group for the international project "Rethinking International Governance" described in the preface and acknowledgments.

Rethinking International Governance

The word *governance,* in the vocabulary of The Group, was never intended to imply global "government" but rather the aggregate of institutions of cooperation, coordination, and common action among sovereign states and nongovernmental organizations that constitute the management of peace.

We decided at the outset to proceed with this ambitious task in three stages. In stage 1, we looked at the requirements for international cooperation through the prisms of four concurrent global revolutions powered by scientific discovery and technological innovation: revolutions of explosive power, of biotechnology, of human-made environmental change, and of fast-spreading information. Stage 2 of the project was to derive from this diagnostic work a fresh analysis of the international functions of the future, that is, the requirements side of the equation of future international cooperation. Stage 3 matched these functions with fresh thinking about the international institutions the world needs with the wider functions made possible by modern science and technology and made necessary by insistent aspirations of the human spirit.

All this proved to be a very ambitious undertaking indeed. It engaged the two preparatory meetings of The Group in 1986 and 1987, hosted and cosponsored by the Johnson Foundation at its Wingspread Conference Center in Racine, Wisconsin, and by Spring Hill Center near Minneapolis.

Between 1987 and 1989, it spawned two workshops (in Lisbon and Hong Kong) and a year-long computer teleconference on the impact of biotechnology, led by Carl-Göran Hedén, then president of the World Academy of Art and Science, our cosponsor for this track; a workshop on "The Implications of Informatization for the International System," hosted and cosponsored by the International Management Institute in Geneva; a special meeting with the heads of some international organizations, hosted in Geneva by the Centre d'Études Pratiques de la Négotiation Internationale; two workshops on "The Global Commons," in Paris (cosponsored by the Lindbergh Fund) and Boulder, Colorado (sponsored by the National Center for Atmospheric Research); and a planning session in June 1989, also hosted by Wingspread, to prepare for the third and final meeting of The Group, hosted and cosponsored by the Generalitat de Catalunya, in Barcelona, Spain, in October 1989.

A paper on the nuclear revolution was prepared and presented at Spring Hill by the Canadian Institute for Peace and Security. A more extensive analysis of institutions for world security was prepared by Professor Lincoln Bloomfield of MIT, a member of the steering committee for The Group. Analytical papers on the world economy were provided by Martin Lees, a member of The Group, and G. Edward Schuh, a former official of the World Bank who is now dean of the Humphrey Institute. Research support was provided throughout by Professor Magda Cordell McHale, who also served on the steering committee. Ambassador Geri Joseph worked with me in Minneapolis as co-director of the project.

Along the way four special pamphlets were prepared for publication:

> Harlan Cleveland and Lincoln Bloomfield, *Rethinking International Cooperation* (Minneapolis: Hubert H. Humphrey Institute of Public Affairs, 1988; 2nd ed., 1989).
> Harlan Cleveland and Lea Burdette, eds., *The Global Commons*, containing papers by Dean Abrahamson, Lincoln Bloomfield, Arthur C. Clarke, Harlan Cleveland, John Craven, John Firor, and Luther Gerlach (Minneapolis: Hubert H. Humphrey Institute of Public Affairs, 1988; 2nd ed., 1989).
> Harlan Cleveland and Mochtar Lubis, *The Future of "Development"* (Minneapolis: Hubert H. Humphrey Institute of Public Affairs, 1989).
> Lincoln Bloomfield, *Rethinking International Security* (Minneapolis: Hubert H. Humphrey Institute of Public Affairs, 1990).

A subproject called What Works and Why was a two-year study at the Humphrey Institute of more than a dozen successful examples of international cooperation and the reasons for their success. A summary version of this unusually upbeat study can be found, together with other findings about the processes of international cooperation, in "The Management of Peace," an article I wrote for the *GAO Journal* (a quarterly journal published by the U.S. General Accounting Office), Winter 1990/ 1991, no. 11.

The work on the global commons was used in July 1989 as the basis for a fortieth anniversary symposium at the Aspen Institute. The result was a book, *The Global Commons: Policy for the Planet,* by Harlan Cleveland, co-published in 1990 by the Aspen Institute and University Press of America.

An effort to integrate all this rethinking activity was presented at Barcelona in October 1989. It was entitled "Technological Change and International Governance." Although it was not published as such, the discussion this presentation provoked at Barcelona served as a basis for some of the analysis in this book. The paper itself is available from my office at the Hubert H. Humphrey Institute of Public Affairs, University of Minnesota, 301 19th Avenue S., Minneapolis, Minn. 55455.

SOURCES, NOTES,
AND COMMENTS

I HAVE NOT USED FOOTNOTES, and I do not think it useful to cite sources when they are evident from the text itself. The following notes and comments suggest where my own thinking comes from, where a fuller discussion of some ideas can be found, and who said or wrote some particularly trenchant comments. The notes follow the order of appearance of the passages to which they refer.

Chapter One: A Hinge of History

The chapter-opening epigraph is from a speech given by Lithuania's prime minister during her visit to Washington and quoted in the *New York Times,* May 4, 1990.

Barbara Ward's summation of what she called "the hinge of history" was expressed in her draft version of what appeared in printed form, coauthored by René Dubos, as *Only One Earth* (New York: Norton, 1972).

Thomas W. Wilson, Jr.'s durable comment about the human race consuming its own environment was originally written for a lecture at the Thorne Ecological Institute in Aspen, Colorado, in June 1984. The lecture was published in the journal *Social Education,* March 1985.

Alexis de Toqueville registered his doubts about democracies in *Democracy in America* (1835). His later comment contrasting democracy and socialism is from his "Speech to the Constituent Assembly," Sept. 12, 1948.

My discussion of China's abortive top-down reform derives in part from notes of interviews with Chinese economic planners and officials during a visit to Beijing in 1988. Psychologist Richard Farson's comment on the behavior of China's leaders was made in a 1989 computer teleconference sponsored by the Western Behavioral Sciences Institute in LaJolla, California.

The quotation from George Kennan is from a December 1988 TV interview with Robert MacNeil. See also Kennan's remarks in "The Inescapability of Politics," *American Foreign Policy Newsletter,* Dec. 1989.

The brief analysis of the 1989 revolutions in Eastern Europe is derived from contemporary sources. Especially useful have been facts and insights available from the *New York Times,* the *Christian Science Monitor,* and the *Economist.* I also had a chance to discuss what had just happened with some of those who had made it happen, during a 1990 meeting of the World Futures Studies Federation in Budapest.

John Platt's comment about real-life dramas on television is from his paper, "Global Trends in the Next Two Decades," prepared for the SSSPI/MIGAS Energy Workshop, Suvabaya, Indonesia, July 1, 1989.

I first saw the quip about the revolutions in Eastern Europe (that they took "ten years in Poland, ten months in Hungary, ten weeks in East Germany, ten days in Czechoslovakia, and ten hours in Romania") in a computer teleconference with Paul Levinson, president of Connected Education, Inc., in New York City. When I asked him to track down the quip, he found that a review by Jan T. Gross of Timothy Gartan Ash's *The Magic Lantern,* in the *New York Times Book Review* of July 22, 1990, quotes Ash as follows:

> Arriving in Prague on Day Seven (23 November),
> when the pace of change was already breathtaking,
> I met Vaclav Havel in the back room of his fa-

voured basement pub. I said: "In Poland it took ten years, in Hungary ten months, in East Germany ten weeks; perhaps in Czechoslovakia it will take ten days!" The reviewer commented that this quip has had "a fantastic career worldwide," but annoyed some of Ash's Polish friends.

At that time the scenario in Romania had not yet unfolded. By the time he used the idea several months later, says Paul Levinson, it seemed metaphorically logical to add the hyperbole of "ten hours" for Romania.

Chapter Two: A World of Difference

My historical comments about fairness were first written for the article "Information, Fairness and the Status of Women," which appeared in *Futures*, Feb. 1989.

The idea of human rights as "new business" in the history of civilization was developed in a paper written by Professor Elaine Pagels for the Aspen Institute Program in International Affairs. The full exposition appears in Alice Henkin, ed., *Human Dignity* (New York: The Aspen Institute, 1979).

The brief comments in this chapter on development and foreign aid and most of the proposals in Chapter Nine were first advanced in one of the pamphlets published by the "Rethinking" project: Harlan Cleveland and Mochtar Lubis, *The Future of "Development"* (Minneapolis: Hubert H. Humphrey Institute of Public Affairs, 1989). Soedjatmoko's comments were made at an Aspen Institute 1989 symposium, as reported in *The Global Commons: Policy for the Planet,* cited above.

Elise Boulding's comment about "the 10,000 societies living inside 168 nation states" was reported in an interview with Kenneth and Elise Boulding in the *Christian Science Monitor,* Aug. 22, 1990, p. 12.

Magda McHale's comment about cultural identity as a collage was made in a personal communication to the author.

The quotation from André Malraux comes from a talk by George Berthoin of France, the European director of the Trilateral Commission, to the Aspen Institute's Distinguished Fellows in Aspen, Colorado, on July 30, 1990.

The tension between the outward push of science and technology and the inward pull of cultural, ethnic, and other parochial communities was discussed in a concept paper for The Group by Lincoln Bloomfield and myself and later published as *Rethinking International Cooperation* (Minneapolis: Hubert H. Humphrey Institute of Public Affairs, 1988, 1989).

Chapter Three: The False Analogy

Much of the comparative history in the early part of this chapter, and the "peace-in-parcels" theme, are based on a paper I prepared for the Aspen Institute, published in 1981 as one of its first Wye Papers as "Governing a Pluralistic World." I am grateful to Sidney Hyman, who edited those papers, for many wise and constructive suggestions.

Thomas W. Wilson, Jr., contributed the description of the policy failure on energy, of which the Iraq crisis of 1990 and 1991 was so dramatic yet natural an outcome.

On the leakage of power from the modern nation-state: the *Economist,* in a June 23, 1990, editorial titled "Goodbye to the Nation State?" predicted a "redrawing of boundaries" and described the leakage this way: "This time the new shapes will appear at two levels: on high, in an acronymic atmosphere where people's lives are run not by national governments but by regional groupings of ECs, CSCEs, ACCs, NAFTAs and the like; and down below, in a basement world of Eritreas, Tamil Eelamas and Uzbekistans."

Chapter Four: The International System

During two recent years, Geri Joseph and I worked with two groups of Humphrey Institute graduate students as bright and creative as we could have wished, studying what seemed to be working in the international system, including the dozen cases sketched in the text. Since this was a graduate course, Ambassador Joseph and I felt no obligation to pose to the students questions to which the faculty already knew the answers. The object of the study was to figure out what these successes had in common, not just how the programs were working but why. In addition to its use as a working paper for The Group, the essence of this student research project was presented at the twentieth anniversary meeting of the Club of Rome, held in Paris on October 25 to 28, 1988, and at the 1988 annual meeting of the American Society for Public Administration in Portland, Oregon. The members of the graduate seminar, whose research and insights were so valuable to the "rethinking" project, are listed here together with the parts of the international system on which each of them worked:

Greg F. Adams	The World Weather Watch
	The Antarctic Treaty Regime
Derrick Chitala	The International Monetary Fund
	The UN High Commissioner for Refugees
Charles B. Finn	Informatization and the World Economy
Scott Graves	International Frequency Management
	INTELSAT: Satellite Telecommunications
Steven Gray	CGIAR: World-Scale Agricultural Research
	Regional Seas: The Mediterranean
Masato Homma	Informatization in Perspective
Sumit Majumdar	Multinational Corporations
	Pacem in Maribus
Roak J. Parker	Law of the Sea
Sharon Pfeifer	Biotechnology and Development
Victor Raymond	Lawmaking in Outer Space
	Citizen Diplomacy

Joanne Swartzberg	Eradication of Infectious Diseases
	Live-Aid
Juliana Tanning	Protecting the Ozone Layer
	UN Peacekeeping
Caroline Truth	ISDN and International Cooperation
	Globalization of the Information flow
Marlys Zoren	Confidence-Building Measures
	The UN High Commissioner for Refugees

Several of these success stories—the World Weather Watch, smallpox eradication, UN peacekeeping, the outer space treaty, the arrangements in Antarctica—are programs I helped start or nurse in their infancy during the time I was assistant secretary of state for international organization affairs in the Kennedy and Johnson administrations from 1961 to 1965.

One part of the Law of the Sea negotiations, that dealing with deep-sea mining, was one of the first examples (the World Weather Watch is another) of the collaborative use of computer modeling. It was Elliot Richardson, then the U.S. ambassador to the Law of the Sea negotiations, who brought to the attention of Singapore's Ambassador T.T.B. (Tommy) Koh, the chairman, an MIT model on the financing of seabed operations. Koh in turn persuaded his Third World colleagues to redesign this model for use in the negotiations. This sidelight was provided to me by Donald Straus, former president of the American Arbitration Association. See "Computer Culture," *Annals of the New York Academy of Sciences,* Vol. 426, 1984; and James K. Sebenius, *Negotiating the Law of the Sea* (Cambridge, Mass.: Harvard University Press, 1984), p. 45.

The full story of the ozone negotiations is lucidly and authoritatively told in Richard E. Benedick, *Ozone Diplomacy* (Oxford, England: Oxford University Press, 1991).

Chapter Five: The Management of Peace

The epigraph about "community learning at the world level" comes from a speech Knut Hammarskjöld, longtime director general of the International Air Transport Association, delivered in San Francisco on June 26, 1990, at a celebration of the forty-fifth anniversary of the founding of the United Nations.

"Flawed premises" of 1945 and guidelines for the next try at peaceful change were developed by Lincoln Bloomfield and myself for The Group. An early version of this analysis appeared in the pamphlet *Rethinking International Cooperation,* already cited.

The theory of legislative-type international bodies attributed to Dean Rusk appeared in an article of his entitled "Parliamentary Diplomacy—Debate vs. Negotiation," in *World Affairs Interpreter,* 1955, *26*(2).

The germ of the extranational institution (first described by Georges Berthoin, a French veteran of the European Community) and the concept of international taxation were the product of an international group assembled by the Aspen Institute under my chairmanship in 1974 and 1975. Our consensus report was *The Planetary Bargain* (New York: Program in International Affairs, Aspen Institute for Humanistic Studies, 1975).

Toward the end of this chapter, some key paragraphs of the United Nations Charter are mentioned. Here, for the reader's convenience, are three important fragments of international law and policy: the charter's Preamble, Chapter I, and Article 55:

Preamble

WE THE PEOPLES OF THE UNITED NATIONS, DETERMINED

to save succeeding generations from the
scourge of war, which twice in our lifetime
has brought untold sorrow to mankind, and
to reaffirm faith in fundamental human rights,
in the dignity and worth of the human per-

son, in the equal rights of men and women
and of nations large and small, and
to establish conditions under which justice and
respect for the obligations arising from
treaties and other sources of international
law can be maintained, and
to promote social progress and better standards of life in larger freedom,

AND FOR THESE ENDS

to practice tolerance and live together in
peace with one another as good neigh-
bours, and
to unite our strength to maintain international peace and security, and
to ensure, by the acceptance of principles and
the institution of methods, that armed
force shall not be used, save in the common interest, and
to employ international machinery for the
promotion of the economic and social advancement of all peoples,

HAVE RESOLVED TO COMBINE OUR EFFORTS
TO ACCOMPLISH THESE AIMS . . .

Chapter I. Purposes and Principles

Article 1

1. To maintain international peace and
security, and to that end: to take effective collective measures for the prevention and removal of
threats to the peace, and for the suppression of acts
of aggression or other breaches of the peace, and
to bring about by peaceful means, and in conformity with the principles of justice and international
law, adjustment or settlement of international disputes or situations which might lead to a breach
of the peace;

2. To develop friendly relations among nations based on respect for the principle of equal rights and self-determination of peoples, and to take other appropriate measures to strengthen universal peace;

3. To achieve international cooperation in solving international problems of an economic, social, cultural, or humanitarian character, and in promoting and encouraging respect for human rights and for fundamental freedoms for all without distinction as to race, sex, language, or religion; and

4. To be a centre for harmonizing the actions of nations in the attainment of these common ends.

Article 2

The Organization and its Members, in pursuit of the Purposes stated in Article 1, shall act in accordance with the following Principles.

1. The Organization is based on the principle of the sovereign equality of all its Members.

2. All Members, in order to ensure to all of them the rights and benefits resulting from membership, shall fulfill in good faith the obligations assumed by them in accordance with the present Charter.

3. All Members shall settle their international disputes by peaceful means in such a manner that international peace and security, and justice, are not endangered.

4. All Members shall refrain in their international relations from the threat or use of force against the territorial integrity or political independence of any state, or in any other manner inconsistent with the Purposes of the United Nations.

5. All Members shall give the United Nations every assistance in any action it takes in accordance with the present Charter, and shall refrain from giving assistance to any state against which

the United Nations is taking preventive or enforcement action.

6.　The Organization shall ensure that states
which are not Members of the United Nations act
in accordance with these principles so far as may
be necessary for the maintenance of international
peace and security.

7.　Nothing contained in the present Charter shall authorize the United Nations to intervene
in matters which are essentially within the domestic jurisdiction of any state or shall require the members to submit such matters to settlement under the
present Charter; but this principle shall not pre-
judice the application of enforcement measures
under Chapter VII. . . .

Article 55

With a view to creation of conditions of stability
and well-being which are necessary for peaceful and
friendly relations among nations based on the principle of equal rights and self-determination of peoples, the United Nations shall promote:

a.　higher standards of living, full employment,
and conditions of economic and social progress
and development;
b.　solutions of international economic, social,
health, and related problems; and international
cultural and educational cooperation; and
c.　universal respect for, and observance of, human rights and fundamental freedoms for all
without distinction as to race, sex, language,
or religion.

Chapter Six: A New World Disorder

Kenneth Boulding's crisp definition of peace, in the epigraph,
is from "Finding the Next Frontiers of Peace," *Christian Science
Monitor,* Aug. 22, 1990, p. 12—a joint interview with Kenneth
and Elise Boulding already mentioned in the notes on Chapter

Two. Boulding's immediately following comment is equally relevant: "War is a very poor form of conflict management."

President John F. Kennedy's much quoted aspiration for American foreign policy comes from his commencement address at American University in Washington, D.C., on June 10, 1963. The full sentence, in effect addressed to the Soviet leadership, was "If we cannot end now our differences, at least we can help make the world safe for diversity."

The T.S. Eliot quotation is from *The Waste Land,* III. "The Fire Sermon": "Like a taxi throbbing waiting, . . . throbbing between two lives."

The figures on nuclear weapons are from "Nuclear Overkill," in Ruth Sivard, *World Military and Social Expenditures 1989;* Lester Brown and others, *State of the World 1989* (New York and London: Norton, 1989); and the *Universal Almanac,* 1990.

Robert McNamara's comment on the nature of the nuclear arms escalation is from *Out of the Cold: New Thinking for American Foreign and Defense Policy in the 21st Century* (New York: Simon & Schuster, 1989).

Admiral John Marshall Lee's study of nuclear use and usability was done for a Minnesota-based public affairs project and can be found in Harlan Cleveland and Lincoln P. Bloomfield, eds., *Prospects for Peacemaking: A Citizen's Guide to Safer Nuclear Strategy* (Cambridge, Mass.: MIT Press, 1987), pp. 25–64.

Richard Garwin's 1988 proposal for deep mutual reductions in Soviet and U.S. nuclear weapons stockpiles appears in his "Blueprint for Radical Weapons Cuts," *Bulletin of the Atomic Scientists,* March 1988, pp. 10–13. Robert McNamara's 1990 insistence that even deeper cuts should be possible appears in his book *Out of the Cold,* already cited.

Roger Hilsman's judgment that with three thousand to seventy-five hundred intercontinental warheads on each side, Russia and the United States still would have a tenfold overkill capacity comes from his editorial article in *News of the Day* ("Perspective" section), Sunday, June 28, 1992.

Helpful information about nuclear proliferation is contained in the 1990 report of the Aspen Strategy Group, a team of non-governmental experts assembled by the Aspen Institute. An article based on that report, "Third World Threats," by William Perry, Bobby Inman, Joseph S. Nye, Jr., and Roger Smith, was published in the *Aspen Institute Quarterly,* Summer 1990, pp. 10–32.

A primary source for the section on chemical and biological warfare is what I have learned from Carl-Göran Hedén of the Swedish Royal Academy of Sciences (a member of The Group) and Raymond A. Zalinskas of the University of Maryland's Center for Public Issues in Biotechnology. I am especially grateful to them for sharing with me in manuscript their joint paper "The Biological Warfare Convention: A Vehicle for International Cooperation," prepared for J. Lundeen, ed., *Views on Possible Verification Measures for the Biological Weapons Conventions* (Stockholm: Stockholm International Peace Research Institute, 1991). Quotations not otherwise attributed are from that paper. See also Raymond A. Zilinskas, "Biological Warfare and the Third World," *Politics and the Life Sciences,* Aug. 1990; and "Terrorism and Biological Weapons: Inevitable Alliance?" *Perspectives in Biology and Medicine,* Fall 1990.

The references to a report of the Aspen Institute Strategy Group and to ballistic missiles as a prime proliferation multiplier are derived from "Third World Threats," *Aspen Institute Quarterly,* cited above. See also "Ballistic Missile Proliferation," Background Paper (Sept. 1990) of the Canadian Institute for International Peace and Security.

On Iraq and Argentina as each other's suppliers of terror weapons, see Eric Ehrmann, "Iraq's Nuclear Wildcards," *Christian Science Monitor,* Sept. 4, 1990. On the chemical warfare negotiations in Geneva, see H. Martin Lancaster, "Unite Against Chemical Weapons," *Christian Science Monitor,* Sept. 12, 1990.

The quotation from the *Economist* about chemical retaliation comes from its leading article "A Whiff of the Unthinkable," Aug. 18, 1990.

Chapter Seven: World Security

What Dag Hammarskjöld said to Nikita Khrushchev was quoted by the then secretary general of the United Nations in a 1961 conversation with the author.

My discussions of information technology in crisis management, anticipating violence, early warning, the role of nongovernments, and the issues that oblige the international community to enter into the internal affairs of sovereign nations are the product of much joint work with and advice from Lincoln Bloomfield. See especially his *Rethinking International Security* (Minneapolis: Hubert H. Humphrey Institute of Public Affairs, 1991), to which the Bloomfield quotes not otherwise identified can be traced.

The discussion of partly incapacitated U.S. presidents is based on historical research done for an earlier book of mine: *The Future Executive: Guide for Tomorrow's Managers* (New York: Harper & Row, 1972). The Lincoln historian cited is Edward J. Kampf.

The comments on remote sensing imagery are based on a study I chaired for the National Research Council: *Resource Sensing for Development* (Washington, D.C.: National Academy Press, 1977).

The idea of a UN satellite monitoring capability was floated in Harlan Cleveland and Lincoln P. Bloomfield, *Disarmament and the U.N.* (Princeton, N.J.: The Aspen Institute, 1978). Arthur C. Clarke's gloss on that idea and his comments on "the Age of Transparency" were given in his 1987 Lindbergh Award speech in Paris and reproduced in the Humphrey Institute pamphlet *The Global Commons* (1988).

An early analysis of UN peacekeeping — and, I believe, the first use of the phrase *soldiers without enemies* — appears in my book *The Obligations of Power* (New York: Harper & Row, 1966), pp. 73–84.

The documents that together constitute the "international bill of rights" are collected in a very useful appendix to the Aspen Institute book *Human Dignity,* cited.

Information and judgments about the International Committee of the Red Cross as an activist neutral are derived from the author's personal interviews in Geneva in September 1991.

The statistics on international terrorism in the 1980s come from "International Terrorism," *Gist* (Washington, D.C.: Department of State, June 1990).

For useful information on international refugees, I am grateful to the High Commissioner for Refugees, the American Refugee Committee, the U.S. Committee on Refugees, and the Refugee Policy Group.

Comments on the post–World War II record of UNRRA are based on my personal experience as UNRRA's deputy chief of mission in Italy (1946–1947) and as the last director of the UNRRA China Office in Shanghai (1947–1948).

Andrew Maskrey's comment relating "natural" hazards to poverty is from a review of his "Disaster Mitigation: A Community Based Approach" (1969), in the *Futurist,* Sept.–Oct. 1990, p. 51.

Chapter Eight: World Economy

In the epigraph, the observation of John Maynard Keynes (he was not Lord Keynes when he wrote it) is from one of the concluding notes in his landmark book, *The General Theory of Employment Interest and Money* (London: Macmillan, 1936), p. 383.

The Geneva workshop of the "Rethinking International Governance" project, held in 1988, considered in depth "The Implications of Informatization for the International System." The discussion paper I wrote under that title for that workshop assembled the thinking of several members of and consultants to The Group, including Albert Bressand, Christian Lutz, and Magda McHale, together with material from earlier writings by Daniel Bell, John McHale, Juan Rada, and myself. Parts of this chapter, including the quotations from Bell, Bressand, and Rada, are based on that paper as modified by comments by participants in the workshop.

This chapter has greatly benefited from careful reading and criticism by my economist brother, Harold van B. Cleveland, a former vice president of Citibank and author (with Thomas F. Huertas) of that bank's definitive history, *Citibank 1812–1970* (Cambridge, Mass.: Harvard University Press, 1985). He also called my attention to an admirably succinct historical generalization by a French economist: "All the great crises of the 19th and 20th centuries have resulted from the excessive development of credit, of promises to pay and their monetization, and of the speculation that this development has caused and made possible." Maurice Allais, *Les Conditions Monétaires d'une Economie de Marchés* (Paris: Association Française de Science Économique, 1989), p. 8. My brother is, however, absolved from responsibility for the judgments and proposals I have derived from his teachings about credit inflation.

Peter Drucker's early perception that knowledge, which he calls "a form of energy that exists only when doing work," had become the dominant resource in advanced societies appears (along with many other inspired guesses about the future) in his 1968 book, *The Age of Discontinuity* (New York: Harper & Row), p. 264. The compression of *worldeconomy* into one word was a rhetorical contribution of Albert Bressand, the French member of The Group, in the title of an article in *Foreign Affairs* magazine.

The impressive volume of foreign exchange transactions, compared with "international trade," was derived by H. van B. Cleveland from 1989 statistics reported in the *Quarterly Review* of the Federal Reserve Bank of New York.

The cultural memory of ruinous inflation has been a major factor in the thinking of German policy makers and therefore on European monetary policy. I was not old enough to experience Germany's 1923 inflation, but I was in China in 1947 while the waning fortunes of Chiang Kai-shek's Kuomintang government were reflected in comparable currency inflation rates reaching 30 percent *per month*. Our UNRRA mission in Shanghai controlled a "proceeds of sale fund," forerunner to the local-currency "counterpart funds" generated in the later Marshall Plan. We persuaded the Chinese government to express these funds in

bales of cotton rather than Chinese national currency to protect them against the runaway inflation. During the first few
weeks after that agreement, the Central Bank of China forgot
to apply to the "Cotton Fund" a rate of interest stripped of the
prediction of inflation, which ballooned the commercial interest
rate. Our Cotton Fund was consequently on track to double
every three months. I called this grotesquerie to the attention
of the governor of the Central Bank; he was first embarrassed,
then his sense of humor took over. "If you hadn't said anything,"
he told me with a smile, "in a very few years the UN would
have owned all of China!"

A particularly useful contribution to the analysis of shifts in international banking in the 1980s is "Bareknuckle Banking," *Time*,
July 30, 1990, pp. 48–50.

My discussion of self-defeating secrecy and the benefits of tech-
nological openness draws on work done as a consultant to Cray
Research, Inc., and a resulting seminar I chaired in Aspen on
U.S. export control policy. *Economic Dynamism and Export Con-
trols: International Technology Transfer in a Knowledge-Intensive World,*
Report and Recommendations of a Policy Seminar, Aspen,
Colorado, Aug. 25–28, 1988 (Queenstown, Md.: The Aspen
Institute, 1988).

I am grateful to my Minnesota colleague Professor Margaret
Dewar, now at the University of Michigan, for help in understanding the often dysfunctional outcomes from government intervention to prop up economic losers in a market system.

Comments on intellectual property derive from my earlier writings on that subject. See especially Chapter 5 ("Ownership:
Knowledge as a Shared Resource") in *The Knowledge Executive,*
pp. 73–86; and "How Can 'Intellectual Property' Be 'Protected'?"
Change (published by the American Association for Higher Education), May/June 1989, pp. 10–11. See also "The Point of Pa-
tents," the *Economist,* Sept. 15, 1990, pp. 19–20, which argues
that "As a way of encouraging innovation, they are becoming
increasingly irrelevant."

Paul Strassman, a former Xerox Corporation executive, has studied in depth the use and abuse of information technology in corporations. The full range of his stimulating thinking on this subject is set forth in his book *The Business Value of Computers* (New Canaan, Conn.: The Information Economics Press, 1990).

Earlier intimations of my argument in this section are to be found in *The Knowledge Executive,* already cited, especially in Chapter 7 ("Geopolitics: The Passing of Remoteness"), and also in an article, "The End of Geography?" *WorldPaper,* Nov. 1991.

The judicious comments of Jan Pronk are from an April 1990 speech at the Special Session of the United Nations General Assembly on International Economic Cooperation, as reported in *ifda dossier,* July/Sept. 1990.

The discussion of trade policy owes a good deal to the comprehensive survey on world trade ("Nothing to lose but its chains") in the *Economist,* Sept. 22, 1990.

Chapter Nine: World Development

The epigraph is quoted from an address by President John F. Kennedy to Latin American diplomats, at the White House in Washington on March 12, 1962.

Many of the ideas and proposals in this chapter are derived from papers prepared for The Group by Mochtar Lubis of Indonesia and myself and integrated in the pamphlet *The Future of "Development,"* cited above.

The arresting figures on civilian war casualties are from an interview with UNICEF Director James Grant, "Child Summit: Moving Towards a Global Ethic," *Development Forum,* Sept.–Oct. 1990; and from UNICEF's *The State of the World's Children 1989.* Alan Durning's booklet is *Poverty and the Environment: Reversing the Downward Spiral* (Washington: Worldwatch Institute, 1989).

Timothy W. Stanley, president of the International Economic Studies Institute in Washington, suggested in 1990 that by 2010, 80 percent of the world's people would have 20 percent of the world's wealth, and vice versa. He was using CIA estimates projected to 1990 and rounded. "Of a global product approximating $20 trillion, the U.S. has about 5, Japan and the USSR share 5, the other OECD members have 5 (of which the European Community contributes 4), and everyone else has 5. . . . Projecting this for 20 years at the economic and population growth rates of the past decade yields the 80–20 economic and 20–80 population ratios foreseen in the year 2010."

The discussion of developing countries' external debt owes much to the insights in an unpublished paper (May 1990) "Debt Relief for Sustainable Development — A Win-Win Solution" by banker Karl Ziegler. The Harvard debt-for-scholarships plan is described in *World Development Forum* (published in New York by the Hunger Project, Nov. 1990).

Efforts to define and measure basic human needs have quite a long history, which is omitted here but can be found in a long introduction I prepared for John and Magda Cordell McHale, *Basic Human Needs: A Framework for Action* (New Brunswick, N.J.: Transaction Books, 1978). This work came out of an Aspen seminar I assembled in the summer of 1977 — forty-five people from eight countries and thirty-three professions, an international task force to analyze the widespread dissatisfaction with the "growth ethic" and guess at what its successor might be. See also John and Magda Cordell McHale, *Human Requirements, Supply Levels, and Outer Bounds* (Princeton, N.J.: Program in International Affairs, Aspen Institute for Humanistic Studies, 1975); and Harlan Cleveland and Thomas W. Wilson, Jr., *Humangrowth: An Essay on Growth, Values and the Quality of Life* (New York: The Aspen Institute, 1978).

Diplomat/author Charles Yost's comment on the limitations of gross national product as an economic indicator appeared in "The Ambiguities of GNP," *Christian Science Monitor,* July 16, 1976.

The underlying statistical basis for the human development index (HDI) can be found in *Human Development Report 1991,* published for the United Nations Development Program by Oxford University Press, 1991. There is a good summary of the methodology in "A New Scale of Progress — Measuring the Human Development Dimension," *World Development,* May 1990.

Chapter Ten: A Global Commons

The comment of Jean-Jacques Rousseau is the opening passage in *The Social Contract*. The full text is conveniently available in Saxe Commins and Robert N. Linscott, eds., *Man and the State: The Political Philosophers*, a book in the series *The World's Great Thinkers* (New York: Random House, 1947).

The comments of John A. Eddy about "an ecumenical movement" in the natural sciences were made in an editorial in the first number of a newsletter entitled *EarthQuest*, published by the National Center for Atmospheric Research in Boulder, Colorado, Summer 1987. The judgment of Frank Press, president of the U.S. National Academy of Sciences, was contained in his 1990 speech to a Paris conference on planet Earth. The prospect of an "irreversible rising of the oceans" is documented in *Sea-Level Change*, a report by the Geophysics Study Committee, National Academy of Sciences (Washington: National Academy Press, 1990).

The report of the World Commission on Environment and Development was published as *Our Common Future* by Oxford University Press in 1987. The conference statement and other documentation from the 1988 Toronto conference "Our Changing Atmosphere" are available from the Ministry of Environment, Ottawa, Canada.

A 1989 symposium organized by the Aspen Institute as part of its fortieth anniversary celebration took as its theme an idea on which The Group had already conducted two international workshops: the emerging concept that "for important parts of the human environment it may be useful to think of the world as a commons and to manage some of its resources in common." The resulting insights were captured in my book entitled *The Global Commons: Policy for the Planet* (already cited), from which the definition of the problem in this text is derived. The quotations from Maurice Strong are from a chapter about his seminal thinking ("The Commons as a System"), pp. 29–31.

The section on the June 1992 Earth summit in Rio de Janeiro is an interpretation of the extensive coverage of that huge U.N.

conference in contemporary newspapers and magazines. Especially useful were in-depth commentaries in the *Economist* and postconference judgments in *Newsweek* (June 22, 1992) and the *New York Times,* which published on June 14, 1992, a useful wrap-up by reporter William K. Stevens. Useful insights were provided by colleagues who were there, especially by Richard N. Gardner and Richard Benedick, who were in Rio as consultants to Maurice Strong. See especially Richard N. Gardner, *Negotiating Survival* (New York: Council on Foreign Relations, 1992).

Senator Al Gore's book on the global environment referred to in the text is *Earth in the Balance: Ecology and the Human Spirit* (Boston: Houghton Mifflin, 1992).

The idea of using the UN Trusteeship Council as trustee for the global commons was considered by The Group. Some members preferred an ad hoc commission on the global environment, along the lines of the follow-up commission actually agreed upon at the Rio conference. My preference for using the Trusteeship Council as the authorizing organ is (a) that the Trusteeship Council is a major constitutional body in the UN system, comparable in rank to the Security Council and the General Assembly, and (b) that the word *trustee* best describes the function: a world body overseeing resources and environments so physically huge and morally significant as to be beyond the reach of the jurisprudence of nation-states.

The "cautionary question" of Lao-tzu is in his *Tao Te Ching,* trans. Gia-Fu Feng and Jane English, number twenty-seven (New York: Vintage Books, 1972).

Chapter Eleven: The Club of Democracies

The full text of Article 1 of the United Nations Charter appears in the references, notes, and comments on Chapter 5. Article 51, which declares "the inherent right of individual and collective self-defense," was what the anti-Iraq coalition used as a basis for its military action in January 1991. It reads in full as follows:

> Nothing in the present Charter shall impair the inherent right of individual or collective self-defence

if an armed attack occurs against a Member of the
United Nations, until the Security Council has
taken measures necessary to maintain international
peace and security. Measures taken by Members
in the exercise of this right of self-defence shall be
immediately reported to the Security Council and
shall not in any way affect the authority and responsibility of the Security Council under the present
Charter to take at any time such action as it deems
necessary in order to maintain or restore international peace and security.

The colloquy between Charles de Gaulle and Dean Acheson was
recounted to me by the former secretary of state when in 1965
I visited Acheson for advice just before taking up my new post
as U.S. ambassador to NATO.

A general theory of international consultation is put forward
in the book I wrote after nearly four years at that post, *NATO:
The Transatlantic Bargain* (New York: Harper & Row, 1970), especially the chapter "The Golden Rule of Consultation" (pp.
13–33). During a 1967 visit to the North Atlantic Council, then
in Paris, Vice President Hubert H. Humphrey proposed the
Golden Rule as a guide to alliance consultation: "that each of
us consult as soon, as often, and as frankly as he would wish
the others to consult." The phrase *a habit of consultation,* used later
in this chapter to characterize the club of democracies, was used
in 1951 by the NATO Committee on the North Atlantic Community to describe the political relations among the Atlantic
allies.

John Gardner's comment about "wholeness incorporating diversity" is from his pamphlet *Building Community* (Washington, D.C.:
The Independent Sector, 1992).

The emphasis in the section "World Politics Is Local Politics"
on domestic motives and obstacles in some key countries is in-
fluenced by an unpublished paper, "The International Management of the World Economy," written for The Group by Martin Lees, a Paris-based British economic consultant.

The Deadlock of Democracy is the title of a book by U.S. historian James MacGregor Burns. The full title is *The Deadlock of Democracy: Four Party Politics in America* (Harper & Row, 1963).

David Calleo's description of the limits of European integration is from his introduction to David P. Calleo and Claudia Morgenstern, *Recasting Europe's Economies: National Strategies in the 1980s* (Lanham, Md.: University Press of America, 1990).

Jean Monnet's dream for European union is best described in his own story, one of the outstanding autobiographies of our time: Jean Monnet, *Memoirs* (New York: Doubleday, 1978).

Georges Berthoin's comment on a European foreign policy, and his later remark on the role of Germany and Japan, were made in his Aspen Institute talk already mentioned. H. van B. Cleveland's skepticism about Europe's political will and ideological ambition is taken from the text of an unpublished speech in 1990. A parallel comment was that of historian John Lukacs: "History is not determined by economies — which is why it is absurd to assume that economic and administrative arrangements in 1992 will amount to a real political union of Europe" (*Harper's Magazine*, Aug. 1990, p. 48).

INDEX